URBAN WATER MANAGEMENT

FRENCH EXPERIENCE AROUND THE WORLD

Edited by
Dominique LORRAIN

Translated from french by Robert Sachs
Supervision: Dominique Lorrain

URBAN WATER MANAGEMENT

FRENCH EXPERIENCE AROUND THE WORLD

Acknowledgements

The following set of texts represents the product of a collective effort that brought together, between June 1994 and July 1995, academics, executives from major French companies and an international array of government officials. The process undertaken was one of an iterative nature. Academics could take account of the reactions from the engineers whose practices shape their research. International experts communicated the observations recorded from their own experiences. Company heads made a special effort to take some distance from their daily preoccupations. Through a detailed review of international organization publications along with participation in various seminars - Louveciennes in June 1994, Washington D.C. and Paris in December 1994, and Montreal in June 1995 - this book's panel of authors was able to assimilate key issues from other countries.

Our thanks go first of all to the host of unnamed contributors to this book; their presence has been felt by the experiences they've transmitted. Acknowledgements are also in order for the members of the French working group that managed this project - Mr. Le Masson (formerly) from the Caisse Française de Développement who has overseen this project since the beginning, Mr. Cadiou from the Seine-Normandy Water Agency, Mr. Loosdregt from the Lyonnaise des Eaux, Mr. Talbot from the SAUR, Ms. Duval-Somveille and Mr. Rossi from the Compagnie Générale des Eaux. Equally deserving of recognition is our group of colleagues and international experts who provided considerable input and whose questions pushed us to sharpen our analyses. And last, but not least, our deepest thanks to Mr. Coulomb from the Syndicate of Water Producers and Distributors who supported this project in the early beginning, Mr Frank Harvelt and Pieter Klop from UNDP, Ranjith Wirasinha from the *Water Supply and Sanitation Collaboratice Council,* as well as Guy Le Moigne from the *World Water*

Council for enabling us to establish fruitful exchanges with representatives from many countries. We would also like to express our gratitude to the organizations which financially supported this book, along with the preparatory series of seminars, received financing from the SPDE, the Seine-Normandy Water Agency, international development banks and the UNDP.

The texts presented herein are not official documents and in no way bind any of the organizations that contributed to this work. Responsibility for the descriptions, analyses and conclusions in the chapters that follow lies entirely with their authors.

Dominique Lorrain
CEMS, CNRS Paris

Contents

Acknowledgements, ... V

Foreword: *Frank Hartvelt* IX

Introduction: *Dominique Lorrain* 1

Chapter 1:   The public environment, *Claude Martinand* 33

Chapter 2:   Lyons: a century of history in public
and private management, *Franck Scherrer* 45

Chapter 3:   Bordeaux –1903, 1993–,
Jean Roland Barthélémy 61

Chapter 4:   Nîmes, political alternation,
Dominique Lorrain 77

Chapter 5:   France's water agencies or 25 years of sustainable
development, *Alain Cadiou* 93

Chapter 6:   Changing the ground rules. Caracas, chronicle of a
missed privatization opportunity,
Henri Coing 109

Chapter 7:   The concession of Buenos Aires' water supply
and wastewater services,
Daniel Faudry 129

Chapter 8:   Two African experiences: Ivory Coast and Guinea,
Jean-Claude Lavigne 149

Chapter 9: Village water supply in Mali,
Hugues Le Masson 177

Chapter 10: Experimentation with privatized water services
in Indonesia - from Surabaya to Jakarta,
Eric Baye 195

Chapter 11: A contract for the production of drinking
water for Sydney, *Jack Moss*.....................................213

Chapter 12: From Macao to China, *Didier Rétali*.........................227

Chapter 13: The transformation of a municipal firm
into a joint-venture company,
Zbigniew Maksymiuk...237

Chapter 14: Italy: the paths to reform, *Marco Venturini*...........255

Conclusion: Lessons from the experience,
Dominique Lorrain..267

Authors' Biographical Notes...287

Foreword

In the years to come, one of humanity's greatest challenge will be to meet the water needs of the world's rapidly-expanding population. The magnitude of this endeavor led water experts the world over to create, in 1990, a forum for sharing and generating new ideas: *the Water Supply and Sanitation Collaborative Council*. At its 1993 meeting held in Rabat, the Council decided to form a working group whose work would be centered on the theme of "Institutional and Management Options". As coordinator of this group and to mark the occasion offered by the publication of this book "Urban Water Management-French experience around the world", I would like to make the following remarks.

This publication which represents a major portion of the working group's achievements, introduces the "French experience" in the private management of a public good: water. Through a variety of case studies, it is demonstrated how this experience has contributed to supplying water to urban populations across a wide range of countries. The examples presented serve to highlight the difficulties encountered by those responsible for providing this basic life-sustaining element. The book also illustrates the cooperation that has developed among professionals from different countries, institutions and cultural backgrounds.

This book is the product of a team effort of academicians and practitioners, most ably directed by Mr. Dominique Lorrain. Also taking part in this effort were heads of companies, government staff and experts from a good number of countries and international organizations who all participated in workshops in Louveciennes in 1994 and in Montreal in 1995.

My sincere expression of gratitude is also in order to those who have contributed their talents to the team involved in producing this book, and in particular for Mr. Hugues Le Masson (formerly) from the Caisse Française de Développement, Mr. Guy Le Moigne (formerly) Water Resources Advisory at the World Bank, Mr. René Coulomb, President of the Professional Syndicate of Water Distributors, and Mr. Pierre Tenière Buchot, Director of the Seine-Normandy Water Agency.

In conclusion, I would like to convey how privileged I have been in taking part in this work, aimed at developing new initiatives to enhance cooperation in the field of water.

New York, June 1997

Frank Hartvelt
Director
Water, Waste Management and Aquatic Environment
Sustainable Energy and Environment Division
United Nations Development Programme

Dominique Lorrain

The socio-economics of water services : the invisible factors

1. The challenge of urbanization

In light of the explosive urban growth of developing countries along with the rising awareness of environmental issues, the problems of water treatment, wastewater, waste disposal and pollution removal have now come to the fore with renewed urgency. Urban utility networks are becoming important and the focus of political debate (World Development Report, 1994, 1992)[1].

The importance of these networks' successful operations in the domain of economic development, just as in each moment of everyday life, can never be emphasized enough. Household water delivery, removal and treatment of wastes, electricity distribution and public transit shape the lives of millions of city residents. Poor performance of these services leads to relatively serious problems: public health, lost time, excessive costs. Conversely, these services fade into the background when in good working order; they simply become second nature and blend in with the rest of the environment. It's therefore a sector of activity that has been pulled by two extremes: forgotten in the industrialized countries, yet inadequate for millions, thereby creating severe problems in developing countries.

---

1. See in France works conduct by reasearch teams of CNRS : GDR 903-réseaux et GDR Interurba

Megalopols, supporting populations in the millions and typically under-equipped in services, are proliferating across all continents. Their names are now familiar to the general public - Mexico City, Jakarta, Calcutta, Bangkok, Lagos - and tensions in these places are mounting rapidly. And how many other cities are also experiencing the same conditions - strong population growth, lack of facilities, water and air pollution, horrific traffic jams. In China, for example, the mere migration of 10% of the rural population towards cities - due to enhanced levels of productivity - has generated 80 million additional urban residents. Similar phenomena have occurred on the Indian sub-continent and in other countries inside the Pacific Zone. Nor have the countries of Latin America and Africa been spared this tremendous concentration of populations within a few urban areas.

The pressures facing cities throughout the world have reached an all-time high. The magnitude of the projects required to alleviate this pressure over the next few years is tantamount to what is normally developed over several decades. In considering the pace at which electric power plants or water purification plants are being built in Asia, as soon as previous shortfalls have been remedied, the continuously rising needs have already exceeded current capacity. For example, in the province of Guangdong, water purification capacity increased by 3.14 million m^3/day during the first few years under the 8th Plan - 1990-1993 - but must still be expanded by another 5 million m^3/day in 1994 and 1995 to simply keep up with demand.

Among the range of infrastructure facility needs, one of the most indispensable is household water supply - one of life's basic components affecting millions of men, women and children the world over. It's only when this need has been met that the resources necessary for providing other household-related services - wastewater treatment, waste disposal - can be mobilized (Serageldin, 1994). As a result, solutions adopted in this sector will serve to incite the development of complementary components of urban infrastructure.

2. The need for a legal and institutional framework for collective action

Up until the present time, the history of urban services across all the industrialized countries has been focused on national companies that were more or less specialized by sector of activity, whether they be public or private.

Today, the intensity of the urban issue is bringing about a change in these sectors' organization. First and foremost, the dynamics specific to the private sector must enter into the equation. The enormous needs for infrastructure have created a market and attracted major growth-oriented firms, leading to missions contracted abroad. The policies adopted by these firms are fundamentally pushed by the needs of big cities around comprehensive technical systems to be designed, built and operated. Secondly, public decision-makers in developing nations also recognize that in order to speed up the pace of service expansion, it becomes vital to change the existing action framework and call upon these major firms by virtue of the various advantages they can offer : i) technological capability, ii) sufficient financial stature to undertake large size projects, iii) reliability over the long run as well as guarantee of continuity, and iv) capacity to draw up a framework for action and to successfully perform within sometimes unstable institutional environments.

A segmented national organization is thus modified by the current trend towards globalized markets; the biggest urban services and utility companies have acquired a global business capacity. They have become integrated into an activity; they have diversified into several public services; and ultimately they have gone international.

Put otherwise, the challenge of modern urbanization requires harnessing as never before human, financial and technological resources. The entry of major firms into the sector of urban infrastructure has ushered in a new configuration in comparison with past formulae.

In light of such a situation, two approaches may be envisioned. The first consists of relying upon what theory has taught us, dating back to a time when equilibrium between the private firm and the public authority was distinctly different, and of acting so that this type of relationship can be reproduced wherever possible. The second considers that the phenomenon of the major urban services company, while relatively recent in the history of city government, is merely a reflection of the trends affecting other markets and that the likelihood of its perpetuation is very strong. Such a prospect makes laying the ground rules that foster a longlasting association of these firms with public authorities more than ever a necessity.

Up until now, two principal kinds of solutions have been explored : management by public corporations, and the regulation of private firms benefitting from a territorial monopoly within a specific sector of activity. New rules for collective action, which would enable creating constructive partnerships - the so-called "win-win" game - between local government and this group of large internationally-oriented firms, obviously still need to be devised.

Let's hold for a moment on this notion of a framework for collective action. An assessment of what's transpiring across the world's industrialized nations, including the most recent ones, indicates that simply transferring contracts is not sufficient to make "things work". Utilizing more sophisticated technical equipment merely because the technology exists is not sufficient either. The quality of the final service, the quality of the relationships between the private firm and the public authority is highly dependent on the context of global regulation, which remains all too often misunderstood. More than in other domains a set of rules has to be set up to incite collective action, since adjustment between supply and demand doesn't happen spontaneously like in other markets. This feature is due to the size of the capital investments, the indivisibility of the utility networks and the nature of the public service doctrine (equal access, continuity). Public services belong, in economic terms, to the category of public goods; their collective optimum cannot therefore be attained from the market by aggregating individual preferences alone. In this case, the market must be shaped. Public authority intervention is necessary to build a framework for action. As long as this step is lacking, the actors in this process won't rally together, and problems will always persist.

In other words, organizing an international tender and then selling off pieces of public-sector corporations, in order to privatize a service, need for a stable, legal and regulatory framework. Collective action is only possible under the condition that the applicable rules guiding the action are stable. If these rules stay poorly defined, or if they are changed too frequently, action in effect cannot be carried out. It is necessary to build the appropriate *socio-political pre-conditions to action*, for example : i) what is the political legitimacy of local elected officials; ii) does a precise definition of public domain exist which would, in any event, authorize work sites on any parcel of land not subjected to ownership disputes?; iii) do applicable legal precepts enable settling conflicts of interest and providing financial guarantees to lending institutions?

It becomes possible thereafter to design the *political and institutional arrangements* to respond to the following straightforward questions: Who is the appropriate authority responsible for a given sector? What is the status of the entity managing the service's network (public, private or mixed)? What are the various types of contracts and methods of financing? How are risks covered? How is the system regulated?

3. The contents of this book

This book is above all devoted to the analysis of this socio-economic component, which remains little known, invisible and yet so important in the resolution of many near-term urban problems. Key questions concerning the choice of a responsible public authority, the methods for awarding contracts, construction programs, adaptation of contractual relationships and rate revisions all therefore need to be addressed.

The contents are heavily oriented around the French experience. Through becoming an urbanized country during the 1960's, actors in France's development process in effect have gained an expertise that can be applied to resolve some of these problems. And yet this expertise, in certain respects, tends to counter intuition.
- Within a country where the State has often taken an active stance as legislator, administrator or entrepreneur, it was expected that the State would play a key role, which is simply not the case.
- Within a country where political criticism has often been focused on private enterprise and where many activities have been nationalized, the presence of large private companies managing urban public services under the responsibility of local authorities is commonly encountered.
- Finally, this experience has lacked, and definitively so, both widespread exposure and a formal description since the implementation of this action framework has resulted more from adapting to problems than it has from applying theory. What a paradox to find in the country of Descartes and of strong public-sector interventionism another model for collective action, one that's more pragmatic and more driven by private-sector actors.
Such a discovery obviously warrants at least a few explanations.

The initial undertaking of this book is thus to present, as clear as possible, the essence of this French experience. To accomplish our mission, we've assembled contributions that describe long-term applications - Lyons, Bordeaux and Nîmes - and that emphasize the relationship between public authority and service operator : how was it created? how has it been evolving? Other chapters focus on the public-sector environment, the role of the State and of the National Water Basin Agencies. The overall perspective provides us with a relatively balanced view of this method which came into being in the mid-XIXth century and has been developing since the Second World War.

Yet, in seeking to highlight some of this experience's key features, our purpose herein is also one of demonstrating how the international debate on this topic can benefit from this work, as a potential solution, or an element of clarification or quite simply the illustration of a problem. To this end, the book's authors have circled the planet in order to convey different system configurations and to show, in accordance with their local contexts, how problems have been approached and solved. These fields of inquiry can be applied then to four distinct scenarios.

i) experiences of delegated management within decision frameworks similar to those developed in France; the Macao and Ivory Coast cases fall into this category.

ii) experiences of delegated management within different regulatory environments; such is the case for Sydney, Buenos Aires and Gdansk.

iii) a water services management experience conducted in a rural setting with a private operator: distributing water to Mali's rural areas.

iv) experiences of delegated management which are in progress or have not yet reached maturity, thereby focusing on the importance of the set of conditions preliminary to the execution phase: Caracas, Guinea, Indonesia and Italy.

Having accomplished these pertinent inquiries, we then proceeded to draw some more generalized conclusions which could serve as an evaluation tool for interested parties across a wide array of countries seeking to enact reforms in this sector.

BOX 1,
Presentation of the case studies

Lyons: Municipal-private relationship dating back to 1853. Succession of contracts in central city, suburbs and metropolitan area for water production, distribution and wastewater. Metropolitan area of one million population.

Bordeaux: Municipal-private relationship dating back to 1903. Succession of missions and contracts. Water and wastewater concession for the entire metropolitan area of 700,000 population. Drinking water production at 272,000 m^3 per day.

Nîmes: Leased water services since 1969, wastewater since 1985. Political alternance of local government, from Communist party to "free-market" right-wing politics back to Communist. City of 125,000 population.

National Water Basin Agencies: Institution created in 1964 to ensure consistent water resource management policies for each given river basin territory. Levies pollution control taxes, redistributes revenue and oversees the programming of all facilities. Assembles the service's various partners: user groups, elected officials, administrators, private operator into a sort of "water council".

Caracas: Failure of privatization effort on two separate occasions, one a discreet approach while the other more programmed in nature. Chaotic experience in elaborating a reform process, serving to highlight the importance of contextual understanding and the conditions preliminary to initiating action.

Buenos Aires: Largest experience to date in delegating water services. Metropolitan area of 11 million population, including 9 million within the concessionary boundary and 6.5 million connected to the water distribution network. 30-year concession for water and wastewater services since April, 1993. 4 billion $US of capital investment slated over the concession's first five years.

Ivory Coast: State-municipal-private relationship dating back to 1960. Several cities within service area, including Abidjan (2 million population). Succession of missions and contracts adapted to both user needs and economic context of growth followed by downturn. Example of a private service provider operating in a relatively poor country.

Guinea: Example of delegated management following the complete political and economic reform of 1984. Separation of service between public ownership and private operations. Experience has been heavily supported and monitored by international organizations, including the World Bank. 10-year leasing contract entered into in 1989. Highlights the need for more time to fundamentally alter current practices.

Mali: Water supply to rural areas through well-drilling program begun in 1975, up to 3,000 wells in 1994. Emphasizes the role of the human factor, in the person of a "missionary-developer", along with the importance of operations to utilize capital investment to its fullest. An approach being gradually oriented towards the introduction of basic economic principles in order to change behavioral patterns: assigning a manager for each facility; determining a price for water.

Indonesia: Accommodating the factors of strong urban growth, need for updated infrastructure, public-sector indebtedness and necessity to call on private capital. Various ongoing experiences demonstrate that these factors are not necessarily compatible; also required are contextual conditions to be met and that parties to the process all agree on the appropriate institutional framework.

Sydney: World's largest B.O.T. contract for water production. 25-year contract term commencing in September 1993. Projected capital outlay of 200 million Australian dollars (155 million $US). Drinking water production at 3 million m^3 per day.

Macao: Concession for the production and distribution of water. 25-year contract term commencing in 1985. City of 550,000 population. Drinking water production at 195,000 m^3 per day.

Gdansk: Leasing agreement for the production and distribution of water as well as wastewater services. 30-year contract term commencing in July 1992. City of 460,000 population. Drinking water production at 170,000 m^3 per day.

Italy: Industrialized nation clearly lagging in the performance of its water services. Socio-economic considerations as the root cause: fragmented organization of operators; public authorities prefer political reshuffling to sound economic principles; a new legislative framework that's slow to be implemented. Reform remains atop the agenda; users have become adaptable.

BOX 2,
This book's guiding themes

1. The socio-economic factors that influence the orientation of collective action, though invisible, do nonetheless play a fundamental role; as long as they're not being taken into account, problems will persist.

2. We're currently traversing a very critical period in our urban history, characterized by sizable population increases across urban areas and by the proliferation of major metropolitan centers.

3. To meet these newly-emerging challenges, mobilizing both the expertise and the resources of large urban services companies, as novel as it may seem in the area of urban affairs, has become an absolute necessity. Performing such a role for the large urban services company, frequently a foreign company, has proved to be no simple feat. It's a role that has modified old habits by introducing a level of competition into sectors previously under the "protection" of nationwide monopolies.

4. This situation has incited establishing a new framework for collective action which is intended to adapt the theories of regulating monopoly markets, developed in the 1930's for electricity distribution and in the 1960's for telecommunications.

5. Urban utility networks - water supply, wastewater, waste, public transit - all exhibit characteristics that differentiate them from telecommunications and electricity distribution networks. Their capital-intensive nature gives rise to a longer period of return on investment. Similarly, their very strong spatial and urban orientation has resulted in close ties with urban growth patterns and, consequently, with city management strategies.

6. Regulation in the area of water supply is not strictly a technical matter and doesn't solely concern this market sector; instead, it encompasses all aspects of city government. It goes without saying that the modernization, in both its technological and financial aspects, of water supply networks is contributing to the reorganization of local power structures. For those countries that experienced, over very long periods, a centralized government regime while State-run companies were being protected by national monopolies, the immensity of the transformation taking place far exceeds the limited mission of household water delivery.

7. The spotlight on operations. The approach of an equipment manufacturer is obviously not the same as that of a construction firm, and even further from that of a service operator. The work herein displays that the operations phase engenders a unique approach, not to be confused with the roles being performed by other actors which invoke specific regulatory mechanisms.

4. The French experience

For over a century now, urban services companies have been part of France's urban history. From modest beginnings, they now play a highly-visible, fundamental role. They began in the area of water distribution and expanded to become involved in all services that comprise the field of urban public works (Martinand, 1986) or what could be termed the sector of "urban infrastructure". A few more recent entrants, primarily construction firms and restructured public-sector corporations, have joined these "veterans" in covering this market.

One would therefore be very tempted to tag the French situation a "model" since from one service sector to the next, the same actors, the same action guidelines and the same working culture are all present. Nonetheless, in overusing this term, the risk is run of deforming its intended meaning.

First of all, the word model can be interpreted to mean "exemplary"; yet, such boastfulness, such self-proclaimed excellence would definitely suggest the complete opposite of a true culture of understatement, which has characterized this sector and insures that both public decision-makers and users alike have their say. Secondly, this term "model" could lead to imagining the conception of a perfectly-reproducible mechanism, a kind of algorithm. In this instance, it's a different characteristic of the system that's being opposed: its flexibility, its adaptability, its capacity to find the appropriate equilibria for a variety of situations.

4.1. The essential characteristics: actors, principles and culture
More than a model, it's a summation of experiences, a sort of pragmatism that's at play herein.

- The primary responsibility is that of the municipalities. The underlying principle in effect is very old; it emanated from the local-specific nature of water resources, was reinforced by the 1884 legislation on municipal autonomy and has been reaffirmed ever since. Municipalities can band together to form "second-tier" organizations whose administrative structures correspond to the necessities of the public service networks. It's a role that cities fill to a great extent; one could even go as far as saying that intermunicipal cooperation in France relies, above all, on the management of urban services.

This principle of municipal responsibility is of utmost importance in that it places elected officials, and in particular big-city mayors, at the very heart of the institutional framework. They are, after all, responsible; they sign the contracts.

- Second principle: cities can operate urban services on their own or they can delegate what's outstanding to the private sector, since it's the public authority that retains ownership of the service networks. This provides the basis upon which today's major firms were able to develop. The fact that this possibility was introduced so long ago attests to the perpetual recognition of a principle of market freedom within the scope of French law concerning public involvement in this domain. From this premise, both public and private management could be treated on an equal footing. A pure monopoly has thereby never taken hold; competition between the two sectors has prevailed right from the start.

- Thirdly, when delegation is consented, the agreement between public authority and private service provider is expressed by means of a contract. Its initial forms were concessions; afterwards, following the Second World War, new forms better adapted to the relationships among actors were established (refer to the case of Lyons or Bordeaux for this legal adaptation). The development of the contract, an act of free will between two parties, brought with it something new from the realm of private law, within a universe where unilateral administrative procedure, hence public authority prerogative, ruled supreme (see the work of the public legal experts Duguit, Ducos-Ader and Laubadère). This contractual principle has introduced into the area of local management the obligation to specify a few objectives, even if this process does remain somewhat modest at the outset. The example of Lyons, illustrates well the lack of clarity in the relationships between city and private firm before the First World War; accounting practices, budgetary control and overall monitoring procedures were all in their infancy.

- Delegation as a recourse did invoke the current principle of a separation between the organizing authority and the operator; in the past, these two parties were referred to as the concession-granting authority and the concessionaire, since the most common scenario was indeed the concession. Without being presented as such and though not entirely perfect, this separation helped to avoid the confusion existing when a public authority makes decisions and executes projects through the intermediary of a public-sector corporation.

- It wasn't until later that the principle of financial equilibrium for public industrial and commercial services[2] was clearly affirmed. With respect to water supply, it has been a long evolutionary process mainly accomplished in the 1920's-1930's. The trend was then generalized to include other utility networks up to becoming at the present time a basic rule in the economics of service provision. Highlighting the reasons behind this adaptation process is not an altogether fruitless exercise. Initially, the services were all part of the local administration; they were financed directly from the budget. Each

---

2. The legal term in french is "Services publics industriels et commerciaux -SPIC-."

step in the evolution taking place at the time tended towards greater economic autonomy of the water supply system from the public administration's hold; the firms active in this sector would also push for more autonomy. A direct, regular payment by the user himself would gradually replace more irregular public subsidies. It's from this revised economic basis that these firms would go on to build water supply pipelines and equip the country. Much later, around 1965, at the beginning of the intense phase of urban growth, the rule of budgetary autonomy would be officially established.

At this point in the reasoning developed, it could be said that the French experience has remained a relatively straightforward one. It relies upon an institutional framework with two main actors: the municipality and the private firm. It gained prominence once a principle of organizational autonomy between municipal service departments and operators had been elaborated and once a principle of financial equilibrium had become effective. At that precise moment in time, the basic principles of a market economy were set up, and the system could then develop. And that's exactly what it did, thanks in large part to its strongest pole and most strategic actor, the group of major urban services companies. Consideration must nonetheless be paid to the role of the State and to the fact that these companies have developed by satisfying the expectations of decision-makers and users alike, as well as by adapting to changing contexts.

The development of this entire water services system cannot be fully comprehended without describing the indirect role of the State and of its senior staff. Throughout history, the State has exerted tremendous influence in designing tools - economic, legal, financial - that make it both legitimate and materially possible to implement this type of action for the public authority. It became essential to elaborate a right of eminent domain, tender procedures for work contracts, etc. A long-term historical overview teaches us that a good portion of the principles applied today in the area of urban public services were originally forwarded by construction engineers belonging to the State Corps; whether in naval construction, canals or railroad building, they carved the necessary economic concepts (Lorrain in Martinand, 1993).

The State has also been involved in the critical construction of the theory of public services (see Claude Martinand's chapter). The French originality lies in positioning this economics of urban services at the intersection of market efficiency - making possible the concessionary approach - and public action - obtained, in this context, by the right of public service. The fundamental idea herein is that urban services cannot be treated like other market commodities. They participate surely to the life of the economy, and they do provide certain economic properties, yet they are also being subjected to the specific obligations of service continuity and equal access which pertain as much to principles of social justice as to their monopoly status. Put otherwise, by developing over long periods of time, the category of "public industrial and commercial services" has been conferred a dual property. These services contribute to a market economy, yet they also help uphold the social link by treating all citizens equitably.

Lastly, the State has been present at those crucial moments when the system has needed a strong boost. That's what happened with the creation of the river basin agencies during the 1960's (see Alain Cadiou's chapter). This intervention provided the means to affirm the existence of the technical water cycle - conveyance, use, disposal - around the principle of "polluter-payer", while respecting the principle of autonomous city management. It had become possible to collect revenue and redistribute it according to a prescribed investment policy. The agencies incited market development by soliciting financing sources and by emphasizing the theme of water purification to mayors; the companies thereafter brought complementary financing along with their specialized sets of skills.

With all this backdrop of rights of public service and rights of concession, one could postulate that the French experience depends, above all, on the work of legal experts. Such a suggestion obviously ignores that this system has historically grown up alongside the local authorities and their problems; so much so that in order to fully understand this experience, a good description of local service problems would be the appropriate place to start. In this sector, the French propensity to legislate has always been offset by the pragmatism of local elected officials and practicing public works engineers. The system has actually developed from a set of unwritten, uncodified cultural principles, which also explains to a great extent the attitude adopted by its various actors.
  - the system is problem solving oriented;
  - operators assume a performance-based obligation; and
  - relationships between actors rely on a spirit of trust.
This informal development has been so prominent that contractual rights have not proved to be constraints; rather it has provided a contingency construction emanating from the questions to be resolved. Furthermore, it's never a prerequisite, just the moment to stabilize a relationship. As testimony to this development are the successive adaptations to contracts in Lyons and Bordeaux, or the Nîmes example wherein an operator adapts to changes in political priorities without any commensurate modification to the contract.

Dominating the scene that depicts this experience are the figures of local elected officials and practicing engineers, along with a few high-ranking State officials and public legal experts in the background. In comparison with other countries, the absence of economists is noteworthy. From the standpoint of academic disciplines, the center of gravity of this cast of characters lies somewhere between political science, contract law and industrial economics.

4.2. The French regulatory environment

Regulation in France tends to resemble certain aspects of the soft-pedal regulation of AT&T between 1938 and 1956 (Simon, 1991). The workings of the urban services market in France demonstrate that self-regulation can exist. What transpires herein illustrates some of the postulates of Hayek or Smith concerning collective action. Some regulatory mechanisms are the product of long-term collective action and, as such, escape immediate notice since they haven't actually been designated. Nonetheless, a true systemic regulation has been put into effect.

From a more formal perspective, three types of regulations can be distinguished.

a. Regulation by the markets.

i) Urban services groups are less industrially integrated than is all too often professed. They are evolving towards a more cellular structure which offers a wide maneuvering range to each subsidiary in carrying out its specific actions. A multiplicity of partnerships with foreign firms aimed at penetrating markets abroad does exist, and to such an extent that the borders which had enabled distinguishing a group from its environment are now more blurred. The result has been to call into question previous assessments of integration within oligopolistic structures. In addition, these are not industrial firms inasmuch as they're not utilizing their monopoly position to impose their own equipment, which is one of the criticisms directed against monopolies (Curien, 1995).

ii) Competition among urban services groups for major contracts does take place since the market is of a nature where entry opportunities are presented intermittently. It would be useful to make the distinction between urban service contracts - B.O.T., concession and other franchises - which are established for long terms and public works contracts, smaller in scope but more frequent. This feature has repercussions on the level of competition experienced among firms. They are not in a position to not compete, for their future growth depends dearly on it.

iii) Yardstick competition, has always been present. It only accentuates as the number of competitors increases with the markets; groups eye one another closely; cities compare themselves. International bankers, committed to the long run, conduct audits and respect reporting procedures. Statistical information flows freely.

iv) Competition on capital markets. By virtue of being quoted on the stock exchange, these firms must consistently expand, satisfy their clientele and monitor their competitiveness, which leads them to be continuously weighing the cost/benefit tradeoffs for their investment policies. Since the cost of money is high, investments must be dosed. This constraint has induced firms to optimize their investment policies and to find a middle ground between oversizing and under-investment. The former is expensive while the latter could jeopardize service quality. This action format limits the risk of over-investment ascribed to monopolistic situations.

b. Global and political regulation. The mechanism is rather simple to apply. As long as the complaints reaching the mayor's office are not extremely serious, the operator is deemed to be performing his work correctly. The issue of profit and the use of profit get relegated to secondary importance. The operator is bound to a results-based objective; once this has been attained, he enjoys a certain margin of flexibility. This flexibility implies that not all service parameters are necessarily subjected to regulation, as in the English experience. This mechanism is, first and foremost, "problem-oriented" in nature. The regulatory scheme evoked herein relies entirely upon a particular socio-political framework. The system so devised works because the mayor wields a lot of power, endowed with political legitimacy, and because there is congruence between the level of political intervention and that of the urban services organization. The fact that this relationship, in the user's eyes, could be publicized by elected officials is testimony to the sociableness of the small town, a heritage passed on from France's rural past. Users would solicit their local politicians who, in turn, would incite repercussions (see the case of Nîmes for an example of strong influence on the part of politicians prior to 1983, even though the service was being delegated).

Now that the general principle has been discussed, a more detailed description of how matters actually proceed is in order.

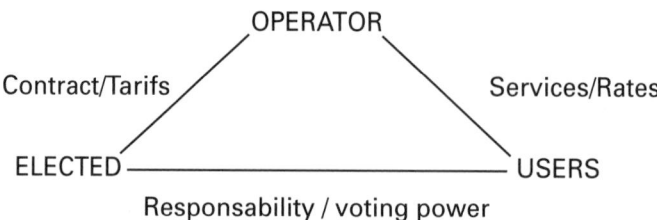

- The local authority-operator relationship. The culminating moment in the relationship is played out at the signing of the contract. Thereafter, contracts take on a life all their own; operators perform their work in constant touch with the public authority and inform the authority of their main decisions - works programs, rate revisions. The delegation of public service leaves great freedom of action to private firms, which nonetheless do not operate on separate terms from the local public authority.

This entire system depends on contracts; thousands of contracts are concluded with local elected officials, themselves being subjected to the oversight of their electorate. These contracts represent the strongest link in the chain connecting the two parties. Such an action framework, completely different from the ten distinct contracts for the ten Regional Water Companies that cover 75% of England, provides flexibility and produces the means to effectively limit monopoly power. Groups are continually renegotiating contracts. A serious abuse of a dominant negotiating position in territory A would immediately be known to all pertinent actors and would impact the renegotiations in territory B or C. It shouldn't be overlooked that if operating activities are legally classified as a monopoly, they take part in a system wherein all actors know one another and information circulates very quickly through political channels, associations of public works engineers as well as the press.

- The elected official-user relationship. Service users are also part of the electorate and clearly perceive their elected representatives as being responsible for urban services policies. As such, recourse at the "ballot box" insures that their opinions get expressed if rates are too high, or if quality is insufficient. Politicians react to what rebounds from users: silence translates into satisfaction; a mounting number of complaints conveys a dysfunction that cannot be ignored.

- The user-operator relationship is structured around a dual exchange: service rendered is remunerated by a service fee. For a long time, companies handled this relationship as professionals, meaning that they would provide the user with the highest quality of service possible. Nowadays, they have become even more quality-conscious by installing user feedback systems, which serve to complement the information transiting through the conventional channels of elected officials: toll-free telephone numbers, centralized information dissemination, heavy publicizing of major service modifications. In short, professionals do communicate.

c. The third regulatory mechanism concerns reputation, or rather the threat of losing a reputation. This "sword of Damocles" instills a real drive for efficiency among firms completely dedicated to the urban infrastructure market and who, as opposed to conglomerates, don't deviate as opportunities come and go. It's a very old mechanism. Mr. Samuel Insull, Manager of Chicago's Commonwealth Edison and President of the National Electricity Light Association, explained to his colleagues around 1907 that it was in their interest to spontaneously accept a regulation (Hirsh, 1991). Furthermore, they should not abuse their position of strength, in order to insure avoiding the risk of nationalization or of municipalization, as practiced at the time in Europe (Simon, 1991). In this case, it was the threat itself that created a principle of self-imposed limitations on excessive power.

BOX 3,
Primary lessons from the French system

1. A wholly-decentralized structure featuring an empowered public authority, the municipality, close to its residents and endowed with a strong political legitimacy. Complementary to this structure are the river basin agencies that coordinate actions on a broad scale and the State, which assists in framing the overall operating environment: legal doctrine, standards, key programs.

2. A great number of contracts, thereby offering a gradient of possibilities for better adaptation to the problem at hand. In all cases, no sale of assets takes place; the public authority retains ownership of the facilities.

3. A variety of regulatory mechanisms that enables avoiding complete dependence on one sole factor.

4. The application of a few simple, yet essential, economic guidelines: organizational autonomy of water service operations, the principle of financial equilibrium, metering of actual consumption and remuneration in the form of service rates.

5. Central role played by large, fully-integrated firms with longstanding practical experience in all phases of the water cycle.

Advantages of this system:
– Involvement of politicians who know their cities and understand their needs.
– Clearly-defined lines of responsibility and ease of comprehension for the user.
– Introduction of the efficiency-oriented methods of large firms.
– A gradient of solutions and learning possibilities.

Risks: the dialectic of strong vs. weak.
– Risk that the dynamic approach of a firm leads to a spirit of overachievement.
– Risk of "hoarding" the sector's state-of-the-art knowledge by a few firms.

Maintaining both a base of technical understanding within the responsible public body and a clearly-outlined split of assignments between public authority and private firm is therefore essential.

Reputation is a general fact of business life; firms must constantly oversee their reputation. This aspect is even more relevant within a growing market with shares to be won. The "mishaps" in one territory could generate repercussions and then negative effects elsewhere. This factor takes on even greater significance in that firms operate within the sphere of the service profession, which nonetheless remains somewhat intangible in nature. The reputation of the name of the firm is tantamount to a brand name in other markets. This feature is of capital importance for the firm.

5. Some outstanding questions

The experience of industrialized nations has been shaped over the ages. It has depended upon a specific legal environment. In Great Britain, Germany and France, the underlying precepts date back to the end of the XIXth century (Garrard, 1993; Haussermann, 1992; Korte, 1991; Stoker, 1995). In France in particular, the existence of a highly-developed civil service workforce along with the general legislation governing public services warrants mention (Stoffaes, 1994; Martinand, 1994; Loosdregt, 1995). These foundations are referred to herein as the prerequisites for action.

These experiences are certainly not transferable in identical terms since history has been accelerating in developing countries and since contexts are not the same. It has thereby become necessary to adapt solutions and devise methods that enable speeding up the learning process. To accomplish this step, it's vital to clarify a few key questions that arise whenever a public authority decides to call upon a private firm.
- What are the project's potential organizational structures?
- And their likely consequences?
- What are the economic advantages associated with a large firm?
- What are the primary choices in terms of global control?

5.1. The major contract types

The general term privatization is actually employed to designate a group of very distinct situations that pertain less to their nation of origin than to the type of solution they apply to the problem of sharing responsibilities between public authority and private firm. This sharing formula becomes effective as of the signing of the contract. A diversity of formulae exists, and the selection only widens as consideration is given to a more international approach to the question.

Two criteria play central roles and allow categorizing the various contractual forms. The first relates to the breadth of responsibilities shouldered by the operator. He may remain simply within the realm of a service provider working with the equipment supplied by the public authority; or, at the other end of the spectrum, he may be financing new facilities, performing management functions and assuming industrial risk. In the former, he is said to be "operating on behalf of the authority", while in the latter, to be "operating at his own risk". The second criterion concerns the duration of validity of the rights granted the firm by the public authority.

This combination of parameters thereby leads to distinguishing the four predominant contractual situations. It is very important to recognize which of these action frameworks would be applicable, since the commitments of the various partners are not necessarily the same and, as a result, procedures for both awarding contracts and exercising control should likewise be somewhat different.

Different stages of private sector involvment

Intensity of private
sector involvment

Large			Privatisation
			Concession
			BOT,
			BOOT
		Lease	
		Affermage	
	Contracting-out		
	Régie intéressée		
	Gérance		
	Marché d'exploitation		
	Delegated management		
Restricted	Operating & maintenance		
Assigned rights	Rights of short-term	Rights ofmid and long term	Rights perpetual
	limited assignment	partial, total assignment	Privatisation

"Limited delegation" corresponds to a situation in which the public authority grants rights for shorter periods - from 18 months to 3 years - to a company operating in accordance with a strictly-defined set of specifications and overseeing only a part of the public service being delegated. Furthermore, the company in this case doesn't make use of a sizable asset base and doesn't assume any risk; it is remunerated directly by the public authority, which retains the commercial side of customer relations. The firm is in the mode of "operating on behalf of the authority". In Anglo-Saxon countries, this situation is indicative of the "operating & maintenance" (O&M), "delegated management" or "contracting-out" type of contracts; in France, the terms "marché d'exploitation" (operations contract), "régie intéressée" (incentive management contract) or "gérance" (management services contract) are employed.

In the realm of "partial delegation", the public authority delegates more substantial portions of the public service. The firm is engaged for terms varying from 7 to 25 years. It carries out capital investment, assumes risks and enjoys freedom of action. Yet, its domain of action remains only partial in scope. On the one hand, the service rendered by the firm stays limited to those facilities already integrated into the existing network operated by the public authority. On the other, this setting of dependency is underpinned by the fact that the operator's remuneration is derived from the public authority and not from the consumer. Lastly, the public authority retains ownership of all facilities, which are ultimately handed over upon expiry of the contract period. In essence, the contract grants only temporary use rights. This situation invokes, above all, the contractual forms of: leases, Build Own & Operate and Build Own & Transfer (B.O.T.).

Once delegation encompasses a wider range of activities, once it covers the entire service, and once the firm is assigned the role of customer relations and balances its accounts directly by collecting service fees, only then can the notion of "total delegation" be appropriate. The firm is committed for terms of anywhere from 10 to 25 years, enjoys freedom of action, carries out its own investment program and assumes full responsibility of the public service. Under French law, the firm is considered to be operating at its own risk. It sets prices, establishes facility work programs and determines hiring policies; it undertakes all measures necessary to provide service and insure service continuity. As with the previous contract formulae, the public authority remains owner of all assets, which are then handed over at the end of the contract period in the case of non-renewal. This situation corresponds to the French versions of leasing agreements ("affermage") and concessionary contracts ("concession").

The fact of the matter is that B.O.T. contracts and concessions have rather a lot in common - length of contract period, considerable extent of firm's involvement and operations at firm's own risk. They do differ as to the source of the operator's remuneration - public authority vs. consumer - as well as to the scope of their mission. In the former, delegation concerns just one component of the service's technical system - one electric power plant or one drinking water production plant - whereas in the latter, the contracted firm runs the entirety of the public service.

The final form consists of service "privatization" through the sale of assets as illustrated in Great Britain for water distribution and electricity. In this case, the public authority transfers ownership of all property and facilities to a private firm that, in so doing, acquires near-perpetual rights. It's a setup whereby the firm exercises tremendous power by virtue of the breadth of its responsibility and of the corresponding long-run nature of the planning horizon. The firm's responsibilities are far-reaching since it oversees the complete water cycle - conveyance, use of drinking water, disposal of wastewater - throughout its monopoly service territory. The analogous example would be combining, in Germany, the missions of several Stadtwerke within a same company, or in France merging several private firms, restructuring municipal water departments at the regional level. This position is, to a certain extent, strengthened by the time horizon factor. According to the Water Act of 1988, Britain's Regional Water Companies were awarded operating licenses for renegotiable periods of 25 years; yet, in accordance with the privatization process, they had to acquire the systems' facilities, which makes them owners as well. Under this fourth scenario, the firm thus finds itself conferred virtually perpetual rights, while the public authority relinquishes the advantages associated with facility ownership along with the potential to recover property at the end of a defined contract period.

5.2. Impacts on several practical problems
This distinction thereby both serves to clarify some of the parameters for deciding among the various action frameworks and generates impacts on the procedures for selecting and overseeing the contracted firm.

a. Potential for gradual choices. Those in governing positions who wish to call upon the know-how of the private sector can make gradual choices and are not confronted with the alternative extremes of public-sector management vs. full privatization. Instead, they are able to introduce partnerships through various degrees of delegation.

The differences between Anglo-Saxon and French law are not necessarily fundamental in nature, even if their means of application do serve to separate them. At each level of partnership, from one case to the next, relevant contract formulae exist. Each country has in effect produced its continuum of legal approaches; the real distinction lies in sorting them into the four major families.

b. Combination of legal controls and industrial economics. Positioning within one family as opposed to another does impact the expectations placed on the private firm. Its behavior will naturally differ depending on the planning horizon of its operating environment as well as on the range of action it is granted. When the firm enters into a long-term contract, it has the possibility to benefit from capital investments in production that reduce operating costs. Conversely, O&M-type contracts tend to encourage adopting more conventional solutions that are well-known and correspond closely with public authority expectations, as defined in the tender specifications. In other words, since this type of partnership involves the firm to an extent that depends both on the freedom of action it has been granted and on the amount of time it has available, the strategic interest of the public authority is best served by implementing an optimal combination of public/private responsibility in relation to the skills possessed by the firm. One such optimal combination may call for contracting a medium-sized local firm over the short run, thereby relying on only a relatively low level of technical skill, whereas seeking to bring a large firm into this particular setting might prove sub-optimal. Choosing from among these categories of partnership, with their associated sets of prerequisite criteria and specific time periods, must be closely tied to the characteristics of the firm.

Noteworthy herein is that the relationship between public authority and private firm must not be solely shaped by legal doctrine and regulatory prescriptions, but also by notions of industrial economics. The key question to be raised in every scenario should be: what is the optimal organization for the socio-technical system that best satisfies users over the long run.

c. This typology gives rise to some practical consequences with respect to the procedures for selecting firms. For a long time, the tradition in France has been that of the "intuitus personae". This practice certainly cannot be generalized, though its implications do merit closer examination since they highlight certain particularities of public service contracts. The freedom of choice entrusted elected officials as well as the informal procedural aspect lead to the conclusion that these contracts are quite distinct from standard public works contracts. This is so for several reasons:

- The length of the contractual relationship and its specificities have to be taken into account. Partners are not necessarily chosen in the same manner, depending on whether the relationship pertains to the acquisition of equipment payable in five years' time or to a service provision agreement covering a twenty-year period. In the latter case, too many elements remain unforeseeable to detail in the contract. There's an overwhelming impetus therefore to make room for a spirit of confidence and for the mutual interest of both parties.

- The number of firms capable of offering this kind of service is somewhat limited. Such was the case in France a century ago, and it would seem that such is also true for international contracts once the formulae of limited delegation have been surpassed. That several large tenders never came to fruition, namely Caracas in 1993, others in China and B.O.T.-framed electric power plants scattered across Asia, is in part due to the limited number of suppliers in these markets. And even when the tender procedures do lead to an outcome, the issue of cost still remains. The cost of the preliminary design studies for the winning consortium in the Buenos Aires project has been evaluated by one of the company's directors at $US 5 million. "Inasmuch as there were four candidates in the running, the global cost can be estimated at $US 15 million", which in itself raises a strategic dilemma: "if $US 15 million need to be spent in order to select the operator of a network serving 6 million consumers, then just what will it cost to satisfy the hundreds of millions left to be served the world over?" Once a global action framework has been chosen, it is undoubtedly more effective to enter into negotiations with those actors most likely to intervene in this capacity.

- If the public authority does call upon a public services firm, it's a clear sign that the authority acknowledges the firm's capabilities. The system of "public procurement", or public-sector contracting, serves to delimit the firm into a strict definition of the problem and into specific solution approaches. In this instance, the public authority is denying itself other solutions that the firm could potentially propose. As a result, for B.O.T.-type contracts, concessions and leasing agreements, the freedom to develop solutions must be accorded the firm as of its initial tender submittal.

From these arguments for which numerous examples can be cited, it becomes readily apparent that selecting a firm within the formula of either total or partial delegation cannot be conducted along the same lines as for a standard public-sector contract, or a public procurement. Consequently, a set of procedures for implementing new options combining administrative transparency with a more flexible formulation of the tender should be established. This development would lead towards the "short list" tendering approach.

d. The classification into four distinct families of contracts does impact to a great extent the forms of global control. The level of public authority involvement varies considerably from one family to the next. The public authority should therefore adjust applicable regulatory mechanisms depending upon its own strengths and the risks it wishes to assume.

In the case of "limited delegation", the authority permanently maintains a wide range of control over operations through retaining ownership of the asset base, through directly collecting all public service-generated revenue, and through entering into only short-term contracts. The forms of control typically associated with this family should thereby be less burdensome and extensively written into the contract; if not, the system becomes too cumbersome to manipulate. At the other end of the spectrum, privatization, wherein many of the public authority's attributes get transferred, requires more regulatory precision since the firm is bestowed perpetual rights. The kind of formulae represented by concessions, leasing agreements and B.O.T.'s, which are positioned somewhere between these two extremes, should thus be handled by other regulatory systems. It's only reasonable to suggest that one focus of a socio-economic perspective would be to refine these systems.

It is also understandable that the mix of regulation emanating from a "privatization" formula with a "partial or total delegation" contract would lead to altering the ground rules. Actors are imposed narrow-scoped and overly-minute control mechanisms that are simply not appropriate given the general action framework. This excessive degree of control engenders extra cost. As a result, prior to choosing the applicable regulatory procedures, it is essential to determine which contract family is relevant. "Privatization" corresponds with a "strict" regulatory environment in that the public authority is being placed into a system whereby it relinquishes a lot of power. "Limited delegation" should be accompanied by more limited controls; and "total delegation" should be implemented under alternative procedures.

e. What is the appropriate degree of precision that should be written into a contract? For short-term contracts, it would seem both logical and plausible to cite the vast majority of potential problems within the contract document itself. For longer terms, the capacity to forecast future scenarios on the part of both contractual parties weakens. The factor of complexity is then too strong. In this case, if the contract cannot be accountable to envision every eventuality, a very detailed written document becomes less imperative. In contrast, it is vital to plan for revision mechanisms that enable perpetuating the contract.

A reading of the Rostock contract, before a notary public, took around sixteen hours! The appendices alone take up more than two meters of archival space. For this particular case, it can be held that the actors assimilated totally new conditions. This city's elected officials along with the water distribution company's executive staff discovered together market economics within a private-sector solution. This event could therefore be analyzed, in economic terms, as the price to be paid for developing a satisfactory action framework. Yet, it is quite understandable that such a legal construction does pose a problem by its sheer weight; its implementation implies a cost, and a risk of inflexibility exists since taking account of the unexpected eventualities would certainly necessitate changing a good number of contract articles that were very methodically written.

Put otherwise, two factors must absolutely be taken into consideration: the nature of the contractor's role - sale of equipment vs. service provision - and the duration of the contractual commitment. They are largely responsible for a contract's internal structure.

5.3. The economic factors of large-firm efficiency
The relationships between public authority and large public service firms are traditionally stamped with the seal of mistrust. One need only look at the results from long periods of unfortunate experiences at the end of the XIXth and beginning of the XXth centuries, when major companies got involved in utility networks. Public-sector intervention has often been shaped as a response either to company excesses or to their inadequacies. The economic theory of monopoly markets has served to reinforce this negative and restrictive vision.

However, an international observation of these markets indicates a growing tendency towards strengthening large-sized firms, whether public or private in nature. Deregulation and privatization policies only partially explain this phenomenon, in that if decision-makers everywhere are reorganizing the framework for collective action, perhaps it's because they consider that these larger firms possess certain advantages. And if these advantages are more obvious today than yesterday, perhaps it's because cities are changing and, by the same token, so are urban problems.

A fundamental movement must be taken into account. The transition from the small town to the metropolis, and then to a networked megalopolis represents a fracture from the standpoint of technical urban infrastructure. The major metropolitan networks are objects which are more complex and more technical, thereby requiring more extensive capital outlays and higher skill levels. For example, experts in the World

Bank's water department have clearly demonstrated a rise in per capita service cost surpassing the proportionate increase in population (Serageldin, 1994; Yepes, 1993). This structural evolution highlights a competitive advantage for large firms that can exhibit the economic factors enabling them to generate productivity gains.

i) Economic arguments
- Economies of scale and the corresponding increase in yield rates. A group that manages water services in hundreds of cities should theoretically perform better than a firm operating one single network, due to the higher yields the group can attain. To reach this stage, firms implement strategies of concentration and vertical integration. Concentration is preferred in the area of water distribution when they oversee a growing number of networks. Integration is opted for when a firm is involved in different parts of the water services sequence of activities: for example, pipe manufacturing, maintenance work and engineering services. This "law" of increasing yields forms the basis of the organization of some monopolistically-run sectors.

- Economies of scope. The know-how required to enter into a particular sector carries with it an acquisition cost which can't simply be measured in technical terms. Understanding contract law and financing techniques is essential; knowing how to handle an ongoing relationship with the user is also essential; gaining access to both local and national decision-making circles is likewise essential, and so forth. Firms are obliged to include this phase of investment. But afterwards, this prerequisite knowledge can then be transferred from one sector to another. This characteristic helps explain why firms can switch easily from water to energy production or to managing cellular telephone networks. These sectors differ with respect to their technical properties yet do retain certain features in common.

ii) Industrial organization arguments
- Transaction costs. The organization of a large group that relies on a great number of subsidiaries and on networks of subcontractors can, by performing work in-house, avoid using the market, with its scheduling constraints, myriad of controls and associated extra costs. These internally-driven organizations, contractually flexible, constitute for some activities a viable alternative to the market outcomes (Coase 1937).
- Optimal technical systems. The mechanism of concession and leasing, which constitutes the very heart of the expansion of French urban services firms, implies the management of an entire technical system. In the sector of water distribution, this system extends from drawing at the source through delivery to the user and includes all the various

facilities for water treatment (plants), for storage (reservoirs) as well as for conveyance (pipes). This global presence allows engineers to design optimal solutions at the system level as opposed to the level of each sub-component. These solutions offer an efficiency/cost compromise which can prove more effective than cutting up the system into a sequence of activities.

5.4. The three paths towards global control: regulator, regulatory mechanisms and principles of self-regulation

First path: regulation by a regulator. Since the end of the XIXth century, it has been commonly admitted that monopoly markets must be controlled to insure that the firm does not abuse its dominant position. It is considered that the development of large firms in oligopolistic situations presents certain risks - excessive prices, sub-optimal technological choices for the locality, and a mix of diverse subsidies that serves to upset the non-monopolistic markets. In this case, the American solutions (AT&T) or the British ones (British Gas) display the most coherence. Nothing new needs to be invented. What's required is to demerge, separate the various components of the sequence, instill competition through new market entrants (as in the example of Mercury with respect to British Telecom), develop competitive tender procedures and establish regulatory institutions. The applicability of this formula (which was primarily set up for electricity distribution and then for telecommunications) to urban utility networks remains a question open to debate.

The regulator initially intervenes in laying out the rules for this two-party game. A classic problem in regulating monopolies is encountered herein, whereby the principle activity of a monopoly subjected to a particular kind of regulation is distinct from ancillary activities - forbidden for some, open to competition for others. Thereafter, the regulator accommodates the policies of the firms in making its presence felt to a greater or lesser extent.

However, it would seem that this vision is susceptible to a few criticisms once it has been applied to the urban infrastructure markets:
- Control implies a cost.
- The independence of the control institution is not assured; over time the risk of capture (corruption, influence, granting favors) appears.
- The set of criteria taken into consideration for control purposes is questionable. Since the controller is not privy to management details, he will tend to use global criteria, which would move urban services management more towards the realm of financial control criteria; nonetheless, this is a sector of concrete physical systems as well. This financial

aspect assumes even greater importance when devising financing schemes for service operations takes on an international dimension.

- The ground rules for the game taking place between controller and the type of control exercised could create a detrimental climate of mistrust and conflict in certain circumstances.

This series of arguments has led to examining other global organizational principles for these markets, even if the solution of an independent regulator remains satisfactory and necessary in a great number of countries.

Second path: regulation by regulatory mechanisms. The idea is that it is necessary to avoid controlling the detailed aspects and instead activate the regulatory mechanisms. A market assessment shows that these regulatory mechanisms actually exist and that they can efficiently replace, within certain contexts, what could be obtained elsewhere by a more specialized regulator, as demonstrated by the French example. These mechanisms fall into three distinct categories (see above for a more detailed discussion).

i) Regulation by the market: competition among products at the time of market entry, competition on capital markets and yardstick competition.

ii) Regulation by the organizing authorities which involves two distinct sub-mechanisms: global and political regulation by users and elected officials, and contract-based regulation.

iii) Regulation by "threat": impacts on reputation.

A third path to raise the issue concerns: formalizing the principles of self-regulation. Control is justified, above all, in order to protect society from the risk that the one in a position of strength - the large firm in a monopoly situation - abuses its advantage. Yet, regulation represents an action framework that classifies the large firm as a potential deviant. Much empirical evidence obtained from market observations across industrialized countries has highlighted that these firms do not behave like the robber barons described to us by the day's economists of the period between the two world wars. Firms do, most certainly, act with the goal in mind of developing, to the extent permitted, given the market's constraints. However, the superprofit associated with a monopoly position is, in fact, not their primary objective. Rather, they tend to integrate more long-term objectives; their staff shares some of the values of the public service ethic. Progress could be made if the major firms, cognizant of the structural inequalities of their position, were making their particular guidelines explicit : code of ethics, self-limitation principle, quality charter, etc. In the United States, the profession of lawyers is predominantly regulated in this fashion; it was also the case for AT&T between 1938 and 1956 with the principles of the Vail doctrine.

In other words, the "right" collective solution is not necessarily positioned where common sense would dictate, by controlling with the limitation principle. The large firm presents advantages for certain sectors under certain conditions of market organization. Market regulation is not always optimized in every case by simply multiplying the number of regulatory bodies. The countries seeking to enact these reforms should be wary of the risk of "institutional mimicking", which leads to importing packaged solutions, originated in and adapted to non-local contexts (Mény, 1993). The appropriate solution is undoubtedly determined by prescribed doses of several mechanisms at once that complement one another, balance one another and connect to the three paths indicated.

6. Références

Annales des Mines, avril 1991. *L'Europe des grands réseaux*. Paris.

Annales des Mines, octobre 1994. *Les réseaux de services publics*. Paris.

Beaud M. et Dostaler G. (1993). *La pensée économique depuis Keynes*. Paris, Seuil, 605p.

Coase R. (1937). The nature of the firm. in Williamson O. et Winter S. (dir.) (1991). *The nature of the firm. Origins, Evolution, and Development-*. Oxford University Press. NewYork, Oxford, 235p.

Curien N., Gensollen M. (1993). *Economie des télécommunications, ouverture et réglementation*, Economica, ENSPTT, Paris.

Curien N. (1995). L'économie des réseaux. *in La privatisation des services urbains en Europe*, Lorrain D. et Stoker G. (dir). Paris, La découverte, 230p.

Garrard J. (1993). *Le pouvoir local en Grande-Bretagne à la fin du XIXe siècle*, conference paper, Salford University, à paraître.

Haüssermann H. (1992). *Les infrastructures urbaines en Allemagne avant 1945*. Flux n°10, Paris, CNRS-GDR réseaux, p24-31.

Hirsch R. (1991). *Regulation and Technology in the Electric Utility Industry, in Regulation (Economic Theory and History)*, Hidh J. (ed.). Ann Arbor, The University of Michigan Press, 191pp.

Korte H. (1991). *Le développement de l'infrastructure dans la Ruhr, 1840-1990*. Paris, Flux, GDR réseaux, N°4 et 6.

Laffont J.J., Tirole J. (1993). *A theory of incentives in procurement and regulation*. Cambridge, The MIT Press, 704p.

Lorrain D. et Stoker G. (1997). *The privatization of Urban Services in Europe*. London, Pinter, 229p.

Loosdregt H.B. (1995). *Service public et gestion déléguée à l'entreprise privée*. Paris, AGHTM, p163-174.

Martinand Cl. (dir). (1986). *Le génie urbain*. Paris, La Documentation française, 294p.

Martinand Cl. (dir) (1993). *L'expérience française du financement privé des équipements publics*. Paris, Economica, 194p.

Mény Y. (dir.) (1993). Les politiques du mimétisme institutionnel, la greffe et le rejet. Paris, L'Harmattan, 285p.

Mintzberg H. (1993). *The rise and fall of strategic planning*. Prentice Hall, 458p

Simon J.P. (1991). *L'esprit des règles, réseaux et réglementation aux Etats-Unis*. Paris, L'Harmattan, 448p.

Stoffaës Ch. (dir) (1994). *L'Europe à l'épreuve de l'intérêt général*. Paris, Editions ASPEeurope, 517p.

Stoker G. (1995). Grande-Bretagne : le volontarisme politique, *in La privatisation des services urbains en Europe*, Lorrain D. et Stoker G. (dir). Paris, La découverte, 230p.

Vickers J. et Yarrow G. (1989). *Privatization, (An Economic Analysis)*- Cambridge, London, The MIT Press, 433p.

Williamson O.E. (1985). *The economic institutions of capitalism*. The Free Press, Macmillan, New York, 447p.

References of international institutions

Alaerts G.J., Blair T.L., F. Hartvelt. (1992). *Une stratégie pour la création de capacités dans le secteur de l'eau*. Delft, IHE/PNUD., 207p.

Briscoe J. (1992). *Pauvreté et alimentation en eau : comment aller de l'avant*. Washington DC. Finances et Développement.

Feder G. et Le Moigne G. (1994). *Une gestion équilibrée des ressources en eau*. Washington DC. Finances et Développement.

Kessides Ch. (1993). *Institutional options for the provision of infrastructure*. Washington DC, The World Bank, discussion paper, 56p.

Klein M. et Roger N. (1994). *Back to the future : the potential in infrastructure privatisation*. London, Oxford University Press, Amex Bank review, 28p.

Le Moigne G., Barghouti S., Feder G., Garbus L. , Xie M. (1992). *Country experiences with water resources management*. Washington DC., World Bank technical paper number 175, 213p.

Richard B. et Triche Th. (1994). Reducing barriers to private-sector participation *in Latin america's water and sanitation services*. Washington D.C. The World Bank, policy research working paper.

Serageldin I. (1994). *Water supply, sanitation and environmental sustainability; the financing challenge*. Washington D.C. The World Bank. 35p.

Serageldin I. and Steer A. (eds.) (1993). *Valuing the environment* (proceedings of the first annual international conference on environmentally sustainable development). Washington DC, The World Bank, ESD series, 192p.

Triche Th. (1994). *Designing water supply & sewerage, oversight institutions to fit the local context*. Washington DC., The World Bank, Lansdowne conference paper.

World Bank policy paper. (1993). *Water resources management,* Washington DC., The World Bank, 140p.

World Development Report, (1994). *Infrastructure for development.* Oxford, New York, Oxford University Press, 254p.

World Development Report (1992). *Development and the environment, World development indicators.* Oxford, New York, Oxford University Press, 308p.

Yepes G. (1994). *Water & sanitation sector, retrospective review of operations.* Washington DC, The World Bank Lansdowne conference paper.

Yepes G. (1993). *Performance indicators; water & sanitation utilities,* set 1&2. Washington DC. The World Bank, TWUWS.

CHAPTER 1

Claude Martinand

The public environment

Water is a vital, natural resource with complex physical, chemical and biological properties. The water cycle utilizes these properties through flows and stocks, thereby offering, in a given place and time, a resource in a quantity and quality more or less suited to various needs. Storing, transporting and treating water insures the flexibility for matching resources with needs, both spatially and temporally, provided the necessary and costly capital investments along with the appropriate management skills are available.

Uses of water have become quite diversified as a result of economic and social developments: drinking water, irrigation and drainage, waterway navigation, energy production (water works, hydroelectric power), water for industrial uses, flood protection, recreational uses (tourism, water sports), environmental protection. These uses often vie with another, are sometimes even conflictual, but they can nonetheless become compatible and complementary if accompanied by the right set of technical, legal and economic management guidelines plus an adapted facility base.

Efficient water management involves large numbers of public and private actors responsible for distinct geographical areas or sectors, often overlapping with one another, and always displaying an interdependence that requires a continual effort of coordination. This interdependence calls on everyone to cooperate in a multi-faceted fashion : each country has opted for unique approaches, suited to their specific historical and geographical contexts as well as to their cultural traditions and level of development.

Ancient civilizations, following the Neolithic Revolution, developed around water control for irrigation and transportation: Egypt, Mesopotamia, China and India. Economic surpluses gained from this development gave the opportunity for these civilizations to build and maintain the necessary hydraulic facilities ; they also guaranteed the needs of the political, military and religious power.

In Ancient Times, Romans became masters in the art of harnessing, conveying and storing water in large, sophisticated hydraulic networks, combining aqueducts, fountains, thermal baths and even sewers ("cloaca maxima"). These initial networks were managed by high-level civil servants (the "Prefect" for water in Rome); they were often damaged or destroyed during the great invasions, but were slowly revived during the Renaissance and during Modern Times. Ship canals and flood protection works were much more extensively built during the XVIIth and XVIIIth centuries.

Hygiene and public health concerns took priority in the XIXth century with the advent of hydroelectric power, industrialization and urbanization. Over the course of the XXth century, major conurbations were progressively equipped with water distribution and wastewater treatment facilities, followed by the rural areas.

Access to good quality water in sufficient quantity has now become a fundamental right. Besides, environmental concerns have led to additional pollution control measures concerning wastewater treatment, dumping in protected areas, storm runoff, which is often as polluted as wastewater. Demands on water quality (purety, taste, cleanliness) are becoming more and more stringent.

This brief historical overview was intended to highlight the multiple facets of water as well as the diversity and changing emphases of service concerns. In France today, there is a general consensus on the obvious public dimension to the organization and management of water resources. This situation does not exclude, and quite to the contrary rather encourages, the emergence of a wide array of private and public actors, both individually and collectively.

In economic terms, this "natural good" became a truly public property submitted to regulation ; then, through establishing a pricing mechanism, it has turned into a commodity, or even more a "product/service" whose proper management is apparently the result of many public interest concerns, thus giving rise to a basic public service.

There are six major river basins in France, each of them very different in nature. Technical know-how owes a lot to the Roman and Italian heritage ; this heritage dates back to the XVIIIth century with the creation of a Corps of State Engineers and the foundation in 1747 of the "Ecole Nationale des Ponts et Chaussées" professional civil engineering school. The colonial experiences in North Africa and Indochina were also a source of enrichment. Germanic-Roman law has served as the foundation for France's legal and institutional framework ; the result has been a system characterized by both its coherence and pragmatism. The 1964 Water Law (amended by the 1992 Law) has proved, through its thirty years of practice, the efficiency of the French institutional, legal, technical, pricing and financial mechanisms.

A true French "school of water management" became known and has gone to receive full recognition at the international level. This school's three basic tenets are : a global-scale policy approach towards water, the central role played by the River Basin Authorities, and the capacity to delegate service provision to private or public operators. Without pretending to portray a model, this extremely insightful experience can nonetheless inspire a meaningful examination of the issue for many countries, provided that the appropriate adaptations to reflect local conditions have been carried out.

o
o   o

Water management calls for establishing a suitable public environment. The public regulation (or this public policy), that meets several objectives at once, is set within the framework of institutions situated at distinct jurisdictional levels (local, regional, inter-regional, national and even international). It utilizes a wide range of regulatory instruments (technical, legal, economic and social norms) and control instruments as well; various actors are involved. Altogether, this produces a system where the principles of public service and the force and rules of market can coexist.

The objectives of public regulation

Water is a natural resource that must be available at all times, in sufficient quantity and quality, to meet the various interdependent needs of individuals and groups alike. This can only happen through at least a minimum set of rules of public order. Different issues are at stake: safety, risk prevention, public health, environmental protection (many external factors, both negative and positive, irreversible damage), well-balanced regional planning, social equality and social justice, and even issues of national defense and sovereignty. Each one of these objectives, as well as the way in which they are met, should be carefully analyzed, justified and defined so as to better match means with ends (principle of proportionality). Furthermore, except when the resource is overabundant, a rare occurrence these days, water should be managed economically, in accordance with the principles of sound economic, ecological and social efficiency, going beyond sheer economic and financial profitability.

The objectives of public regulation can also be examined within three principal dimensions:
- a temporal dimension : developing policies that accommodate the market's short run, the medium run of planning programs and the long run of resource management and sustainable development ;
- a spatial dimension : developing policies that accommodate different uses of space corresponding to different scales, spanning from the local to the global; the spaces being delimited could be next to one another, overlapping or interconnected;
- a social, or societal, dimension: from simple citizen to national Government or international institutions, including a host of intermediate bodies and the society at large, seeking to reconcile objectives of social equality and integration within different territorial dimensions, with objectives of freedom of lifestyle choices.

When the objectives to be weighed involve some very serious issues, only a truly democratic debate can guarantee durable, well-balanced, well-understood and well-accepted outcomes. However vital the role of the expert may be, politics can never be left out of these debates altogether.

Appropriate levels of jurisdiction for public regulation

Networks are found everywhere, in every spatial dimension; major networks serve to structure space. Therefore, natural river basins would appear the suitable choice for administrative jurisdiction over water management; interdependence between the various entities throughout the basin lend justification to this choice. However, this raises two kinds of problems:

- These natural geographical areas rarely coincide with the administrative and institutional boundaries specific to an empowered public authority. Besides, these zones often overlap several regions or sometimes several States; the river itself can even form a border in some cases;

- These geographical areas, for major rivers anyway, are too big to allow a refined management approach to meet the needs of various water consumers whose ultimate conflicts, or common concerns, can only be expressed locally.

Here's the reason, therefore, that for urban services based on the notion of local-level provision, like water distribution or wastewater collection, the administrative jurisdictional reference be local. In France, this fundamental role is played by the "commune", whether they be former church parishes or municipalities. Two explanations behind this situation: water is easier to store than to transport; and both water distribution and water treatment networks are essentially local in nature. The appropriate level for equalizing water prices should also be highlighted as a signal of social equality within these basic administrative jurisdictions. However, because of economies of scale, it is often useful to extend the selected jurisdiction to encompass several "communes" through intermunicipal cooperation which is particularly adapted to this kind of action.

The institutional, legal, technical and fiscal framework is usually created by the State and partially, by supra-national organizations, more specifically the European Union in the case of technical standards or rules on competition.

In fact, three, or sometimes four, levels of regulation are useful, even necessary, with each of them having its own scope or sharing responsibilities in accordance with the principle of "subsidiarity": deal at the lowest level possible with the maximum number of issues, only climbing to the next level when it is absolutely necessary. This complex situation implies a strong level of cooperation among the regulatory authorities in order to rectify the appropriateness of historical boundaries and to allow a global management of interdependence at the suitable level (usually at the level of the river basin). This cooperation among levels does not come naturally; it requires taking efficient and precise measures.

At the national government level itself, it is equally essential to set up coordination programs between divisions of different ministries that tend to favor their own sectorial points of view (health, environment, planning, transportation, agriculture, tourism, local authorities, civil safety, budget, economy, etc.).

Therefore, the emergence of a ministry that would "steer" or lead seems as necessary as it does fragile to implement. It's only recently that the French Ministry of the Environment has been performing this role.

Regulatory Instruments

In general, market and competition regulatory instruments are set apart from, or even opposed to, general regulatory instruments, "global control". It should be mentioned that the French term "régulation", in contrast with its English equivalent is not strictly limited to the field of regulatory policy.

Non-specific instruments include:
- technical, social and fiscal standards as well as the control over their application;
- technical and economic information, especially statistics, made available to all actors in order to direct or facilitate a rational decision-making process. This information provision obligation is itself a type of public responsibility that the government must usually assume;
- private or public authorities that incite useful concertation, debate and cooperation to take place, on the basis of shared information;
- general rules organizing the market and competition (especially anti-trust, abusive market leadership practices and illegal government assistance) and control measures.

The market, along with fair and longstanding competition among the economic actors, doesn't come about naturally; it is a complex social structures relying on a shared set of culture values and ethics serving to create a true mechanism of self-regulation that can become a most effective instrument.

Specific regulatory instruments include:
- planning and programming infrastructure projects of national interest;
- rules for entering the market of service suppliers: exclusive vs. special rights (notably in the case of a natural monopoly), approvals, permits, agreements or contracts, specifications highlighting the rights and obligations of operators, terms for potentially auctioning these rights or contracts, statutes of the operators granted the running of facilities or services, etc.;
- rules concerning pricing and eventual public financing (this key issue will be addressed later on);
- rules allowing, or even encouraging, cooperation among actors as well as complementarity among water uses;
- different kinds of incentives: positive ones (public contributions, incentive clauses in contracts) or negative ones (taxes, fiscal measures like "polluter payer");
- methods of participation, association or consultation among the various actors involved in the regulatory system and resource management.

An advanced and quite global form of regulation combines different instruments, both specific and non-specific, in a spirit of efficiency and equity, resulting from a harmonious balance among the variety of possible concerns. It seems that the key issue is to coordinate the market with the public service, as well as to find an equilibrium between competition and cooperation among actors.

Regulators

There are three main types of regulatory mechanisms besides the self-regulation mentioned above. Two of these three mechanisms can be considered conventional:

- the administrative model of regulation wherein the public authority delegates to its own services, under the control of its executive and procedural bodies, the responsibility for drafting the rules, making specific decisions, negotiating contracts, etc. This model tends to dominate in France for nationalized firms, may lead to confusion between regulator and public-sector operator, in the case of in-house management, and, more often, between regulator and overseer or majority shareholder of State companies; and
- the independent expert model of the English "regulatory authority" type or the American "regulatory commission" type.

In both cases, it is hard to avoid the risk of the regulatory authority being held captive by the operator, in light of the structural asymmetry of information and expertise between the two parties, thereby shifting this relationship between accommodation and permanent conflict. This the reason why it seems appropriate in the case of water management is to assemble the parties concerned for a detailed comparison of the vying interests and points of view, thus encouraging movement towards a more balanced situation or a realistic compromise agreeable to both sides.

The 1964 Law that created of the River Basin Authorities was specifically aimed at bringing together the main parties involved in water management policy within the framework of a more modern form of regulation, comprising:
- the various user or customer categories through their representatives;
- the same categories broken down by polluter vs. beneficiary, both reliant upon the same water resource;
- taxpayers through their elected officials from individual municipalities;
- third parties, either impacted by positive or negative external factors, or representatives of future generations whose interests must be taken into consideration.

This regulatory authority is based on implementing both economic incentive instruments and the "polluter-payer" principle; its objective is to solve, within a given river basin territory, specific problems related to the enhanced value, protection and management of water resources.

Similarly, conventional administrative regulation can be improved at the local level through the consultation and participation of the various actors involved: not only customers/citizens but also staff and management of the operating company itself, as well as environmental protection groups (fishermen, etc.).

The central role of rate structures in the public regulation of water

The pricing of water reflects the primary strategic orientations within an overall water management policy:
- the importance of social justice for all users subjected to the same pricing structure;
- achieving a balance between user and taxpayer;
- achieving a balance between taxpayers at the local, regional and national levels; mechanisms for equalizing financial resources and the ensuing redistributions;
- achieving a balance between users who pollute and third parties who are penalized;
- achieving a balance between short-term and medium-term objectives through self-financing and borrowing mechanisms set up to finance future investments;
- major economic signals, giving directions to the economic actors, while not constraining them (as happens all too often in a regulatory context), thereby leading to efficiently managing an often-limited resource.

In fact, the "real cost of water" includes both internal and external cost components:
- internal costs: ascribed to a specific management unit (investment and operations, depreciation rules not being easily identifiable because of the facilities' very long life cycle and the different techniques employed for financing through taxes, self-financing or loans);
- external costs: ascribed outside the management unit, more or less integrated through additional taxes borne by users.

The pricing policy therefore represents, in most instances, a compromise between financing entirely through taxes, regardless of consumption level and direct costs yet guaranteeing everyone equal access to the resource (the notion of an "individual service"), and financing entirely through user and polluter fees for up to the full cost. While the latter may be more economically efficient, it nonetheless remains difficult to implement for lower-income users and certain consumer groups.

The mechanism that was adopted in France is a mixed one; it guarantees some level of social equity both at the local level, where the rate structure guarantees equal access to the resource, and at the river basin jurisdictional level, through a formula of rate equalization. In addition, the State level provides another source of social equity through several transfer mechanisms in the subsidies channeled by government to the municipalities (adjustment of the most blatant disparities) and through incentive funds for the development of water networks, especially in rural areas.

In practice, the compromise that was chosen at the municipal level (or by the municipalities that join together reflects a choice amidst a hierarchy of the following objectives:
- economic (to avoid waste);
- financial (to balance budgets);
- social (to insure service to lower-income households, protect health concerns, hygiene and public order);
- ecological (to protect the natural environment and our long-term future).

Indeed, the price of water still varies greatly, and it should remain that way (up to a 30-fold variation): for physical and geographical reasons (quality and availability of the resource, fluctuation of the needs and the resource, geographical dispersion of users, etc.); for financial reasons linked to the size and length of investment programs.

Standards on water quality, as well as on water effluent discharged into the environment upon treatment, are also major factors of pricing trends, along with consumption levels. The price of water is expected to double in France within the next ten years as a result of recent European Directives concerning wastewater.

Another equitable balance among various user groups (farmers, households, industries) can also lead to heated political debate, especially when it comes to adjusting existing rate structures that are simply unacceptable in the long run (the case of mineral pollution in aquifers through the use of fertilizers).

As opposed to the field of electric energy, there are no practical applications as of yet to modulate water prices with respect to use patterns at different times during the day, depending on the availability of the resource; such a measure would probably be more effective than the conventional, more restrictive measures taken during droughts. However, this could only be envisioned with the implementation of metering systems that are more sophisticated than the ones currently in place. Varying the price of water within a given geographical area would lead to dismantling the process of local price equalization; however, this option should not be totally ruled out in the long run for large water consumers.

Finally, the price of water, which is in fact a service rate because it's not the simple result of an adjustment between supply and demand (given the monopoly-run distribution system), must be fixed with regulatory authority oversight and eventually approved, since the commodity in question affects the areas of health and public hygiene.

The long-term contract as a tool for organizing the regulator-operator relationship

The French experience in delegating urban services is a longstanding one; it is diversified and has globally been qualified as effective. "Leasing" or "lease agreements" and concessions are the two conventional forms of delegation, but each contract is in fact a unique, context-specific case, which serves to highlight the great flexibility of the French model.

This model is aimed at combining the following elements:
- management and operational efficiency of having a service run by an independent private or public company;
- control exercised by the local public authority over major decisions, especially pricing structures and capital investment programs;
- retention within the public domain of facilities, even in the case of a true concession, that might have been financed, in all or in part, by a private concessionary company, (whose ownership can never be granted to the operator);
- a financial balance by assuring an equitable split between the rights and obligations of the operator, as stipulated in the contract's specifications, including mechanisms to readjust responsibilities in case of "force majeure" or to handle requests to modify the contract's general conditions; and
- implementation of a competitive bidding process for public procurements particularly since the promulgation of the 1993 Law. Indeed, there is, in the long run, a real level of self-regulation and an obviously competitive environment among the major French service operators, which does explain their success abroad, on every continent. This competitiveness is spurred by the strength of a rather efficient public sector involvement.

The guiding philosophy behind service delegation is based on the notion of long-term confidence and partnership, and should, in no way, be confused with the attributes of conventional public works and supply contracts. This philosophy implies a high level of technical, financial and legal competence on both sides, resulting from longstanding traditions and common cultural values. Both the role of the State's public function, its mobilization and its breadth of experience, along with the role of the local public service, strengthened by the 1982-83 decentralization legislation, constitute key conditions for success.

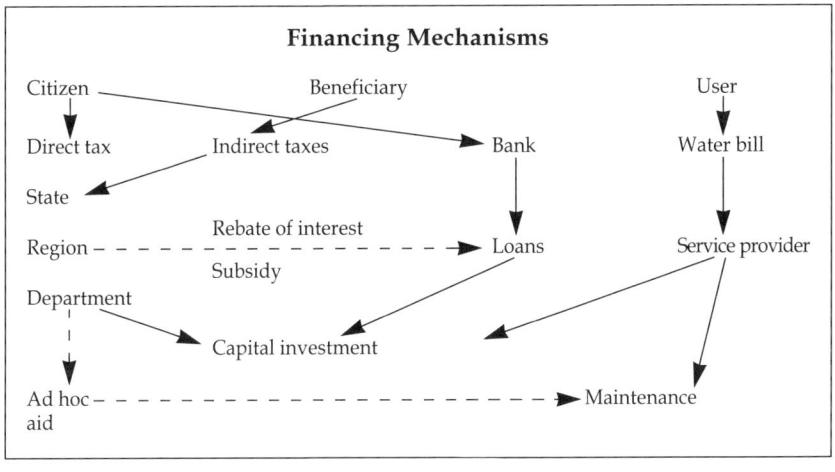

Financing Mechanisms

○
○ ○

At an initial glance, the French model could seem to present a level of complexity and cultural specificity to hinder its applicability to foreign contexts, such as in countries with an Anglo-Saxon-inspired legal system (as opposed to the "Latin-type" legal system) or in the developing nations. However, the experience has, in fact, shown itself not only to be flexible and pragmatic, but also conceptually rigorous and capable of evolving, thereby yielding:

- a source of reflection and inspiration for all policy matters related to water, provided that the vital stakes have been well-defined and the appropriate transformations and/or simplifications have been carried out; and

- a decisive factor in the success experienced by French public service operators throughout the world within a wide variety of contexts.

Yet, no approach is ideal, and the continuing internationalization of markets in these sectors will undoubtedly give rise to further developments in the competing public service provision models and, ultimately, to their convergence.

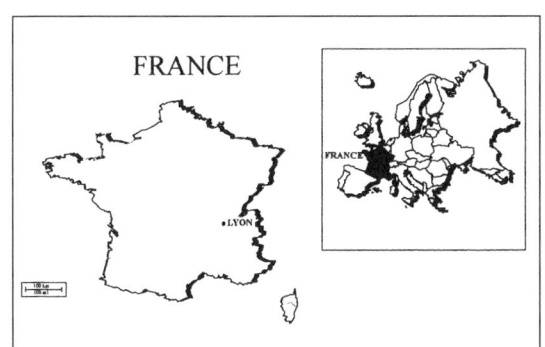

CHAPTER 2

Franck
Scherrer

Water service in the Lyon metropolitan area: A century of history in public and private management

The Lyons metropolitan area, France's second largest, with a population of one million plus, has over the ages developed a reputation as being a serious and relatively discreet place. The public services sector of water supply -the invisible factor- keeps perhaps more than elsewhere an especially low profile. The city is served by a proximate source of water that's both plentiful and high-quality, thanks to the collection points located within the Rhone River's alluvial groundwater table. Since 1986, operations of the water supply network have in essence been leased to the Compagnie Générale des Eaux (C.G.E.) under the effective and strict control of the Metropolitan Government Council (the "Communauté Urbaine"). In many respects, this contract which represents C.G.E.'s largest contract in France outside the Paris Region is exemplary for the international urban services group not only for its technical management requirements, but also for the contractual and day-to-day working relationships it has fostered with the concession-granting authority. Foreign clients have looked to the Lyons contract in order to understand how the requirements of a public service can be successfully reconciled with a private-sector management approach, styled as the "French model".

The current situation is the vestige of a long and somewhat troubled history. It is often overlooked that C.G.E. was specifically created in 1853 to establish and operate Lyons' very first water supply network and that this company has been present continuously, in one form or another, in the Lyons area for the past century and a half. Even if an explanation were required for this rare display of staying power, the relative serenity of today's situation cannot, in any event, be projected into the past quite so easily. The history of the relationship between C.G.E. and the City has had its share of ups and downs, as the principal defining trait of this relationship testifies: after having lost the concession in 1900 for the City of Lyons, to a municipally-run agency, following a half-century of consecutive service, C.G.E. would perservere all the way until 1986, when it became once again the area's water services operator, thereby accomplishing a stunning yet low-key return.

It must be kept in mind that during the XIXth century, the City of Lyons and C.G.E. were quite distinct from what they've become towards the end of the XXth century. This feature makes the continuity of their relationship seem even more remarkable. The parameters associated with the distribution of drinking water (environmental aspects, hygiene measures, type of housing, lifestyle and consumer demands, regulations, etc.) have been constantly evolving throughout this century. Over the same period, the "water services profession" has also undergone significant changes in both its technical and financial aspects. Furthermore, although Lyons had already confirmed its status as a major city during the last century[1] its first "industrial"-type water supply service was on a more modest scale, and even more so in the suburban areas, which at the time were composed of small villages and settlements. What follows in this presentation will hopefully provide a better understanding of the evolutionary forces that helped shape this remarkable history of continuity.

In addition to its interest from a local perspective, the history of Lyons' water supply highlights the importance of relationships over the long run, which for a variety of reasons (the spreading of infrastructure construction programs and return on investment over time, the slow reconciliation of satisfying needs, accommodating urban growth and advancing a complex technical network) tends to be the most appropriate time scale to fully appreciate the evolution of this sector. Such a long-term horizon cannot be neglected when performing evaluations and analyses that frame the ongoing debate between public and private management approaches.

---

1. The Lyons area counted some 250,000 residents in the mid-XIXth century

Following a succinct overview of the city itself, this century-old story of Lyons' water supply services will be told in the simplest manner possible in order to glean a few lessons:

- on the capacity of a private operator to adapt to quite varied situations,
- on the importance of the transitory and evolutionary aspects of the contractual relationships between public and private actors,
- on the time lags encountered in the evolution of the roles of the main actors, and finally
- on those features directly attributable to the current situation.

A few historical and geopolitical highlights

Ever since its founding by the Romans in the first century B.C., Lyons has consistently benefitted from its outstanding geographic position at the crossroads of very distinct forms of transport. In fact, the city's development and its span of influence have only breifly been on a par with this exceptional locational advantage: at the beginning of the XVIth century, when Lyons was hailed as the intellectual capital of the French Renaissance and as the port of entry for powerful Italian mercantile dynasties. This prominence was also apparent during the XIXth century, though to a lesser extent, when its industrial strength gained recognition. Lyons now does not wield the clout of the capital city of a major principality or a city-state like Barcelona, Milan or Frankfurt, with which it is often compared; it has definitely established itself as France's second-largest metropolitan area, yet does not enjoy a dominant role at the European level within this category, in terms of economic might, as do the others.

The longstanding limitations imposed on Lyons' development because of the centralization of national power in Paris can be traced as a rather complex relationship between City and State during the past two centuries. Deprived for a long time of its municipal autonomy in the XIXth century, Lyons gradually wrested control away from the central government's oversight as of the XXth century, most notably by developing its own design capacity and expertise in the areas of planning and public works. Up until the past thirty years or so, the city hadn't yet procured the financial or budgetary resources commensurate with its size, while the State only invested heavily in the area's growth and development over two brief spans: under the Second Empire (1852-1870) and during the 1950's and 1960's. The history of municipal water and wastewater services has been characterized as much by the need for autonomy in design and decision-making as it has by a lack of budgetary maneuvering room and by a stretched-out capital investment timetable.

The final geopolitical feature specific to the Lyons area would be the tight physical constraints on its central city's land area. Since the beginning of this century, the major share of population growth and industrial development has been located within neighboring municipalities, especially the city of Villeurbanne. Over this same period, several projects to incorporate these adjacent municipalities into the City of Lyons, while not necessarily fruitful, would nonetheless serve to stamp the relationship between central city and suburbs as one of longstanding mutual distrust. Along the same lines, problems pertaining to the intermunicipal development of infrastructure facilities and urban services did necessitate a bit earlier on than elsewhere (around 1930-40) the creation of municipal cooperation. Even though in the area of water supply the boundary between central city and suburb had been rather well-defined up until 1969, as shown later on, cooperation in terms of wastewater services and, to a lesser extent, public transport would provide the training ground in establishing a metropolitan area-wide government. Today's "Communauté Urbaine" (Metropolitan Government Council representing 55 individual municipalities) has benefitted from this initial experience.

1853, 1900, 1928, 1970 and 1986

These five dates highlight the most significant stages in the political and economic history of Lyons' water supply services.

The creation. The first of these five dates, 1853, places us within the general context of France under the Second Empire, an authoritarian regime during which one priority of government intervention was urban renewal. This political focus is especially well-known through the example of the major urban works programs undertaken by Paris's Prefect Haussmann - laying out an entire network of large thoroughfares, creating new parks and gardens, widening the coverage of water supply and wastewater service areas, etc. Its impact would be felt in France's provincial cities as well. The Prefect Vaisse, Lyons' counterpart to Haussmann, who also enjoyed widespread powers, launched within a span of a few months a grandiose redevelopment project: the renovation of central Lyons by introducing new thoroughfares in addition to laying out the city's first ever networks of wastewater collection, public transit and water distribution.

With respect to the area of water supply services, Vaisse took only a few weeks to rule on an open public debate that had gone unresolved for thirty years on the best means of substituting a true water distribution system in place of the former system of public fountains and private wells that had previously prevailed. He intervened directly in the creation of the Compagnie Générale des Eaux de France (at the beginning of May 1853), which submitted for his approval a few days hence a water supply plan for the city that had been prepared several years earlier by a brilliant public works engineer; the plan was quickly adopted. In 1859, the underground tunnels that would enable drawing water from the Rhone River's alluvial groundwater table, along with the water treatment plant and an initial piping network, were operational. Operations of Lyons' very first water supply system, built by C.G.E. at its own expense, was granted to the company through a 99-year, full-risk concession with the possibility of buyout by the City after thirty years.

From the outset, operating conditions proved to be unsatisfactory for both parties concerned. Neither of them foresaw that household water consumption was going to increase so rapidly[2], and although the choice for a water source would turn out to be an astute one[3], water production using the means available in that period quickly became insufficient. In addition, those politicians concerned with spreading to the widest extent possible the benefit of water distribution deemed that the company was applying excessive rates; meanwhile, the company was complaining that the City was being wasteful in its use of water for street cleaning purposes. A new fixed-fee rate structure proposed in 1874 would be responsible for generating a dramatic rise in household consumption and exacerbate the water shortage problem[4]. Between 1862 and 1874, the new capital investments required to increase the volume of water produced were carried out with public monies, thereby altering the incentives for the City in the current concessionary arrangement.

---

2. 10,000 households were connected after ten years, 20,000 after twenty years, or one-sixth of all residences. The initial agreement called for a daily production of 20,000 m^3, half of which was for the city (decorative fountains, street cleaning, etc.). Five years after the beginning of service operations, daily needs were estimated at a minimum of 45,000 m^3, and twenty years after at more than 250,000 m^3.

3. The Lyons metropolitan area has always been chiefly supplied by aquifers in the alluvial groundwater table of the Rhone River. The primary zones for drawing water have been moved since the XIXth century, yet are still located within immediate proximity of the metropolitan area.

4. The initial service subscriptions proposed a volume-based service rate thanks to metered faucets that dispensed at least 100 liters a day for 22 francs/year. The new fixed rates were higher (from 36 francs), yet since the Lyons-area households were used to leaving the faucet open, actual consumption skyrocketed.

Beginning in 1878, Lyons eventually won back its municipal and political autonomy: local elected officials, for the most part Republicans and from the left, rejected the vestiges of city management from the Second Empire, that had included the concession of its water services. Thus, at the date specified in the contract (1885), the Municipal Council decided, in consideration of the service's inadequacies, to buy back the concession. Yet, since the City was lacking both the human resources (its public works staff was just starting to take shape) and financial means (budgetary flexibility was extremely limited) to support its decision, the concessionary contract with C.G.E. was, in reality, being renewed from one year to the next.

A 15-year period (1885-1900) thereby ensued, a period during which the water supply issue would provide a recurrent and important topic for public debate. Grandiose water supply schemes would be pitted against one another (from piping in water from the Annecy Lake to exploiting the sources of the Ain River Valley[5]) all in the name of public hygiene precepts and general welfare of the citizenry, which were major political themes at the turn of the century. In addition, the vested interests of various financial groups, from both Lyons and elsewhere, were also taken into consideration. The plan presented by C.G.E. won support from the State (represented by the Prefect and the Corps of Civil Engineers), the Public Hygiene Advisory Committee (as well as the City's Public Works Office, under the direction of a member of France's illustrious Civil Engineering Corps). Given the strained state of relations existing between City and State as described above, this support served in greater favor of C.G.E. in the opinion of a majority of local politicians, who, during heated debates, considered the company arrogant with respect to the Municipal Council and over-confident of its endorsements from well-placed officials.

While seeking to preserve its entrenched interests, C.G.E. undertook a new, more decisive strategy. Beginning in 1867, and even more aggressively as of 1885, it set out to incorporate the Lyons suburbs into its service territory and, one municipality after another, built (up until 1926) a vast concessionary zone whose networks actually encircled entirely the central city. The mayors of the suburban communities felt in no way concerned by the conflict between the City of Lyons and C.G.E. Short of invoking the term prescience, this territory would nonetheless go on to become the backbone of the urban expansion areas during the XXth century.

---

5. The Ain River Valley ends at a distance of 30 kilometers from Lyons.

Municipal management. The City of Lyons gradually abandoned its grand urban schemes, contented instead to extend the zones of water extraction and to seek a compromise solution with C.G.E., in the form of an incentive management contract[6]. At the end of 1899, the Municipal Council, during a heated electoral campaign, forced the Mayor into a minority position on this issue and voted to transform the city's water services into an in-house municipal department (direct public-sector management) as of January 1, 1900. This surprise decision on behalf of municipally-controlled management, which led the City and C.G.E. to battle in court over the appropriate buyout compensation, would become, a few years later, the ideological "spearhead" for backers of "municipal socialism". It was Edouard Herriot, Mayor of Lyons from 1905 to 1957 and a key political figure during the Third Republic, who initially led this movement.

Lyons' Municipal Water Department ("Régie des Eaux de Lyon") thus became exemplary of public management of public services being more efficient, more cost-effective and more "socially conscious" than its private counterpart[7]. The concern over achieving exemplarity steered the City towards massive capital investment programs (on the order of 22 million francs) in the 1920's, which didn't necessarily correct the continual deficiencies in the service. The Mayor of Lyons proclaimed that it was virtually impossible to limit water consumption for residents of a city served by two abundantly-flowing rivers. Between 1931 and 1934, the widespread use of water meters in dwellings instead of unmetered faucets marked the end of Edouard Herriot's dream to supply water plentifully and nearly free of charge to his electorate. In fact, the measure to introduce meters along with the economic downturn combined to reduce water consumption drastically[8] and, at least temporarily, eliminate the prospect of shortages. In accepting thereafter to simply manage the existing situation, the Municipal Water Department would assume a dormant posture for over thirty years.

---

6. The project covered by the incentive management –"Régie intéressée"– contract included buying back facilities from C.G.E., which would have kept just the status of a fixed-fee management service with a commission on profits realized.

7. The water service rates previously proposed by C.G.E. varied depending on the number of household members and began at 36 francs per year (for a household of one to three members). The new rates proposed by the Lyons Municipal Water Department varied in relation to the rent paid for housing and began at 12 francs/year (for a rent of less than 500 francs).

8. from 236,000 m^3/day in 1931 to 160,000 m^3/day in 1934.

Suburban intermunicipality. At the same time, the suburban network, being operated by C.G.E. in 26 municipalities, began a new phase in its evolution. 1928 is, in this respect, a critical date; it was in October of this year that a deadly typhoid epidemic (quickly halted by the adoption of emergency public health and safety measures) struck the residents of suburbs served by C.G.E., which had distributed contaminated water. Though the company's responsibility was only indirect, its reputation nonetheless suffered tremendously[9]. During the same year, the municipalities served by C.G.E. formed a Suburban Intermunicipal Water Services Syndicate in order to better stand up to a sole operator. Interestingly, aside from their mutual mistrust towards C.G.E. and of what they perceived as a certain lack of transparence purposely built into network operations, the area's industrial and working-class communities to the East and the rural and agricultural communities to the West actually had very little in common.

Lengthy negotiations were held to substitute one unique concessionary contract for the multiplicity of individual municipal contracts; they weren't terminated until 1949. Actually, this new concessionary contract with C.G.E. was, in part, more similar to a leasing agreement ("affermage"), in that the investments programmed to accommodate growth at the urban fringe would be at the expense of the localities themselves. The signing of the contract coincided with the implementation by the Syndicate of a bold plan to extend and modernize both the service and the network. Fifty years, after affecting the City of Lyons, the issue of water supply would become a major political battleground for suburban municipalities, symbolizing not only their coming of age in the modern urban world, but also the affirmation of an identity distinct from that of the central city.

With this new program in place, the suburbs took a 15-year lead over the City of Lyons, which would require the stark warning of January 1963 (when the main pumping station was shut down due to freezing temperatures) to realize the extent of its service's inadequacies. Incited by its newly-elected mayor, nurturing a growing reputation as a "great builder" (Louis Pradel), the City of Lyons took its turn at launching an investment program of mammoth proportions (new water sources, new water purification plants, etc.)[10]. Nonetheless, the cost

---

9. A small creek that crossed a zone of water extraction, which was merely dammed up by C.G.E., gradually transformed into a natural sewer by virtue of the nearby urbanization, thereby contaminating the river's groundwater table.

10. As opposed to his predecessor, Louis Pradel would rely heavily on borrowing. This program was ultimately completed in 1994.

of catching up after thirty years of inactivity by "accelerating" system development was particularly onerous, and the future metropolitan authority, the "Communauté Urbaine", would find itself overburdened by debt during the first half of the 1980's.

The metropolitan organizing authority. Following a law passed in 1964[11], the Lyons metropolitan area was obliged to accept the creation in 1969 of a supra-municipal administrative entity, the "Communauté Urbaine" of Lyons, that comprised, in addition to Lyons city proper, the 28 member municipalities of the former Suburban Intermunicipal Water Services Syndicate plus a good number of other peripheral communities, which represented a complete reorganization of the existing administrative framework. Water supply did become one obligatory responsibility of the newly-formed "Communauté Urbaine" (which assumed authority in the place of existing municipal agencies and syndicates) and, along with wastewater services, was the least contested politically, given the longstanding experience of intermunicipal cooperation in these public service areas.

Initially, the planning and public works staff of the "Communauté Urbaine" was composed, for the most part, of City of Lyons personnel, since they were by far the most numerous and competent in the entire metropolitan area. Many plans, designs and methods specific to the City of Lyons were therefore simply transferred to the metropolitan level of government. Such was the case for the water services department, which essentially consisted of staff from the former Lyons Municipal Water Department. It was clear that all water services for the metropolitan area were not going to be placed under direct public management; so with the intention of standardizing water rates over the entire metropolitan area's territory, a new leasing contract was signed in 1970 with C.G.E. that reduced summarily its role. Just as in 1900, those facilities (treatment plant and suburban distribution network) still belonging to the company were bought back, its operations responsibility over the water extraction zones and treatment plants was also lost to the new Water Services Department of the "Communauté Urbaine". Only the leasing contract for water distribution to the municipalities it had previously been serving was retained. The pendulum would take fifteen years to swing back.

---

11. As was the case in the United States and Great Britain during the same era, the 1958-72 period was marked in France by the political concern over rationalizing local government structures through measures to incite cooperation or even to merge municipalities.

The delegation on the metropolitan area. As of the 1980's, with the legitimacy of the "Communauté Urbaine" firmly established, water supply was no longer a hot political issue but a technical one instead. Preoccupations then turned to management efficiency, inasmuch as the level of indebtedness of the "Communauté Urbaine" in the area of water supply was quite significant.

Against this new, more favorable political backdrop, C.G.E. once again took to the offensive on two fronts. First of all, the company, acting in a very timely fashion, seized the current themes of urban ecology and ecological risks and raised awareness to the real problem of assuring drinking water production if the main aquifers serving the metropolitan area were contaminated by Rhone River pollution descending downstream. In 1984, C.G.E. submitted a proposal to the "Communauté Urbaine" to construct a "turnkey" backup water purification plant and act as concessionaire.

Immediately thereafter, and once again in keeping with the times (in France, the issues of deteriorating urban infrastructure and quality of service began emerging during the 1980's), arguments concerning the vulnerability of some of the network's key pipeline sections, which were already somewhat deteriorated, and the standardization of service to users were strongly forwarded during negotiations. In 1986, these negotiations eventually led to C.G.E. obtaining from the "Communauté Urbaine" executive committee a leasing agreement for water supply operations throughout nearly all the Lyons metropolitan area[12], thus bringing to an end the 86-year existence of the Lyons Municipal Water Department.

This water services privatization decision was officially confirmed during the period 1990-1992 with the ratification of several technical and financial adjustments to the contract, as negotiated by the "Communauté Urbaine".

The new executive committee then set up a well-structured team, to insure control over the execution of the leasing agreement and to carry out certain vital missions that had not been delegated (new construction work).

---

12. Water supply to a few outlying municipalities is leased out to other operating companies, SDEI and SEREPI. These companies, previously independent and specialized in water distribution to rural areas, were both recently bought out by Lyonnaise des Eaux.

C.G.E.' s hundred-year adaptation

What lessons can be gleaned from this complex history broadly summarized herein? An initial inquiry concerns the continual presence, ever since 1853, of a private-sector service provider, a presence that represents considerable staying power in light of changes in both the local and national contexts. One hint of a response to this line of inquiry lies in C.G.E.'s capacities to adapt to a wide variety of situations.

From the beginning, C.G.E. benefitted from, thanks to its first 99-year concession, what could be called an "imperial privilege". Unfamiliar to the city and to the local investment community, the company was perceived as arrogant by Lyons' elected officials. In addition, it was unable to satisfy the increasing demand for water. It narrowly escaped, in Lyons at any rate, the graveyard where a whole host of XIXth-century private urban services companies eventually wound up.

The first active, as well as decisive, strategy that appeared around 1870-80 was territorial in nature: the gradual conquest of suburban municipalities, lasting up until 1926. It most certainly took the form of a growth extension strategy; forecasting suburban growth rates for the next century was obviously impossible in the XIXth century. Providing service to small, rural communities, especially those located at higher elevations (to the west of Lyons), with relatively low volume demands proved a costly venture.

The precariousness of the Lyons situation, beginning in 1885, amidst a year-to-year renewable contract and the threat of buyout, also served to incite the company to geographically diversify its activities. Upon close examination of the map depicting this "suburban conquest", the premise behind such a statement is strengthened, and the overall strategy employed begins to resemble that of a classic board game: surround the opponent, being the City of Lyons, in order to bolster those advantages already acquired, or in this case to remain an indispensable partner to the metropolitan capital. Unable to reach this objective in 1900, C.G.E. did nonetheless wind up owner and operator of a surprisingly vast peripheral ring network.

In the suburbs themselves, two distinct characteristics would favor the staying power of the company: firstly, the conditions of individual municipal concessionary contracts remained confidential, particularly with respect to rate structures and levels, which varied from one locality to the next. It was difficult to determine whether one community was paying for the advantages accorded another.

Secondly, since the concessionary contracts were signed one after the other over a period of more than fifty years (from 1867 to 1926), concession expiration dates (or buyback dates) were all well-spread over time. It was therefore both difficult and costly for any one of these municipalities to decide on its own to renounce or buy back the concession, given that they were all part of the same network.

The creation in 1928 of the Suburban Water Services Syndicate represented a direct response to these characteristics, as elected officials suspected the company of over-exploiting its position (the press at the time referred to the syndicate as a defense agency). Yet, weakened by a lack of political focus in the pre-World War II years, the Syndicate only really started to take shape in the 1950's, thanks to the financial support of the State's post-war reconstruction and redevelopment efforts. From that point on, a drastic change in the concessionaire's attitude, which corresponded perhaps to a more general change in C.G.E.'s corporate strategy at the national level, can be observed. The concessionaire began assuming a distinctly low profile in line with the intermunicipal authority, which alone reaped the glory and the dividends from an improved service. The operator, remaining (very) discreet and efficient, at the ready to serve local authorities, would then appear; such is the image that has remained up to this very day the distinctive trademark of this company.

It's through relying on this profile, at any rate, that C.G.E. has benefitted from the transition in 1986 to the private management of the entire water supply network for the Lyons metropolitan area. One additional feature that appeared in the 1980's should perhaps be added to this profile: that of the multi-service firm (from water supply to public transit, from communications to urban development projects), able to propose "turnkey"-type neighborhood development projects to cities. By virtue of the changing environment for public service companies during the mid-1980's, C.G.E. was also present in Lyons both as operator of the cable television service and as real estate developer for a prestigious and politically-sensitive new business center project within the "Cité Internationale". From then on, it has become difficult to distinguish between what pertains strictly to a business diversification and what is really some form of "commercial benefit" as part of the price for running the water supply services.

The capacity to change behavior or approach depending on historically-variable contexts, while perhaps not a sufficient argument by itself to explain the durability of C.G.E.'s presence in Lyons, does nonetheless stand out as a characteristic specific to this type of operator.

The contract and the transition

This aspect of evolution and adaptation is also pertinent in the contractual relationships existing between public and private actors, which have over time tended to become a lot less rigid than a straightforward legal interpretation would suggest. This history has shown that the moments of major decisions, taken to settle key issues of public vs. private management principles, were in fact not the most crucial over the long run, or in any case less crucial than the somewhat drawn-out transitionary periods.

It has already been mentioned that the decision in 1900 to create the Lyons Municipal Water Department was, in large measure, due to the economic climate of the time, as the municipality's left-wing politicians jumped on this occasion to undermine the position of an "opportunistic" mayor, who was about to lose his seat.

In contrast, the 1986 "privatization" decision seemed altogether justified by a number of arguments: vulnerability of water supply sources and degradation of the distribution network, consistency in service provision and indebtedness. The decision was the outcome of a classical political debate, yet it must be pointed out that this privatization scheme was neither a stated objective during the previous electoral campaign nor a determinant element of the program initiated by the newly-elected President of the "Communauté Urbaine". The preliminary negotiations were actually conducted without much media fanfare. Without going as far as labeling the decision accidental in nature, the hypothesis could nonetheless be forwarded that, as in other cities, the executive committee exploited this opportunity first and foremost to redirect its actions towards objectives heretofore considered more strategic and less debt-ridden than metropolitan water supply.

From another vantage point, it would appear that the nature of contractual relations between service operator and local authorities has continuously been evolving. The concession, in the strictest sense of the term, has only really existed in Lyons over a nine-year period, from 1853 to 1862. From 1862 through 1900, public financing stepped in to relieve the investment pressure on the private company for new facilities; C.G.E. then only retained responsibility for their operations. This mix of public with private investment and of concessionaire with lessee is encountered repeatedly: in the suburbs between the 1950's and 1970's, and still to this day (a leasing agreement covering the extent of the distribution network, and a concession for the backup plant).

From now on, whether subsequent agreements between C.G.E. and local authorities are called concessions or leases, a certain number of features are recognizable from this evolution. First among them is a long-term convergence towards more balanced relationships concerning the status of leasing arrangements, through a series of empirical and progressively "fine-tuned" adjustments. The agreement of 1970 alone has already been amended ten times, thus an average of one amendment every two and a half years. Put differently, both the concept and the application of delegated management practices have been maturing and slowly molding for a century now; it's an evolution wherein the Lyons example displays, and to a certain extent benefits from, today's well-balanced situation.

A multiplicity of actors and their applicable time scales

This history of Lyons' water supply services can also be characterized by the many time scale differences exhibited in the evolution of the different actors. This feature pertains to both their numbers and their varying nature, especially within the Lyons metropolitan area, which has spanned for long periods a wide array of municipalities. Furthermore, the time scales applicable to these actors - in terms of action, decision-making, etc. - are truly distinct from one another.

Local public-sector actors - around thirty municipalities along with local offices of State-level agencies involved specifically with water supply - take a decidedly different stance from that of the operator, be it public or private, on one vital point. For the former, the issue of water supply only occasionally arises as a key political debate, spaced by rather long periods of indifference. In contrast, the operator must project itself into a longer-run perspective not only because of the size of its capital investments, but also from the standpoint of maintaining durability and continuity of service. The close association between short run and long run is typical of the operator's role. It's also a valid explanation for why C.G.E., during the 1950's and 1960's, maintained, under delicate operating conditions, a "temporary" water source without which supplying the daily needs of a part of the metropolis would not have been possible. The population of this particular area, though sparse at the time, did show strong long-term development potential.

Furthermore, the various municipalities comprising the metropolitan area all exhibit their own unique time horizons. The important public debate held on Lyons' "water supply issue" between 1880 and 1914 therefore did not resound into the suburban municipalities, relatively undeveloped at the time. Alternatively, when the City of Lyons was not involved in this public service area (from the 1930's to the 1960's), the issue then became a major political theme in the suburbs.

Within the Suburban Water Syndicate itself, the sense of urgency to improve service was not felt with the same impact by the rapidly-expanding industrial suburban communities to the east and south as it was by the western rural areas prior to their own spurt of suburban development. The very same situation in fact applies to the "Communauté Urbaine" of the 1970's between the outlying sectors subjected to development pressures and the inner ring of built-out suburbs.

It was possible to observe, over the first half of this century, that C.G.E., thanks to its global position of public services operator and the efficient control of schedules that this position implies, was able to exploit these differences in time scales. Afterwards, the existence of stable intermunicipal cooperation, as a means of calibrating the various development schedules, eventually proved to be one condition for insuring the durability of the company's activity.

The importance of this heritage

Another lesson that can be drawn as a conclusion to this historical analysis is that the factors of heredity or of heritage actually play a far more active role than one would imagine in the contemporary context of water supply for cities in industrialized countries, such as Lyons. In this particular case, the role that water supply was able to play in the history of C.G.E. helps explain why this company has always maintained, even during difficult periods, an active presence and, by regularly renewing its aggressive commercial campaigns, eventually benefitted from the opening created in 1986. In addition, the dual experience provided by the existence, over the past one hundred years, of a major municipal water services department in Lyons plus the longstanding history of intermunicipal cooperation within this domain has undoubtedly enabled preserving a unique set of skills. Above and beyond coping with the changes that can occur from one generation of politicians and technicians to the next, this experience has provided a distinctive level of competence along with the capacity to evaluate and control, key characteristics of the metropolitan area's public authority.

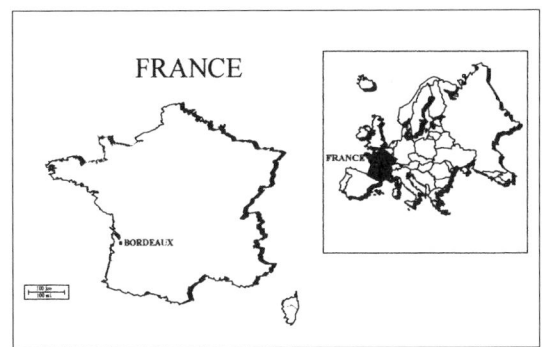

CHAPTER 3

FRANCE

Jean Roland
Barthélémy

BORDEAUX –1903, 1993–

Management of water and wastewater services for the Bordeaux Metropolitan Area, the nation's fifth largest, has been conferred since 1993 to the Lyonnaise des Eaux company. A new stage in the relationship between city and corporation, initiated some ninety years earlier, had thus begun.

Located in southwestern France, a short distance from the Atlantic Ocean, the city of Bordeaux stretches across both banks of the Garonne River, at the beginning of the river's estuary. Its right bank is rather hilly, then gives way to calcareous plateaus; the left bank, on which the city has more prominently developed, is completely flat, composed of sandy alluvial soil.

These geographical conditions explain the particularities of Bordeaux's water supply and wastewater services position. Being situated on a plain was the cause of frequent water pressure problems, due to the inadequate slope; yet, the lay of the land could easily accommodate human settlement. The groundwater table, while easily accessible, only enables meeting the needs of lower-density demand sources. The rising level of ocean tides into the estuary has resulted in the occasional reliance upon more distant water resources, sources or pumping sites located further upstream. Periodically, effluent was actually carried back upstream by the tidal motion. Lastly, Bordeaux typically experiences long rainy seasons in autumn and winter; during the summertime, violent thundershowers cause water flows that require monitoring, even if for only a few days a year.

From a political and administrative standpoint, the metropolitan area (700,000 population) is divided into forty-four different municipalities[1]: Bordeaux (with 210,000 residents) and forty-three others (varying in population from 1,000 to 35,000). Urban development patterns are very spread out, minimally organized and sparsely concentrated because of the absence of both topographical constraints and a nearby major city. Some of the area's municipalities feature suburban residential development while others contain either public housing districts or zones with a mix of rural with single-family residential uses. Only twenty-seven of these municipalities were grouped to form a "Communauté Urbaine" (Metropolitan Government Council); the others preferred remaining autonomous over fear of increased taxes.

This backdrop also includes certain political considerations, linked to the mayor of Bordeaux himself, a figure on the national scene for almost fifty years. His range of political influence extends over the entire region, and his political alliances are far-reaching. For many years, the City of Bordeaux had been the driving force behind the "Communauté Urbaine" and the stabilizing focus for the metropolitan area, as well as for the whole region. Today, as a result of political changes and greater municipal autonomy, this role could be perceived by the smaller municipalities as carrying the risk of being dominated.

All the conditions have therefore been combined to make the issue of water services a tricky and conflictual one. Yet, it has seemed up until now that the management approach utilized has constantly been adapted to overcome these obstacles. Water supply equipment, and soon wastewater facilities, is being decently built, with relatively consistent price structures positioned within the average range for comparably-sized cities.

The origins of public policy on water services

The history of water and wastewater services in Bordeaux pertains to two preoccupations: securing water sources and battling against floods.

---

1. However, the employment and residential basin covers 322 municipalities, or just about the entire administrative department, comprising 1 million population.

The construction of aqueducts and public fountains began with the Roman era. Centuries later, in 1521, mention is made of a master fountain-maker coming from the Normandy city of Rouen; he signed a contract with the city's aldermen to build three fountains supplied by water conveyed from outside sources. In 1759, another project, consisting of nine fountains located along the waterfront, was completed. A leasing agreement, initiated during the 18th century, conferred responsibility for operating the city's hydraulic facilities upon an independent entity.

Towards the beginning of the 19th century, the inadequate flow generated from city sources gave rise to a serious water shortage. Private wells and water conveyance systems became more widespread, though the shortfall could not be overcome. In 1841, "Bordeaux counted 120,000 souls and provided a total, from its public fountains, of the equivalent of 3.5 liters a day for each inhabitant"[2]. The quality of the water delivered proved very inconsistent.

In 1838, an ambitious project was launched to convey water into the city from outlying sources; its implementation proved difficult however due to: water pollution, leaks, the collapsing of a reservoir, and so on. Beginning in 1854, public efforts became more pronounced with the completion of entire systems of pipelines (including one 40 km. long) and a treatment plant, followed by a network of 400 water posts, 248 km. of water mains, etc. The municipal water agency was created in 1880 as the quality of water was improving noticeably. These sources finally reached the production level of 200 liters a day per capita in 1887.

Lyonnaise des Eaux began its service in the suburbs

It's within this context that, in 1903, the Lyonnaise des Eaux et de l'Eclairage company was engaged on behalf of two suburban municipalities (Caubéran and Le Bouscat), which formed a syndicate to create a drinking water delivery service. Water was drawn at a distance of 15 km. from the city, then distributed by a network of 30 km. of cast iron pipes connected to a major water tower.

Even though these facilities, which are still in service to this day, did constitute the base foothold for Lyonnaise des Eaux within the metropolitan area, it wasn't until 1925 that further missions of water delivery to adjacent outlying municipalities were conferred upon the

---

2. extracted from the document, "Eau, réseau général de la CUB (Bordeaux Metropolitan Council), note technique", May 1979.

company: first were Mérignac and Pessac, followed by Bègles (1926), Saint-Médard (1928) and Bruges (1933). In 1933, the company was called upon to intervene on the other side of the river, for the Port Authority and the Carbon Blanc Syndicate; ultimately, five more municipalities plus the airport, which were easily accessible from the existing network on the river's left bank, also requested service.

This incremental evolution does seem justified from a technical standpoint. Against the backdrop of recurrent water shortages, Lyonnaise des Eaux offered a simple solution, thanks to the sources it had already developed and the technical tasks it had carried out in the western part of the metropolitan area. From 1930 through 1947, six wells were dug into the aquifer, aqueduct capacity was doubled and iron-removal equipment was installed.

In the meantime, the City of Bordeaux, which was still running a municipal water agency, was accumulating its share of difficulties and relying, at least partially, on Lyonnaise des Eaux's water resources in order to withstand the shortages periodically experienced. Efforts to set up water supply lines connecting the ponds located on the hillsides and to place pumping stations on the Garonne and Dordogne Rivers would successively fail one after the other. To its credit, it must be highlighted that the Municipal Water Agency was, at the time, providing service to a very large proportion of the area's population (253,000 residents). Water shortages were fairly frequent during the summer months; pipeline losses were significant and water pressure insufficient. Yet, the main wells could not be maintained adequately, as these sources were in such demand.

The creation of a water syndicate to ensure continuous supply

To confront this lack of sufficient water resources, SIBADE, an intermunicipal syndicate devoted to piping water into the metropolitan area, was created in 1949. The primary objective of this reorganization effort was to resolve the issue of procuring adequate water supply. From 1950 on, an additional 15,000 m3 per day were being drawn from new wells, while the capacities of the various local networks were being combined. The renovation and protection of the oldest sources, followed by the restoration of the aqueducts, allowed increasing flow rates and reducing leakage. A new reservoir enabled expanding coverage to the western sectors as well as to sites located at elevations of 60 meters. Thirty new wells were also drilled on the left bank.

Lyonnaise des Eaux was then designated to manage the entire metropolitan area's water service operations, under contract with SIBADE.

Such a decision is understandable if one considers that, outside of the city of Bordeaux, Lyonnaise des Eaux had been granted concessions in twelve of the syndicate's member municipalities. In light of this fact, a new contract was applied. Lyonnaise des Eaux relinquished its status of concessionaire in order to manage, within the scope of an "incentive management contract" ("régie intéressée" or, more precisely, a "cost plus formula", plus a results-based incentive payment), the service throughout all municipalities, including Bordeaux. The syndicate assumed responsibility for capital investments by means of a surtax levied on the price of water.

This first effort to combine service also provided the opportunity to initiate a water billing system based on actual costs. Meter reading was introduced into customer billings. Then, during the 1960's, separate budgeting for water and wastewater services became legally mandated.

The success of this particular stage is demonstrated by essentially putting an end to the period of water shortages. As a result, Bordeaux's outlying areas along with its western suburbs, which comprised the full extent of the syndicate's coverage, were opened up to urbanization.

The "Communauté Urbaine": a technically-sound rationale

The real change in intermunicipal relationships came about some twenty years later, in 1968, with the creation of the "Communauté Urbaine" of Bordeaux (Metropolitan Government Council). This intermunicipal-based government organization, consisting of twenty-seven localities, was mandated by the law of 31st December 1966, which conferred upon the newly-empowered political body certain obligatory responsibilities, including drinking water delivery and wastewater services. The Communauté Urbaine took control of the activities performed by SIBADE, and entered into a "management contract" with Lyonnaise des Eaux. Some of the Communauté Urbaine's member municipalities though continued to be served by external intermunicipal syndicates. Yet, Lyonnaise des Eaux actually went on to conclude a lease agreement with one of these syndicates. The management strategies employed have therefore proved flexible with respect to the divisive local political context while, at the same time, did fulfill a role of unifying the service.

A large portion of the metropolis' built-up area still remained outside the jurisdiction of the Communauté Urbaine. Over the ensuing years, Lyonnaise des Eaux, drawing strength from its recognition within the metropolitan area, would enter into lease agreements with two nearby municipalities and two syndicates. To the west, the rival Compagnie Générale des Eaux started to stake out its position. To the north and south, a local joint public/private corporation, E.S.G. - tied to the utility giant Electricité de France and initially created for the distribution of electricity -, took over running the water services for communities that were part of the metropolitan area. Only three small syndicates and one municipality remained under public-sector management control.

The objective of this revised metropolitan organization was immediately stated: to definitively resolve the issue of water supply. The Communauté Urbaine was intended to provide the means necessary to implement both the construction of a drinking water purification plant[3] and the "100,000 m³ a day" program that Lyonnaise des Eaux had previously studied and proposed to SIBADE to accommodate the rapidly increasing level of demand. In 1971, the plant was completed, and the drilling of twelve new wells had begun. Twenty-nine additional wells were located outside of Communauté Urbaine jurisdiction, followed by ten more along the water supply pipeline; a pumping station enabled servicing the right bank as well. The target of 100,000 m³ a day was just about reached by the end of the 1980's.

Wastewater services: responding to emergencies

The creation of Bordeaux's first wastewater network dates back to 1842; at that time, a major cholera epidemic necessitated the construction of a 75-km. network of connecting sewers[4].

In 1949, a specialized wastewater syndicate was formed to act in conjunction with the one devoted to water supply; however, it was

---

3. This lant accomodates a flow of 1,100 m³/hour and treats a clayey, yet good quality, water by floculation/decantation (Degrémont's Pulsator system). This quality justifies relying on such a distant water source, in comparaison with the very polluted water found within the metropolitan area. Treated water is then conveyed by pipe 41 kilometers with a drop in elevation of 4 meters, all the way to the Bordeaux suburbs, where it arrives some 48 hours later! The plant is controlled, to a great extent, remotely and only necessitates one half-time staff assignment.

4. of the 275 kilometers of utility network recorded at the time. In "The History and Life of Bordeaux's Sewers" (University of Bordeaux, Doctorate thesis in medicine, 1958), M. Gaudin provides an interesting description of the perpetual procrastination between the general public interest, the slowness of decision-making and the difficulty of obtaining collective discipline. To a certain extent, a good number of currently-debated issues, wherein a clear-cut decision is only made in cases of absolute necessity, are well-represented by this depiction.

somewhat lacking in resources and only built a few facilities towards its beginnings. An incentive management contract, similar in nature to that for water supply, was signed in 1969 between Lyonnaise des Eaux and the Communauté Urbaine, covering wastewater operations.

It took two heavy deluges in 1982, causing a meter of flooding in the downtown within a span of two days, before decisions in the domain of wastewater services could finally get enacted. While during its first few years, the Communauté Urbaine "was satisfied with simply protecting its smaller streams", a comprehensive flood control program was laid out under the management contract framework. As part of the sewer system operations contract, Lyonnaise des Eaux's design office became involved in this effort at the time of drawing up final plans and overseeing the construction phase. Bordeaux had become the first wastewater service that Lyonnaise des Eaux managed in France, and helped to earn it the reputation as a pioneer in both system design and "professional" development specific to the field of wastewater. This program, financed by local taxpayers, enabled withstanding without any damage the torrential rains of August 1992, during which the city was subjected to 131 mm. of precipitation in 24 hours.

Learning from the past

From a technical standpoint, the intermunicipal framework has provided the means for rapidly expanding sources of water supply as well as improving water quality, in accordance with the projects and plans drawn up by Lyonnaise des Eaux beginning in 1950. The framework of "contracting out" management functions or a "delegated management contract" does indeed invoke a system that incites technological advances, since the private manager is not being asked to cut costs. Remuneration is simply based on actual expenses within the limits specified in a contract. By calling upon the specific capacities at his disposal, the manager is in a position to propose solutions that optimize the quality of service from a more technical standpoint. For this reason, some professionals today feel that this period was financially advantageous for Lyonnaise des Eaux. Yet, to the contrary, it should be emphasized that the metropolitan government agencies lost tremendous interest in the water issue at this time, considering that the topic was no longer critical and that the manager alone could handle any potential problem.

This system was also adopted in order to equalize costs between the area's central city and its periphery, extending beyond the boundaries of the Communauté Urbaine's territory. Lyonnaise des

Eaux's development outside the Communauté Urbaine actually occurred during the 1970's and towards the beginning of the 1980's, in competition with the two other leading service groups (C.G.E. and E.S.G.) active in the Gironde department. Some of these contracts, particularly those in the rapidly-growing "urban fringe" municipalities, proved to be operating at a deficit due to the low contract price negotiated. These losses were compensated by the profits generated from the Communauté Urbaine contract. Bordeaux area residents, while protected by the Communauté Urbaine, did indirectly pay for the works carried out in these more distant zones experiencing strong urban growth. To a certain extent, the approach to equalize costs across municipalities was in itself a factor in the development taking place at the outskirts of the metropolitan area. The private operator did benefit from a commercial advantage in the provision of wastewater services, in that the map showing the locations of leasing agreements signed for wastewater services would correspond almost identically to that drawn for water a few years prior.

This set of features also helps explain the evolution to come...

The transition to a concession

On 1st January 1992, Lyonnaise des Eaux was awarded the concession for the Communauté Urbaine's water services. One year later, it signed the leasing agreement for the provision of wastewater services to twenty-three municipalities as well. This turn of events[5], whether it was dictated by the economic context or not, does nonetheless display both the confidence expressed by the elected officials in Lyonnaise des Eaux and the limitations of the previous system, which was too narrow in delegating responsibility. This evolution occurred with practically no resistance from the politicians, as they were solely concerned with avoiding a major increase in the price of water. The transition to a concession resulted from the constraints imposed by the past situation, for Lyonnaise des Eaux as well as for the Communauté Urbaine.

For Lyonnaise des Eaux, the incentive management contract status was an uncomfortable one, even if it did turn out to be a financially attractive[6] and risk-free one. In fact the contract stipulated a means-

5. the upcoming completion of the service management contract, along with the wishes on the part of both sides to renegotiate it within an amicable setting, without being subjected to quantitative tender criteria.

6. between 5 and 10 million francs of gross earnings. It's this surplus that enabled covering the deficit of the region's rural municipalities. The Communauté Urbaine absorbs the bulk of capital investments and assumes operations risks.

based obligation, often out of sync with the real needs of the time, to be overseen by agencies within the Communauté Urbaine which were not in touch with what was happening in the field. The net result was reliance on an oversight authority that often proved to be awkward and counter-productive. To take but one example, maintenance of the wastewater collection network was contractually based on the number of jobs carried out per month, a number that might have been either insufficient or excessive, depending on the particular case. The services "under management contract" were strictly separated from the remainder of Lyonnaise des Eaux's regional activities. Wastewater services, water service operations and capital investments were all treated distinctly. In sum, the impression left by the employees suggested that only the Communauté Urbaine benefitted from the efforts undertaken by Lyonnaise des Eaux, whereas the latter absorbed the criticism.

Water Distribution in the Metropolitan Area.
1970...53.0
1972...51.2
1976...56.2
1977-1984 ....variation between 51.8 and 53.8
1985-1989 ....value around 56.0
1990...55.6
1991...54.5
1992...52.4
1993...55.7
Reference : Communauté Urbaine in million of m^3

For the politicians, two events served to change the course of the system in place. For one, renewed increases in water consumption beginning in 1985, which culminated in the drought year of 1989 at an all-time level (272,000 m^3 a day), approached the designed security limit. The Office of Geological and Mineral Research (a public geological research organization) warned of the risks of an overly-strong drop in the groundwater table level[7] and the possibility of infiltration.

---

7. It's wasn't until 1989 that BRGM (Office of Geological Research) developed a mathematical model for groundwater sources, while a groundwater management committee was being set up. Previously, it had been difficult to make forecasts of this nature, and to motivate elected officials on this subject.

Secondly, the implementation of European norms, in the domain of drinking water much like those for wastewater, would impose a resumption in capital outlays. The aquifers located to the north of the metropolitan area exhibited excessive fluor and sulfate contents, thereby requiring new, replacement sources to be exploited. In addition, the Communauté Urbaine has already laid out plans for the development of new infrastructure - underground rail, facilities to enhance economic growth potential - which necessitates restoring its debt capacity.

The negotiation of the new contract has essentially been focused on controlling prices and water resource commitments. Herein lies the formula designated a "concession", which in fact is a leasing agreement for existing facilities coupled with a classic 30-year concession for all new capital investment. Lyonnaise des Eaux took over repayment of the Communauté Urbaine's outstanding loans and accepted, within certain limits, a performance obligation: responding to current needs and demands for quality in return for a fixed price, being responsible for maintenance and equipment renewal. The company must, within the scope of a master plan being prepared, procure an additional 20,000 m3 a day over ten years, raise storage capacity by the same amount and eliminate all water supply not up to standard. Such are the objectives that adhere, more or less, to the terms of the National Water Basin Agencies' Sixth Program.

Naturally, these commitments are not entirely perfect. As far as the Communauté Urbaine is concerned, preparation time was cut back, due to the "deadlines" imposed on deliberations. Thus, the majority of the technical components are defined in a complex set of appendices and often only made known at the very last minute. Some aspects therefore have taken on the appearance of being poorly defined in the contract document: the tax on withholdings not being included in the price per m^3; a poorly-written specification for the quality of materials within the planned investment program; the absence of sanctions for failure to furnish ongoing documentation (summary reports, plans, etc.). This rush in negotiating the contract would cause a few temporary difficulties - followed by compromise - in the relationship between the service department and the Communauté Urbaine.

The transition to a concession for water servcies signifies, first and foremost, the transfer of investment and renewal obligations onto Lyonnaise des Eaux, which then becomes responsible for all the facilities[8], not just operations.

---

7. It has only retained ownership of two well sites.

Yet, this new contract also strongly signifies a change in the mind-set on the part of the concessionaire, who now benefits from greater autonomy for day-to-day management. Coordination with the metropolitan government's technical staff becomes less tight, a fair number of decisions are taken at the group level (discount purchasing center for supplies), and verbal commitments weigh less heavily than in the past. In other words, group policy is felt to a greater extent, and the contract is sacrosanct; these trends are only being accelerated by more frequent changes in the executive staff, in accordance with the group's human resources policy.

Lyonnaise des Eaux has proceeded with reorganizing into a more decentralized structure, exploiting its regional stature for economy of scale advantages and offering a unique palette of services to its clientele. Its activities have been divided into six independent operations centers covering water and wastewater services, with a "customer" service field office. The net result has meant substantial cost savings: consolidation of equipment and of executive workforce, multi-skilled personnel and multi-purpose premises, special relationships developed with the end user. The Regional Office houses the functional departments (personnel and design office, marketing). This evolution is indicative of a turning point for the group towards more commercial preoccupations. It also corresponds to a heavily-backed effort to modernize management (simulation and monitoring system, investment optimization, property performance modeling, etc.). Several of these tools are truly innovative, and therefore contribute a great deal to the city.

The price of water, however, has only barely risen (14.47 francs in 1994); the bulk of capital investments had already been completed, yields were already relatively high (on the order of 80%), and water quality had already reached satisfactory levels. Price has therefore progressed as expected, in proportion with the contract's indexes. The organizational reshuffling which followed the incentive management contract term would enable Lyonnaise des Eaux to assess its pricing policy and to gradually incite the Communauté Urbaine's peripheral municipalities to raise their prices. This move would serve to balance operating costs by emphasizing improvements in the quality of service. Ultimately, the politicians' primary concern seems to have been attained.

In the area of wastewater services, the situation would appear somewhat different: the leasing agreement limits the responsibility of Lyonnaise des Eaux to operations and equipment renewal alone (in coordination with the appropriate Communauté Urbaine departments). Initially, this setup resulted in an operating deficit, because of the increase in heavy maintenance expenses (which rose from about 10 million francs to 40 million) in an effort to reduce the maintenance schedule delays previously accumulated. Investment needs were decisively greater than the capacity of the Communauté Urbaine[9] which nonetheless has decided to retain control over the investment program, as a means of assuring relationships with the individual municipalities. This decision does correspond with the body's scope of responsibility, which covers infrastructure renewal programs and higher-priority capital investments, including wastewater facilities. Maintaining close contact with elected officials is also a prerogative that the Bordeaux Communauté Urbaine prizes.

Privatization: a flexible tool

An assessment of these ninety-two years of private sector involvement in the Bordeaux metropolitan area provides some rather instructive lessons.

Without a doubt, the first among them is the flexibility of the various forms of public/private partnership. It may be considered that the politicians were consistently in the process of changing their set of objectives. They initially sought to resolve the issue of water resources by "stamping" an approval on their own project. The incentive management contract enabled marshaling the technical capabilities of the private firm, which remained in the background while the politicians held control, and thereby monitoring the capital investments undertaken. In contrast, during the more recent past, politicians have declined to exercise their oversight authority, yet have nonetheless sought to better control prices. Adapting formulae beyond standard contract prescriptions was streamlined since the contracted party was a large industrial group, and one that was present across a number of public service sectors (waste disposal, funeral parlors, etc.). As a result, minor adaptations to a contract could be compensated within the context of a much wider range of service sectors. Nonetheless, this flexibility was only made possible through the framework of limited competition and direct relationships between the firm and the public authority.

---

9. needs ranging from 100 to 250 million francs have been cited, in comparison with a capacity of 40 to 50 million francs. Since the elected officials could not decide on the appropriate response, the leasing agreement wound up with a 80%/20% split with the lessee.

Flexibility is also drawn from the special relationship between private service provider and elected officials. The feeling of trust that both parties seek to maintain corresponds to a practically implicit contract that allows settling many "special cases" appearing peripheral to the actual contract. The following examples are pertinent: standard practices for individuals facing particular difficulties, negotiations for preferential rates in cases of industrial relocation. Yet, the "extra efforts" that the concessionaire also undertakes must be included as well, especially when it is felt that they simplify matters. Lyonnaise des Eaux thereby cut by half the users' security deposit. In addition, it has remitted to the Communauté Urbaine the profit realized from the debt renegotiations led by one of its specialized subsidiaries. This has served to highlight one particular application of its "commercial policy", which reveals the respect of this private group for certain public-sector goals.

The transition to a concession demonstrates two distinct facets: on the one hand, a more responsible and economically-efficient management structure, and on the other, the necessity for Lyonnaise des Eaux to affirm its commercial stature, with respect to the end user, within a "stabilized" market environment. As such any municipalities are left to conquer outside of a rural zone in the southern part of the department. However, the service manager does remain the primary target for complaints when problems arise, as was the case in 1994 when the issue of water prices was forwarded by user associations and the media. The previous system, in which relationships nurtured with the public authorities produced a climate of confidence in settling differences, was replaced by the direct involvement of the public. Here we're no longer that far away from a system where calling upon external arbitration as a recourse could be demanded. For example, the application of European directives were an important factor in opting for delegated management formulae, due to the fears expressed by officials of being held accountable for their own services, without full possession of the resources necessary to be properly informed and to perform technical design.

Lastly, the presence of a large private company has been clearly welcomed to manage urban growth against the backdrop of municipal fragmentation, fairly typical of French planning. Beyond the tailored responses it has generated for each individual municipality, Lyonnaise des Eaux has had to demonstrate its capacity to cover a large service area, by progressively incorporating the territories of adjacent municipalities, just as it had to prove its technical capacity in the past. Coverage today encompasses, with the exception of fringe areas, nearly the entire metropolitan basin. There's no arguing that this kind of coverage provides considerable advantages in equalizing costs, managing resources jointly[10] and standardizing prices progressively, which is part of the competitive bidding prerequisites. The reference used in pricing municipal water services is more often being fixed with respect to contract prices for neighboring areas, taking into account obviously the specificities of the local context. We have seen that the efforts of Lyonnaise des Eaux in this regard are oriented towards price standardization, as a means of avoiding the deficits of past experiences.

The local political situation was paralyzed by the conflict between the rural municipalities, subjected to a left-right confrontation, and the "system" implemented by Bordeaux's mayor, which resulted in relative unanimity within the Communauté Urbaine. Can a supra-municipal political body succeed in reconciling these competing stances? The department of the Garonne is strongly positioned on the left of the political spectrum, the Aquitaine region on the right, and the municipal syndicates are too small in size. The "Aquitains" (residents of the Aquitaine region, whose capital is Bordeaux) are renowned for their capacity to rally together, in spite of their differences, to defend regional interests. Within this context, the role of Lyonnaise des Eaux has, in particular, enabled covering the whole of the metropolis' land area with one single management system, whose importance is valued not only from an economic standpoint. This coverage has also facilitated accessing certain types of resources[11], pooling equipment and connecting networks. The private service provider finds itself in as good a negotiating posture as the local authority for purchasing new sites and procuring approvals for operating water sources located in nearby municipalities. Even within Communauté Urbaine territory, Lyonnaise des Eaux plays a positive role in raising the level of technical competence, as compared to the previous situation wherein methods for allocating budgets were based solely on population and not on needs. Finally, the company has also been instrumental in treating problems from a global perspective, by encompassing both water and wastewater services, and thereby completing the water cycle.

The Bordeaux example is therefore representative of a special case, in which the most economical solution of municipal services

---

10. notably, the remote centralized resource management should be cited, along with a mobile laboratory and a specially-equipped truck to detect leaks, ready to intervene rapidly in case of emergency.

11. The majority of water sources are located in the outlying areas; only one municipality refused this pooling of resources.

management could not be maintained, for lack of flexibility on the part of the public system. This absence of flexibility was combined with a rigid intermunicipal institutional framework (both the syndicates and the Communauté Urbaine) as well as with a slow decision-making apparatus. This situation has resulted in decisions always being taken amidst a state of emergency: flooding, peaking consumption or even, in the past, epidemics. To these emergencies, a standard public system would react with an overly-delayed response time, often exceeding a year. This system would stir the various intermunicipal adversaries at each important voting session. In this sense, the different forms of private-sector management have, in Bordeaux, provided responses to very specific situations.

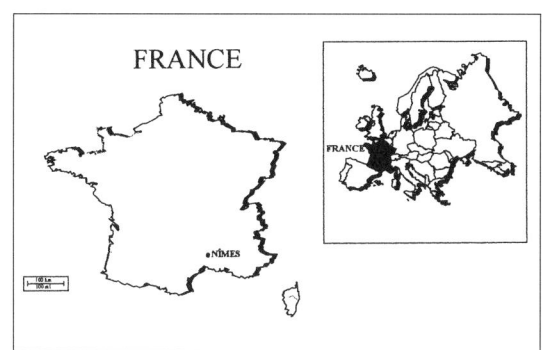

CHAPTER 4

FRANCE

Dominique
Lorrain[1]

Nimes, political alternation

The city of Nimes, population 125,000, has over a long time been a stronghold for the left within France's local political scene. From 1965 to 1983, the city was led by a high-profile Communist mayor and member of Parliament, who was elected following a run of consecutive Socialist mayoral terms that had begun in 1947. The political ideology practiced had largely been tempered by a southern-styled sociability, by the attachment of elected officials to their localities and by the capacity of the mayor to meet the everyday expectations of his electorate. Nimes' Communist mayor represented, during his reign, his party's dynamic and progressive wing (Pronier, 1983). In 1983, the coming to power of a mayor, well-known businessman and decidedly-liberal in his stance, sparked a triple upheaval within the locality: a political upheaval, an upheaval in the conventional practices and approaches, as well as an upheaval in local city management techniques. The history of Nimes can thus be interpreted as an extreme example of both the forms of political alternation and the capacities of adaptation between a company and city officials, since the same water services operator has in fact spanned this entire period.

---

1. In conjunction with Mr. J; Kimpe, Director of Municipal Services, and Mr. Pottin, SAUR Director.

This history is also representative of the water supply situation in the Mediterranean Basin, with its characteristic drought season and sudden downpours. The city, surrounded by seven hills, actually takes the appearance of a bowl at the edge of a break in the hillside slope between the scrubland to the north and a piedmont. In the scrubland, water runoff is only temporary and is divided between two drainage basins. Rainwater drains by following the course of mildly-sloped valleys, which remain dry for more than eleven months a year, yet can turn into virtual torrents at times of heavy precipitation. These short-lived, sudden runoffs only last a few hours and tend to dry up almost as quickly as they appear, in much the same fashion as in North African countries. In terms of surface water supply, only one permanent source exists upstream of the city; however, several aquifers are present under the ground.

1969-1983: The municipality's Communist period

The idea of conferring the management of water services upon a private operator took shape during the 1965-1971 mayoral term owing to the deficiency of both water production means and the quality of the service itself. The water system's technical configuration at the time consisted of an extremely old pumping plant, located at a distance of twenty-five kilometers from the city, and two pipelines. One of the pipelines, made in cast iron, dated back to the end of the XIXth century, while the other, referred to as "the Bonna pipeline" after its manufacturer, was in concrete and installed in 1904[2].

"All three of these facilities were built during a period when the level of household water consumption tended to be quite a bit less than that of the 1960's[3].

The most striking problem had to do with the irregularity in serving some of the city's districts. Pumping capacity was insufficient given constantly-increasing water needs due to the influx of population. The 900-mm diameter "Bonna" pipeline lost almost 50% of the water transported "during its run" and endured around two hundred

---

2. The "Bonna" pipes were developed through the application of a patent for a concrete-fabrication technique that entered the French market in order to compete with the cast-iron "Pont-à-Mousson" pipes. They were ultimately taken over by the Compagnie Générale des Eaux during hte period between the two world wars. The company is still in business, whereas Pont-à-Mousson remains the world leader in cast-iron pipes and has since merged with Saint-Gobain.

3. Director of Municipal Services.

service interruptions a year, necessitating frequent repair work to be conducted by the City's water department under somewhat variable response times. During these periods, residents would naturally be forced to go without any municipal water.

In order to provide a more detailed setting, let's recall what was happening in France in 1962. The signing of the Evian accords brought an end to the Algerian War and, along with it, the return of a million "repatriates". A considerable number of these new arrivals relocated in the southern part of the country, where they found the climate, geography and way of life much closer to their former context. This exceptional influx served to reinforce the already powerful movement towards urbanization. Nimes' elected officials had but one simple observation in mind: rising needs coupled with an outdated technical system and unquestionably limited in-house resources. In light of the sensitivity raised by the water issue, it's understandable that a Communist mayor during that era would decide to call upon outside expertise. This kind of situation illustrates the non-ideological side of water services management.

The municipality conducted a relatively-open initial tender procedure based on a set of specifications stipulating a minimum water production level of 72,000 m^3 per day, no matter the means employed. Several proposals were received. The solution developed by the SAUR company involved constructing a new pumping station on the same site as the existing one since this location, though a considerable distance from the city, did provide the advantage of supplying high-quality water. In addition, SAUR proposed realizing savings in the replacement of the "Bonna" pipeline through installing a flow accelerator on the 800-mm diameter, cast-iron section. By this process, it became possible to maintain water pressure throughout the entire network while performing the necessary repair work, thereby eliminating all service inconveniences for the local population. This solution proposal was retained by the city's elected representatives undoubtedly because it enabled saving on a costly capital investment not at all deemed a priority by residents in comparison with other municipal needs.

For the SAUR company, this contract, signed in 1969, was an extremely important one. At the time, their division covering this part of southern France was providing service to only about 40,000 residents, so that being awarded the operations for a city of 100,000 population translated into a tripling in its number of accounts. Even to this day, Nimes remains the sole major French city operated by this company.

SAUR was organized into eleven regional divisions, and corporate strategy dictated that this operations assignment be handled by the corresponding regional office. This approach was later modified by local officials who feared not being able to fully exercise their control if the Nimes operating accounts were being held along with those of other municipalities within the same accounting system. As a result, the company SODEN, a wholly-owned SAUR subsidiary, was created to operate the city of Nimes exclusively; the contract was ultimately signed with SODEN. Over time and as the working relationship evolved, the officials' preconceptions tended to wane; consequently, SODEN actually came to be managed like SAUR's twelfth regional division, displaying the same accounting practices and the same internal procedures, yet maintaining its own identity, legal status as well as an autonomous financial and accounting system.

The contract signed for a thirty-year period was qualified as a leasing agreement, even if it did exhibit certain characteristics that brought its true status into question. While the City furnished the service with the existing facilities, the contracted firm's initial primary mission was not only to operate the network and collect user fees, but also to carry out some heavy capital investments - new pumping station, installation of a pressurizer - which greatly surpassed the realm of a leasing agreement. From this standpoint, the contract could have been classified as a concession. Though its specific qualification was not reconsidered in legal terms, the contract did nonetheless evolve along with the day-to-day realities to incorporate changes in the operating environment. Given the investments slated plus the need to renovate the networks and extend them to new districts of the city, the leasing agreement framework gradually took the form of a concession.

As far as staffing was concerned, one hundred and fourteen municipal employees, both technical and administrative, were transferred to the company on long-term assignment following lengthy negotiations. The personnel thereby benefitted from a special status, combining the advantages and guarantees of civil service with those of the collective bargaining agreement covering SAUR employees. Executives of the service organization remained attached to the municipality's administration and were assigned the objective of retaining expertise and oversight capabilities at the local government level.

The price of water was contractually set during negotiations held between the municipality and the operating company. The contract's specifications included the provision for a price revision clause, based both on a fixed component and a variable component that incorporates the service's main operating parameters (labor, fluid flow systems and electricity, piping networks, materials and miscellaneous items).

Thanks to the company's contributions, these assigned objectives could be met rather quickly. Such contributions are broken down into three categories:

- The company proceeded immediately with investments in water production, which helped improve the quality of service[4]. The installation of the water pressurizer enabled repairing the "Bonna" pipeline without any service interruption. This solution would be favored up until 1989, at which time the new 1,000-mm diameter pipeline would become operational in replacement of the "Bonna".

- Investments in work site equipment enhanced the performance of the maintenance crews. Customer service was likewise improved thanks through quicker response time for hook-ups and through leak-detection efforts.

- Lastly, a climate of change was felt both in commercial policy and in the relationship with customers/users. Customer account records were updated; billing was computerized, and a greater level of rigor was introduced throughout this part of the operations.

With respect to the relationship between the firm and the local authority, which pertains specifically to the workings of the leasing agreement, we are presented herein with an illustration of the pragmatism of water service operations whatever the effective legal status. Two distinct interpretations of the spirit behind the leasing agreement framework may be forwarded, depending on the history of the network preceding the agreement's application and the expectations expressed by local politicians.

- The leasing agreement could have originated as a concession that was transformed following the financing of a major capital investment by the local authority. It's this type of scenario that often arises when the construction of drinking water purification plants becomes necessary while the distribution system is being run under a former concession. In such a case, practices stem from the concessionary framework, which tends to draw actions towards an all-risk formula wherein the operator retains a broad autonomy over management functions. Once roles and responsibilities have been

---

4. The same characteristic is encoutered in the foreign examples of delegated management analysed in this book: Buenos-Aires, Gdansk and Macao.

adopted and even if the contract changes, operators keep their "relative" autonomy.

- The relationships between operator and local authority in the Nimes example are completely different. Though the leasing arrangement applicable to this case resembles a concession due to the firm's involvement in capital outlays, the prevailing spirit of the agreement is nonetheless closer to that of a fixed-price management services contract. The management contractor is held to report all actions carried out directly to the authority. "We were like part of the municipal staff given a special status. The city provided the asset base which was then made available to the firm; we were at the service of the mayor's office." The operator considered that he was performing the same function as a management contractor, with the only difference being the accounting and tax reporting procedures adopted.

This kind of relationship was perhaps a necessary prerequisite for a Communist-run city government to accept the notion of service delegation without experiencing the feeling of a disembodied public service. In reality, ties between operator and authority were quite strong.

- Exchanges were programmed on a daily basis with the city's public works staff. "They would come to oversee service operations; they'd spend their days in our office, but I wasn't bothered because our work was getting done efficiently."

- Conversely, the firm was being consulted for the scheduling of construction work that did remain under local authority jurisdiction "since the City exercised thorough control over investments just like over rate-setting." Working meetings were organized every other week with the mayor, the deputy-mayor responsible for utility networks and the public works office. These sessions provided the means for keeping the mayor aware of what had been accomplished as well as the opportunity for outlining the works program. Over the years, a climate of trust was instilled in the relationship between the firm's engineers and city representatives, being both the elected officials and the public works staff.

It was during this period that a street-improvement plan was established calling for work to be conducted by the municipality over a time frame of nearly twenty years; as of 1987, the plan had yet to be completed. This planning effort also enabled coordinating work on several utility networks: water, wastewater and, in some instances, electricity.

The level of decision-making authority held by city hall can be highlighted in its attitude concerning the renovation of the "Bonna" pipeline. Since the pipeline system was down constantly, the firm had proposed its replacement on two occasions to the city. While council members didn't definitively reject the idea, they did consider that the state of municipal finances couldn't warrant engaging in such an investment. They felt further support for their decision by the fact that no problems were actually apparent thanks to the cast-iron pipeline's pressurizer, insuring that "the population didn't even realize when repair work was being performed". Moreover, in 1971, one of the Bas Rhone Languedoc Company's plants began supplying an additional 20,000 m³ of water. Yet, this supply complement was not of absolute necessity; the situation had not turned so dramatic, and it would have been possible to wait. The classic public-sector decision-making criteria - visibility, crisis management - are clearly present in this illustration.

Considering public works and procurement, the measures stipulated in the Code for Awarding Public Contracts were applied. The major capital improvement projects were awarded to local contractors; SODEN itself held onto "the small-scale work", more specifically equipment renewal and emergency repairs. Though the annual amount of work assigned the company remained less than the programs undertaken by local contractors, SODEN's input did nonetheless allow, over several years, modernizing a good portion of the networks serving the city's various districts.

1983-1995: The municipality's liberal period

A new municipal team was elected in 1983, thus ushering in a break with past local tradition. The break was, first and foremost, political for this city that had been under left-leaning municipal control since the end of the XIXth century. This event occured pass just two years after the country elected a Socialist president and a left-wing coalition was formed to lead the French government. Within this national context, the 1983 elections marked one step in an overall comeback strategy. The city of Nimes, much like Grenoble and certain cities within the Paris region, would come to symbolize this comeback. The break was also one of style. The new mayor came from the fashion industry where he had built a reputation with the company Cacharel, created in 1964. The Nimes' mayorship represented his first political mandate. He set out to apply a businesslike approach to city management. "Sell the city of Nimes like a company" would become the rallying cry around his policies, thereby echoing the day's national slogan, "Govern France just like a company". At the time, Nimes was among the French towns receiving the most widespread media coverage.

Furthermore, the change brought about in 1983 had an economic dimension. The victory of a businessman undoubtedly signified an understanding on the part of residents that it was vital to broaden the city's economic outlook away from a narrow focus on wine-growing activities and the tertiary sector. While the economic downturn along with the level of unemployment worsened in Nimes, its neighboring "sun belt" cities were recording strong growth rates. The mayor, thanks to his dynamic spirit as well as his network of personal contacts, would go on to open up a city that had heretofore been managed meekly along the lines of the "old school": "Things are fine here, we all know each other." This motto was no longer appropriate given the seriousness of the employment situation. "The election of a mayor with deep-rooted liberal ideals was therefore a sign of hope in the battle against unemployment and in the return of economic growth to the area."

In order to redevelop the city and attract companies to the area, the newly-elected municipal team would argue that infrastructure facilities needed to be improved and that municipal institutions needed to be freed from the burden of their day-to-day management obligations as well as from direct production responsibilities. Beginning in 1985, Nimes gained notoriety through a wave of service delegations - school cafeterias, street cleaning, parks and open space - which broadened the range of private-sector involvement in the provision of public services. Previously, this involvement had been concentrated solely within the utility networks - water, district heating and waste collection.

For the water services operator, under contract since 1969, this political change may be interpreted from two vantage points. On the minus side, it was necessary to adapt to a new decision-maker whose intentions to strip and revamp the current state of affairs had clearly been announced; 1983 was to be a crucial year. On the plus side, the policy of urban development forwarded by the new mayor foresaw substantial infrastructure expansion, which, in turn, would provide business growth potential for SODEN.

Political changes. The mayor had championed in his campaign platform the remunicipalization of water services, pointing out that "the entity that manages the provision of water holds real power"; it has direct contact with the user through administering the billing system and carrying out any required additional works; in short, it knows the city extremely well.

The new term thus started off on the path of mistrust. The new, more liberal-oriented team of politicians had the impression of coming to power in March of 1983 amidst a hostile environment. This would explain why the mayor brought in outside executives to run city departments and why a policy of "privatization" was enacted, as much to prove the superiority of corporate-style management methods as to diminish the influence of trade unions closely tied to France's Communist party. An in-depth assessment of the city's financial management performance and its human resources[5] was conducted once the new team took office. Yet, it was equally understandable that, within such an environment, the idea of remunicipalizing water services appeared completely out of step with the times and had little chance of success. Moreover, it ran against the day's political winds and against the liberal emphasis boasted by the municipality's newly-developed policy.

In addition, local officials recognized rather quickly that SODEN was performing its work well, that the system was functioning above all else on a professional basis. "Things were going fairly smoothly and the mayor had other, more priority matters to attend to; we considered ourselves as partners to the local authority." SODEN accomplished its mission in a spirit of professionalism, dedication and consistency. It was also the little symbolic acts that counted in shaping this perception in the eyes of the elected officials. One Friday evening, the mayor - president of the company Cacharel - was putting on a fashion show. Two hours prior to the event, a water main burst; there was water everywhere! Even before the mayor's office could alert SODEN, a company crew was already on the scene repairing the pipe and cleaning up the roadway so that at show time, all was ready to go. The idea of municipalizing the service never actually came back to the fore. It was decided to retain the existing operator after some minor changes, pertaining to the personality of the new local management team and to their managerial methods, be carried out. The contract remained unchanged. The company was fairly directly associated with the service's capital investment programs.

The new relationship with the local authority. The new rules were clear: i) The local authority established water and wastewater policy through including SODEN in its decision-making framework. Oversight by the City was no longer applicable to the settling of more minor problems on a day-to-day basis; ii) The company, granted greater autonomy and no longer subjected to ongoing control, was assigned responsibility for managing the service's daily operations, covering the areas of facility maintenance and customer satisfaction. This separation between decision-making and execution was further strengthened by SAUR's complete takeover of SODEN.

---

5. For example, over a span of ten years, the number of microcomputers in use would increase from three units to six hundred.

Nonetheless, the operator did lose its direct relationship with local elected representatives, who were heavily involved in the management function, and could thereby receive service information from sources other than municipal staff. Negotiating works programs and planning their execution were both, from then on, conducted between the city's technicians and the company. The role of the City Manager (Municipal Services Director) was to resolve stalemates in negotiations and to propose adoption of the works program. "The relationship with the elected official, if it were to last, would be confined to verifying that the proposals being submitted to the city council jointly by the firm and the City Manager's office actually respected the council's policy orientation." Put otherwise, this revised organization had transformed a direct and personal elected official / private firm relationship into one that's overly-publicized by municipal departments.

From water to wastewater. As of 1975, SODEN has been assigned technical management responsibility for the city's 31,000-m3/day capacity wastewater treatment plant ; this plant was divided into four sections, and never really performed well. Different contractors were involved in the construction of each of the four sections. Not one among them was able to last the project; ultimately, the plant was operated by municipal employees, yet the level of water purification proved unsatisfactory. Residents complained of odors; maintenance of the various basins remained inadequate.

Shortly thereafter, the company set out to remedy the environmental nuisances. A fifth section was approved by the City. Pre-treatment phases were improved. SODEN devoted its attention to the nuisances and saw to it that treatment processes were soundproofed. Nothing extraordinary or spectacular was undertaken, rather a full series of simple adjustments. The company was able to upgrade the plant's productivity by operating with five employees instead of the previous eleven.

1985 was marked by a major campaign of public service delegation. Public transportation, district heating, waste collection and disposal along with water services management were all reexamined closely in order to establish new formulations in line with the City's "search for both the economic and social optima". SAUR was thus awarded the operations, under a leasing agreement, of the city's wastewater services following a competitive tender open not only to the nationwide industry specialists but also to local construction firms.

Later on in 1988, as a means of accommodating the city's growing population, a new plant, with a capacity of 100,000 resident equivalents (20,000 m^3/day), enabled serving, through a gravity collector system, the entire metropolitan area and hooking up outlying villages located at higher elevations, some of which had been discharging untreated wastewater.

This new plant was built by SAUR within the framework of a partial concession, during which the concessionaire provides complementary financing in conjunction with the Water Agency. The length of the contract was thus set at 30 years in order to allow full depreciation of the plant. A second section of the same capacity is targeted for the future, to replace the old facility once a 5-km connecting collector has been completed.

The price of water from 1983 to 1995					
	Total	Operations	Investment in Water	Investment in Wastewater	Taxes
1983	5.78	4.11	1.32	–	0.35
1984	7.04	4.45	2.24	–	0.35
1985	7.56	4.75	2.39	–	0.42
1986	7.94	4.32	2.51	0.66	0.45
1987	8.39	4.54	2.64	0.71	0.50
1988	8.66	4.70	2.69	0.73	0.54
1989	8.87	4.86	2.73	0.74	0.54
1990	10.68	4.99	2.81	2.33	0.55
1991	10.91	5.14	2.84	2.37	0.56
1992	12.71	4.38	3.65	2.86	1.82
1993	13.44	3.91	4.33	3.12	2.08
1994	15.55	5.20	4.98	3.39	1.98
1995	17.15	6.30	5.08	3.68	2.09
Source: Municipal Public Works Office					

in franc, current price.

Replacing the "Bonna" pipeline took place at the end of 1985. SAUR was not directly involved in conducting the actual works. Rather, the company was commissioned by the local authority to act as its engineering consultant, to coordinate the tender procedure and to oversee the execution of the works. A dual technical solution was retained: cast-iron pipes over the five-kilometer section through the urbanized area and concrete pipes for the line's passage through agricultural land. Fabrication was to be carried out by the company SADE (part of the C.G.E. group) at a re-fitted production site located within the same geographical department. Job creation would prove to be a decisive factor in the selection. This solution corresponded to a total investment of 103 million francs, which represented the largest project of its kind at the time. SAUR assumed responsibility for the successful completion of the project, given the objective of not impacting the price of water by more than 0.90 francs/m^3.

October 1988: A natural disaster

On the 3rd of October 1988, during a torrential thundershower, record precipitation was unleashed on the city and its surrounding rural areas. As the rains had been falling ever since the previous day onto especially dry ground, two air masses, one hot and humid while the other cold and high-pressure, met and stopped abruptly above the scrubland just north of the city. This cumulo-nimbus column, reaching a thickness of upwards of ten kilometers, would come pouring down on the city for seven hours uninterrupted, up to a volume of 400 ml/m^3 on higher ground. "The result: an intensity of flooding surpassing anything ever experienced in this century"[6]. "The sky literally fell in on the heads of Nimes residents"[7]. Fifteen million m^3 of water rushed through the city, with flow rates attaining 2,000 m^3/second.

"On the morning of October 3rd, a stream of muddy water began gushing down the hillsides, bringing along everything in its path: tree trunks, cars, street fixtures and miscellaneous objects. In the heart of the city, a veritable cataclysm was unfolding: nine dead, 95% of small shops and businesses destroyed, 2,000 housing units flooded out, 45,000 disaster victims, cemeteries and schools ravaged, 6,000 vehicles destroyed, four billion francs of combined public and private property damage. Certain districts found themselves completely inundated under 3.5 meters of water and mud. Though Nimes had already lived through numerous catastrophes of this nature, all previous records were unfortunately soundly broken on this occasion. The net result was simply frightening".[8]

The city would be declared a natural disaster area by the State and thereby generate a tremendous outpouring of relief support from throughout the country. City hall would receive seventy million francs

---

6. "Midi Libre", editorial from October 11, 1988 special issue, cited by Ch. Dourlens (1991).

7. "Libération", 5 October 1988, cited by Ch. Dourlens.

8. Director of Municipal Services.

of donations from individuals alone - out of the 127,500 personal checks sent - along with an additional forty-two million francs of assistance from other localities. Banks also pitched in. The National Savings Bank ("Caisse d'Epargne") made the first move; it announced the award of a one hundred and twenty million-franc, no-interest loan in favor of the disaster victims. The BNP bank followed suit in offering fifty million under the same conditions, and the Crédit Lyonnais bank another thirty million.

Repairing the utility network was naturally a vital step. SAUR's contribution in this respect proved very important since it was able to mobilize 280 people and one hundred and forty machines by calling up reinforcement personnel from all over France. "These resources in manpower exceeded by far what the city could have mustered on its own within the framework of its municipal functions." Assistance from other municipalities and volunteer workers was also considerable, accounting in total for over 5,000 volunteers as well as 750 public works machines that took part in the clean-up effort, under the supervision of the City Manager's office. It should be highlighted that at this time of crisis, city hall became the crisis control center, even though during the very first hours following the deluge, the State's response teams were the ones most concerned.

The mayor would rally the efforts of those around him to erase, within one week's time, the visible signs of the disaster. He issued the challenge the day the drama occurred and was, generally speaking, able to meet it.

In-depth actions. In 1985, the city had conducted a study which projected the construction of retention basins at the foothills of the scrubland in order to protect the more densely-populated parts of the metropolitan area. The initial phase of the project had already gotten under way when the torrential downpour struck. Unfortunately, those basins still unfinished at the time were, at least partially, destroyed.

On the 16th of October 1988, the city created a water resources commission whose objective was to devise a plan to protect the city against forty-year flood levels in its northern districts and hundred-year flood levels in the south. This effort, approved by the State in March of 1990, became the focus of many public hearings during the year 1992, prior to its adoption.

Moreover, the city council undertook, at the beginning of 1989, the implementation of a risk-exposure plan. The subsequent measures gave rise to significant modifications in the land use planning code and a revision in the works program to protect the municipality's water system. "The last project comprised: fifty-eight kilometers of conduits and pipeline, retention basins with a capacity of 10.5 million m^3, resulting in a total cost of 670 million francs at constant 1991 values. To this day, six retention basins have been built along with the partial completion of conduits, at a cost of one hundred million francs." To provide an order of magnitude, the 1996 program was set at eighteen million francs.

A steering committee, representing all actors concerned with issues related to the risks and management of the municipal water system, laid the groundwork in 1990 for the creation of an emergency network.

Lastly, the city initiated a very sizable program of renovating the utility networks which was executed under the format of a specific concession contract. The scope of work entailed 170 million francs invested by the company and balanced by an increase of the water price over a period of 17 years. This program, was executed in junction with a large program of roadway and street lighting reconstruction, directed by the city.

o
o   o

June 1995: a repeat in political alternation. During the past round of municipal elections, Nimes' incumbent mayor was beaten by an electoral list headed by a Communist. How much of this defeat can be attributed to personal rivalries? how much to the general corruption climate? how much to increases in public service rates and in local taxes? and to unemployment levels? Nimes residents wanted to punish their mayor, symbol of the corporate management approach. A new team took office with its own political style as well as a host of other priorities. And the story goes on...

References.

Barthelemy J.R. (1991). "Le cas de Nîmes", in L'Autonomie une troisème voie. Rapport Fondation des Villes, Plan Urbain, Ministère de l'Equipement, Paris.

Bernié-Boissard C. (1994). Nîmes, le choc de la modernité. L'Harmattan, Paris.

Didier M. (1990). "Evaluation des performances de divers modes de gestion des services publics locaux", in Performance des services publics locaux, UNSPIC, Paris.

Dourlens Ch. (1991). "Nîmes, la domestication d'une catastrophe", in Regards de chercheurs sur une catastrophe. Dossiers des séminaires TTS. Ministère de l'Equipement, Paris.

Hoffmann-Martinot V. (1988). Nîmes, gestion moderniste de l'image d'une ville. Annales de la Recherche Urbaine, n°38, Paris.

Pronier R. (1983). Les municipalités communistes (bilan de trente années de gestion). Balland, Paris.

CHAPTER 5

Alain Cadiou

France,s Water Agencies or 25 Years of Sustainable Development

The current interest for the French water services management model pertains specifically to two of its parameters: the management of public water services being delegated to the private sector, and the efficiency exhibited by France'sWater Agencies. While the former has been greatly developed in the other chapters we will seek herein to explain the reasons giving rise to the latter.

The problems related to the management of water quality have started appearing relatively recently. The solution adopted by a majority of governments has consisted of transferring into this sector the responses deemed appropriate from other public service sectors. In this fashion, the issue of pollution, considered as environmentally harmful, has been the focus of more repressive-type legislation, based on the notion that the party causing the adverse impacts is fundamentally delinquent and thereby must be punished. The systematic application of a syllogism, seemingly so straightforward, has not always however proven to be effective. Though such an application has yielded quite satisfactory results in Northern Europe and America, the same cannot necessarily be stated for other parts of the globe, where merely promulgating a new piece of legislation does not ensure automatic compliance.

The French approach presents radical differences. It doesn't intend to constrain the polluter, rather to incite the polluter to diminish the impacts his actions generate on water resources. This incentive system has been founded on the Anglo-Saxon-derived concept of "polluter-pays principle", which consists of charging the party responsible for causing the resource's pollution with the financial cost of the resultant environmental degradation.

Since the threat imposed lacked ample disuasive force, the French legislator sought to temper the penalty-oriented nature of this measure by adding an incentive-driven quality: financial compensation would be awarded for positive efforts towards improving the quality of water resources. The significance herein is to recognize pollution no longer as a crime but as a plague that society, as a whole, must strive to eradicate.

This financial consideration is, in general, the only one known to foreign professionals interested in the role of France's Water Agencies. Their success can in reality be attributed to the synergy developed among several factors, which will be highlighted.

Set of fundamental principles

Immediately following the Second World War, France experienced over a few decades the most profound transformation in its entire history. Whereas it had remained a primarily rural country ever since the Middle Ages, an unprecedented wave of migration of populations towards cities and their surrounding areas could be observed, bringing with it a whole myriad of new problems associated with demographic concentrations within limited geographical spaces.

Infrastructure facilities had to be adapted to this affluence of rural residents attracted by the employment opportunities afforded by industries and nearby-located services.

The corresponding increase in the standard of living stimulated a whole new set of needs for water and wastewater services with respect to what had existed beforehand. The development of industrial production likewise raised the demand for water, which was becoming all the more rare and whose quality was definitely deteriorating.

In zones of heavy agricultural activity, the thoughtless use of fertilizers and pesticides destined to upgrade output, along with the more widespread use of irrigation systems in these same regions heretofore contented with rainfall, also led both to a reduction in the quantity of the resource and to its progressive contamination.

The applicable French legislation at the time dated back to the end of the XIXth century and had become completely inappropriate in coping with this unprecedented level of demand. In addition, conflicts among users could no longer be settled by the pertinent administrative bodies, whose span of authority simply covered a single sector within the spectrum of water services management. No less than twelve Ministries could be counted having some level of jurisdiction in managing at least one aspect of the problem, depending on the territorial borders, which happened to correspond poorly with the water courses' natural boundaries.

The law passed on December 16, 1964 displayed a distinctly revolutionary characteristic, that still exists even 30 years after. This law was based on three guiding principles:
– the water resource management boundary is the natural hydrographic basin,
– inclusion of each basin's user groups into the policy-making arena within the Water Basin Committee,
– application of the "polluter-payer principle " and "user-pays principle " across France's six major basins.

FIGURE 1:
Map of France's Water Basins

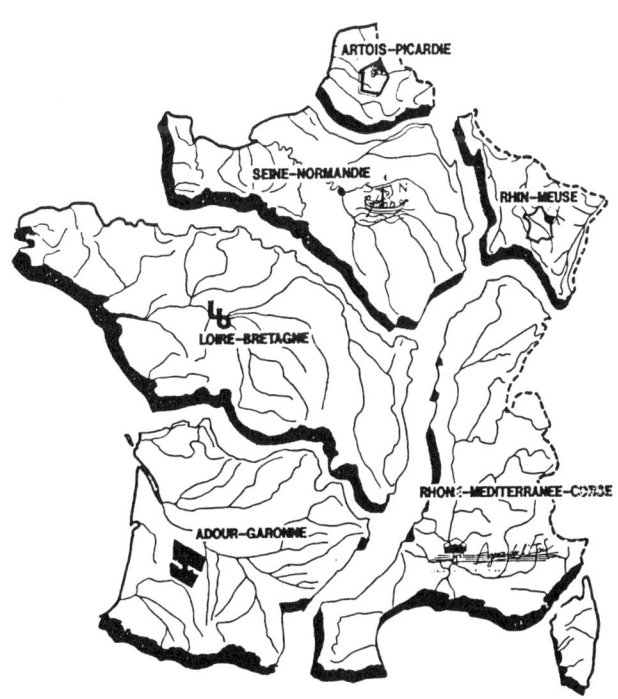

Institutional framework

The Water Basin Committee or "the water forum": This novelty introduced by the 1964 Law is, without a doubt, the most important as well as being the most difficult to apply for those countries seeking to utilize the French model. In fact, the key feature herein concerns a real decentralization of power, and thereby the State yielding a portion of its span of responsibility. It could be considered as a realistic interpretation of the principle of subsidiarity which seems to be gaining ground in the area of water services management.

Each of France's six river basin jurisdictions has been set up with its own Committee on which the legislator has included representatives of all parties with a stake in the provision of water services. The following table indicates the composition of the six Water Basin Committees.

FIGURE 2: **Composition of France's Six Water Basin Committees**					
Catchment area	Elected officials	Water users	Socioeconomic professionals	Public administration	Total
Adour Garonne	30	30	6	18	84
Artois Picardie	25	25	2	14	66
Loire Bretagne	42	42	8	22	114
Rhin Meuse	22	22	3	14	61
Rhône Méditerranée Corse	40	40	6	21	107
Seine Normandie	38	38	7	20	103

The electoral college for elected officials (mayors, members of parliament, senators, county councilors) is required to include one elected official from each administrative jurisdiction (departement) along with the mayors of the water basin's largest cities.

The electoral college for users to the committees contains representatives from all heavy water-consumption industries, as well as from environmental protection associations, fishing and outdoor sporting groups, farmers, water distribution companies, etc. The mission of this college, in addition to that of the elected officials, is to expose the problems encountered throughout the basin and to provide a forum of expression for those who observe and for those who simply endure.

The socioeconomic professionals participating are appointed by the Social and Economic Affairs Committees of each administrative region located within the basin's jurisdiction.

On the Public Administration side of this composition, all Ministries with some connection to the field of water supply (Agriculture, Budget Office, Economic Affairs, Environment, Health, Industry, Interior, Maritime Affairs, Public Works, Tourism, Transportation, Youth Affairs and Athletics) are represented; to this contingent would be added the State's regional representatives (Prefects).

It's this forum-like setting, where divergent interests often compete with one another, that constitutes the keystone to France's system of water services management. For it happens to be the melting pot wherein the basin's overall water policy is derived, concerning both underground water sources and surface sources.

Figure 2 highlights that, within each Basin Committee, the majority of seats is held by water service users (in that the elected officials do actually represent the consumers themselves) and not by the State. This fundamental point exhibits the originality of our system that's the hardest to accept on the part of heads of other countries who are seeking to set up similar structures, since this feature implies that the State, in general the sole institution holding power, must yield at least partially its span of control.

The Board of Directors. As an analogy to the governmental institutions making up a nation, the Basin Committee represents the legislative branch, while the Agency's Board of Directors performs the role of the executive branch. Each basin's Board is composed of 26 members, of which 24 are elected directly by the Basin Committee. The Board's President is appointed by the national government.

The breakdown of the members is as follows: one Chairman, eight electoral representatives, eight users' representatives, eight representatives of the Civil Service and one representative from the Water Agency's staff. The Board of Directors retains authority over all aspects concerning the running of the Agency, especially with respect to the budget, water use taxes, subsidies, regularly-scheduled programs, etc.

The Water Agency. The Water Agency is the executive arm of the two previouslydiscussed entities. It holds the official status of a public-sector institution endowed with a civil service mission and financial autonomy. Its General Manager is appointed by the Prime Minister. The Agencies' collective goal is to improve both the quality and the quantity of the nation's water resources.

The Agencies' set of general objectives can be summarized as follows:

- preserving the natural resource,
- protecting public health, and
- reconciling economic activity with environmental protection
(this notion applies to the Sustainable Development issue raised in
Agenda 21 at the Rio de Janiero Conference).

In organizational terms, the Water Agencies display relatively
light administrative structures (comprising for the Seine-Normandy
Agency, by far the largest of the six, a staff size of 380). Their domain
of competence encompasses both technical and financial matters.
They exercise no policing power whatsoever over the use of water (which
remains the role of the State). They do not act in the capacity of a facilities
owner, nor do they provide water supply or wastewater services (under
the control of municipalities).

FIGURE 3:
Map of the Seine-Normandy Water Basin)

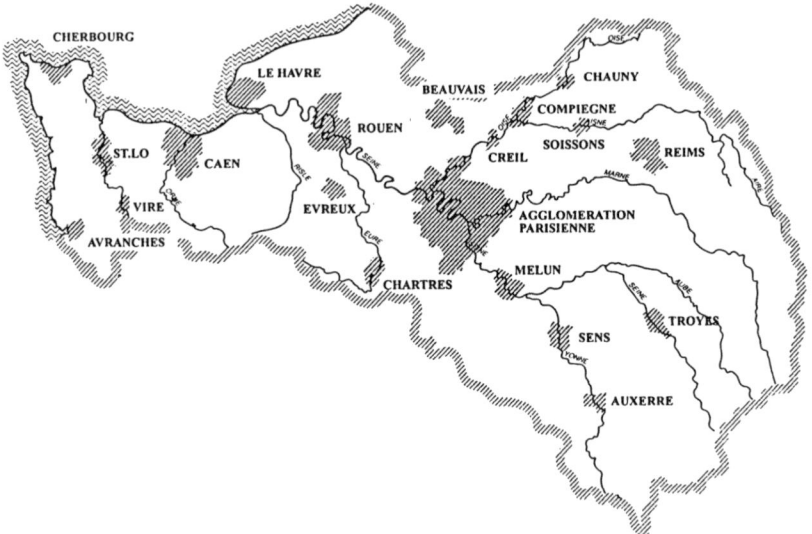

Economic instruments

Water fees. In order to implement the policies developed by the
corresponding Basin Committees, the Agencies are authorized to
charge all water consumers with a fee. Such a fee can take on two forms:
a water intake tax designed to augment the quantity of water available,
based on the volume being extracted from either underground or surface
sources, and a water pollution tax levied to upgrade the quality of the
resource, based on the weight of pollutants discharged.

Residents, industries and farmers are all required to pay water intake
taxes. Concerning agricultural uses, negotiations held between the

government and farming organizations have resulted in paying the volume-based extraction component of the use tax only for irrigation purposes and the pollution component solely by cattle breeders. The tax corresponding to the pollution engendered by an excessive use of fertilizers and pesticides has yet to be collected.

The use tax rates, which were held very low at the outset, climbed until 1991. From that point forward, political decisions at the national level have stimulated a strong surge in these taxes that's clearly visible in Figure 4 shown below.

FIGURE 4:
Progression of water use taxes for the Seine-Normandy Agency, in Millions of constant francs, 1994.

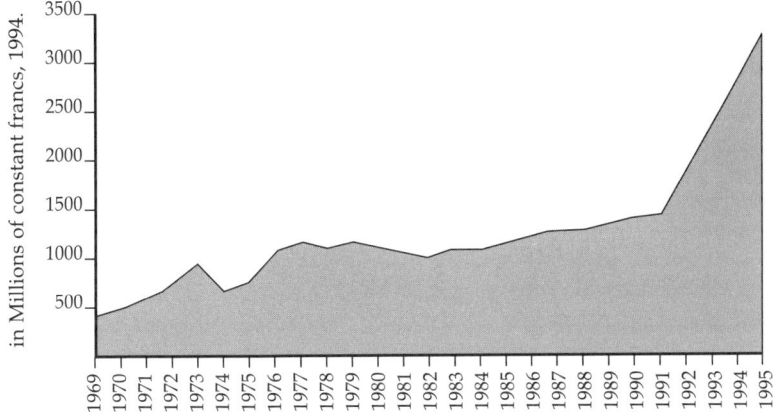

In 1996, the contribution of each resident of the Seine-Normandy Water Agency jurisdiction amounted to about 40 US dollars, which served to generate a total figure of 680 million dollars. An additional amount of approximately 70 million US dollars was provided by industries.

Subsidies. The theory behind the principle of "polluter-pays" assumes a high enough tax level to dissuade the polluter from discharging without ensuring any treatment. When the Water Agencies were being set up, an analysis concluded that applying this premise blindly would seriously jeopardize the profitability of the firms operating within this sector. A redistribution of taxes was therefore envisioned, in the form of subsidies targeted at combatting the very same environmental impacts that had motivated imposing the tax in the first place. To the axiom "Whoever pollutes should pay", a rather significant corollary had been added: "Whoever purifies should receive financial assistance". It's most certainly this last principle that facilitated the enactment of the 1964 Law and that enabled making up for the lag France had accumulated with respect to waste water treatment plants.

The two types of charges collected have given rise to two types of involvement on the part of the Water Agencies: resource improvement in quantity terms and resource improvement in quality terms. It had quickly become apparent that the need for quality improvement was decisively the more pressing. In the Seine-Normandy basin in particular, this trend has been accentuated, inasmuch as nearly 90% of all financial assistance is being earmarked for pollution abatement.

Financial assistance takes the form of subsidies (for 2/3 of the total) and very low-interest loans (1 /3). They serve to finance a portion of the necessary service facilities.

Examples of facilities financed by the Water Agencies

- dams-reservoirs,
- drinking water treatment plants,
- wells and borehules,
- connections between water supply networks,
- waste water treatment plants,
- wastewater collection networks,

- protection of wells area
- industrial waste treatment,
- autonomous wastewater equipment,
- run off pollution control equipment,
- assistance in the operation of waste water treatment plants,
- etc.

Financial assistance provided by the Agency, while not substantial at the outset (1969), has become, over time and thanks to increases in the water charges, a vital element in the projects undertaken by facilities owners. As an example, the graph below indicates the evolution in constant francs of financial assistance granted by the Seine-Normandy Agency ever since its creation up through the end of 1996 forecast.

Figures 4 and 5, in displaying the evolution of water charges revenues collected and financial aid dispensed since the start-up of the Agency, respectively, highlight a significant rise since 1990, which happens to correspond to the State's withdrawal from the water services sector in France.

Incentive bonuses. The third economic instrument being utilized consists of incentive bonuses. For individual households, the Agency charges a use tax corresponding to a fixed level of pollution ascribed to each resident. In return, it transfers to the local authorities that operate water treatment facilities a bonus determined by the amount of pollution being removed. This compensation enables lowering the operating expenses being born by local authorities.

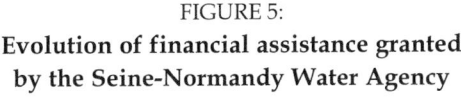

FIGURE 5:
**Evolution of financial assistance granted
by the Seine-Normandy Water Agency**

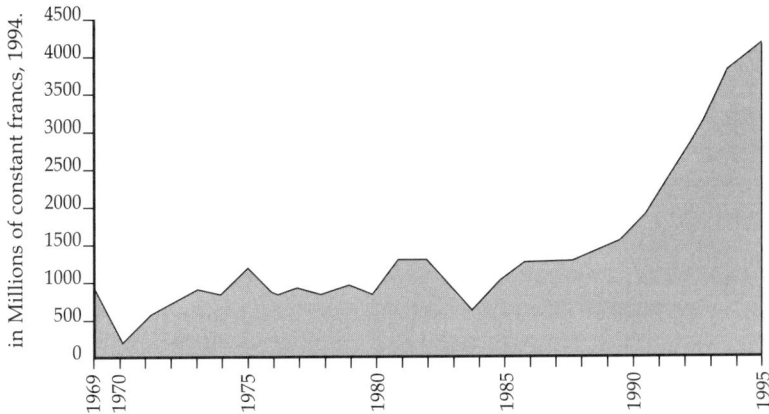

As far as industries are concerned, they are only requested to pay the difference between the amount of pollution produced and the amount of pollution being treated. These incentive bonuses for water treatment have taken a much greater significance over time : in 1996, they represented 46% of the Seine-Normandy Agency's budget (including the bonuses transfered to industries).

Other means of action

Planning. The Agency is operated on the basis of five-year programs that outline the water use tax rates to be charged as well as a set of objectives to be achieved. The outcome of a compromise between what is truly desirable and what is actually possible, these programs are heavily debated within the Basin Committee commissions, and involve a good number of external professionals.

The Agency's Sixth Program, covering the period 1992-1996, is a particularly ambitious one: it calls for 4 billion $ in assistance being accorded by the Seine-Normandy Agency, which would translate into a minimum of 6 billion $ worth of construction work in the field.

Instituting a contractual framework. Since the Agencies can't exercise any real coercive power, they had to institute an incentive-based strategy. It's in this perspective that they have increasingly been calling upon the use of contracts by means of entering into agreements with the representatives of interested local and regional authorities. Two types of contracts are most frequently encountered:

– river basin contracts with local authorities devoted to a rational management scheme of a specific water course, in terms of the water supply plan along with the wastewater discharge and overall environmental quality control program.

– urban area contracts in which either the mayor or the head of a group of municipalities undertakes a water resource improvement program, with respect to quantity as well as quality.

In both cases, the Agency agrees to provide, as a priority, subsidies and ultimately the loans necessary for financing the implementation of those measures stipulated in the contract.

Results

The Water Agencies are the only pertinent bodies able to produce an overall vision of the problems affecting the provision of water services. Their range of actions over the past 25 years has enabled, in addition to upgrading the level of drinking water distribution, develop the construction of water treatment plants which at the time of the Agencies' creation were extremely limited. As an example, Figure 6 exhibits the rapid growth in the number of public water treatment facilities within the Seine-Normandy Water Basin territory (the Agency's actions commenced in 1969).

FIGURE 6

**Evolution of the number of waste water treatment plants
in the Seine Normandy Basin**

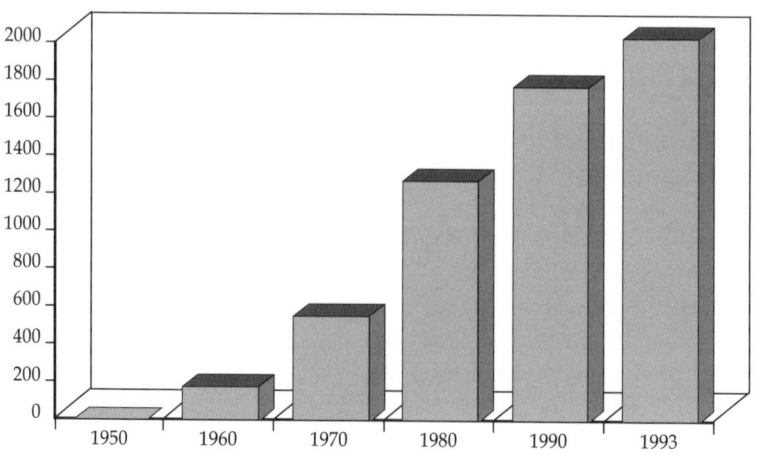

Improvements registered in the quality of effluent being discharged by localities is less remarkable, since the wastewater treatment plant itself constitutes but one link in the chain of the entire process; furthermore, it's the rationalization of the collection networks that most significantly impacts the overall level of efficiency. Herein lies the essential reason why a major portion of Agency financing resources are currently being devoted to efforts carried out in collection network improvement.

Industrial pollution clean-up initiatives have yielded by far the most tangible results: the quantity of pollution being eliminated either through treatment facilities or through modifications introduced in manufacturing processes has improved from roughly 10% in 1968 to 90% in 1996.

These successes are, to some extent, counterbalanced by the semi - failure encountered with the agricultural community. Following long years of negotiations, authorities were in fact finally able to persuade farmers to pay the water charges corresponding to the pollution caused by breeding activities; however, such an agreement has not yet been reached concerning the pollution generated by fertilizer and pesticide use. This specific issue have been very central to the discussions held in preparing the Agency's Seventh Program (covering the period 1997-2001).

The future : reconciling man with nature

Setting up the Water Agencies was carried out first and foremost by water supply experts, and then chemists were included on the professional team. Today, also being called upon for their valued expertise are biologists, naturalists, landscape architects and the like. This trend reflects an evolution in how the Agencies are examining the whole water services management issue.

As for the elected officials, they have for a long time considered the Agencies as a valuable technical and financial resource without any great policy implications. This period is now over; the sheer size of the budget (1474 million US dollars for the SeineNormandy Agency alone in 1996) along with the ever-increasing awareness on the part of the public have served to alter the attitude of both elected representatives and water users alike regarding this policy instrument. It'sone that remains under their joint control as well as one that they hope not to be stripped of by some central government authority.

Concerning the technical and financial aspects, charges collected on the volume of water extracted represent a continually declining share of the budgets being adopted by the Agencies, which are becoming more heavily committed to combatting pollution. As a result, a multiplication in the number of pollution-charges, as well as in the number of parameters utilized to base the tax amount computations, can be observed. A summary of current trends is structured as follows:

Management of water facilities. The Agencies' financial system has enabled the creation of many water supply-related facilities. The efficiency of these facilities implies constant attention being paid to overseeing their operations. The incentive bonuses allocated to facilities owners have contributed to reducing operating costs, and this allocation should rise over time.

Bacteriology. The pollution-removal efforts undertaken by local authorities has, up until now, concerned pollution of a carbonous, nitrogenous and toxic nature. Studies conducted over the past few years have highlighted the persistence of a bacterial pollution, on which the treatment facilities in place exert no impact whatsoever. Additional taxes have been envisioned in order to treat this type of pollution.

Nitrates. Increases in the rate of nitrates found in underground water sources, due to the uncontrolled use of fertilizers, worries service managers who have only been able, for the time being, to observe the phenomenon without putting a halt to it. Efforts made on the part of the Water Basin Agencies to implement a specific nitrate pollution charge have met, up until now, with hostility from the agricultural community, whose attitude has largely been motivated by the economic difficulties currently being experienced.

In fact, nitrates are merely the tip of the iceberg in terms of the pollution emanating from agricultural activities, wherein the use of pesticides presents a much greater danger to the survival of all aquatic species as well as of mankind. In order to be able to provide a response on this topic, new charges have been proposed; however, the bases upon which they'll be computed have yet to be defined.

Pollution caused by rainwater runoff. The concentration of population in urban areas along with the increasing impermeability of soils have given rise to a higher level of water runoff during major storms. The harsh cleansing of polluted soils and the overflow of wastewater collection networks into water courses located downstream can engender a considerable level of pollution that's capable of completely negating in the span of a few hours' time the extent of pollution-removal efforts. It's most likely that in the future, a special charge fund will be established to cope with the enormity of the capital investments to be carried out, and in particular those within France's largest metropolitan areas (the Paris region in the first place). The basis for this taxation still remains to be defined since no logical correlation exists between this source of pollution and the water user.

Individual wastewater treatment. Some municipalities inside the water basin jurisdiction contain fewer than 100 residents, a feature which makes implementing a collective wastewater system an extremely costly, in addition to a highly inefficient, venture. The future solution retained will most certainly consist of standardizing and collectively managing the individual treatment systems currently in place.

Physical improvement projects for the basin's rivers. Non-navigable waterways do not, in general, benefit from systematic maintenance programs. When high-water levels have been reached, the obstacles that hinder the river's natural course tend to cause flooding. In addition, the haphazard growth pattern of brush and trees along the river's banks prevents sunlight from penetrating through, thereby diminishing the water's selfpurification capacities. The Agencies are presently devoting a small portion of their budgets towards improving the current state of rivers' physical appearance, yet a more durable solution would necessitate a special tax.

Protection against flood waters. In France, material damage related to flooding is in theory covered within the scope of national disaster-relief programs. The increasing withdrawal of the State in the area of financing water supply infrastructure facilities will most likely lead to the application of special taxes, which would at least enable financing more prevention-oriented equipment.

Conclusion.

As Water Agencies have been experiencing great success at home, their fundamental principle is now beginning to be exported to several other regions throughout the world. It should be noted that this principle has not necessarily impacted the privatization of water and wastewater services. In France itself, the private management of services has actually expanded significantly, in proportional terms, since the Agencies were set up (see Figure 7 below).

The success achieved by Water Agencies relies, first of all, on the harmonious marriage of an economic incentive instrument with a political

FIGURE 7:

**Evolution of the private management of water and wastewater
services nationwide Millions of residents served**

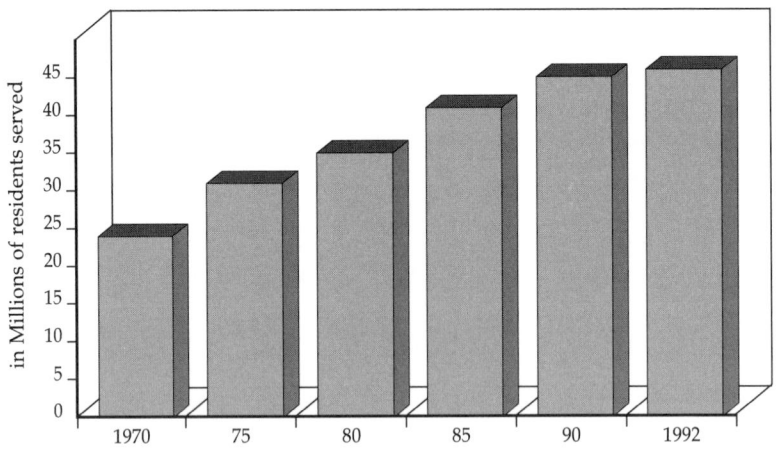

institution. The consensus reached among the various actors involved
in the domain of water services has paved the way for a much easier
acceptance of decisions on the part of those to whom these very
decisions apply. As a result, the polluter is no longer considered as
a delinquent, but rather as a partner with the Agency in pursuing the
least expensive solution to resolving a common problem. Ultimately,
both the flexibility and speed with which the Agency reacts represents
a decisive element in maintaining their reputation. The organizational
framework retained for the Agencies is relatively light (a workforce
of roughly a thousand across the six agencies), well located throughout
the nation's territory, and composed of specialized technicians in the
field of water, capable of advising each type of user on the most
economical solution approach to his particular set of difficulties.
The goal of the Agencies is to optimize the use of non-extensible budget
resources through a maximum of actions undertaken.

Up until now, the Agencies have, first and foremost, enabled
developing infrastructure facilities. It would seem that their role
with respect to financing the operations of these facilities will be
increasingly requested to expand. Such a trend has now become
more generalized, and in the future, expenditures earmarked for
the environment will be more often allocated to management
assignments.

Nonetheless, even though spectacular results have been obtained,
it should not be inferred that an incentive-based system is sufficient
to win the battle against pollution. Also involved in the effort are State-

run services for policing the use of water, whose actions are coordinated with those undertaken by the Agencies. A recent law has allowed reinforcing the range of their scope of action. This additional assistance will enable perfecting later on the endeavor initiated a quarter of a century ago, so as to instill within the sector of water services that character of purity it never should have relinquished, either in Nature or in the mind of Man.

CHAPTER 6

Henri Coing

Changing the Rules Caracas: Chronicle of a Missed Privatization Opportunity

Caracas, the 7th of August, 1992: on this day was held the solemn opening of the bids submitted by the five candidate consortia for the concession of water and wastewater services in the Greater Caracas Metropolitan Area. Present at this bid disclosure were the Minister of the Environment, heads of the organization overseeing the privatization program (FIV), members of Parliament; the absence of two of the three mayors concerned was definitely conspicuous. The press was also in attendance, as were representatives from various political parties and organizations supporting the political opposition, all voicing loud and clear their desire that this call for tender be nullified.

The companies presented their bid envelopes: three of them merely contained letters of apology, announcing their withdrawl from the competition; two others contained offers, whose conditions nonetheless were, as everyone knew, unacceptable. The call for tender was then declared null and void : what an unexpected blow, coming after months of negotiation between the government and the candidate consortia.

Beyond the anecdotal value of the story and the controversies undoubtedly stirred by such a turn of events, a few lessons can still be drawn from the experience; their value serves less for a debate on the virtues of privatization or the delegation of public services than it does for an assessment of the ground rules in effect, their coherence and their stability. The choice had been made to delegate the service as a concession, in place of the previous national-level, public-sector management system, or instead of in-house municipal management. This implied the resolution of at least three sets of problems: defining a stable system of financing water services; deriving a new model for regulation and control; and clearly identifying the concession-granting authority's role and clarifying the relationships between the State and the local authorities. These are the three themes that will be examined herein.

The provision of water in Caracas poses some complex problems: this city of four million population relies on water resources located at greater and greater distances, up to 250 km. away at the Guarico River; pumping is then required to compensate for an elevation difference of one thousand meters. Water distribution itself is very costly in terms of pumping, with the city being spread out over altitudes ranging from 850 to 1,450 meters. The service's facilities are hindered by a lack of homogeneity (due to a later integration of private utility networks) and a certain dilapidation; the physical state of the network has caused continual ruptures in the pipes, as well as a high rate of losses. Service flaws are therefore less due to an inadequacy in water resources (as the capacity for water conveyance and treatment enable meeting the demand) or to a delay in extending the network (with a connection rate of over 85%) than they are to a real deficiency in maintenance, renewal, operations, commercial management or cost recovery, etc. As far as the financial situation is concerned, it can be described quite simply as catastrophic. In sum, the poor quality of service (scarcity of water resources, delivery interruptions, continual degradation in the level of service) has illustrated the breakdown in a particular financing model, coupled with a breakdown in an enterprise-management model.[1]

The service had been provided by a national-level, public enterprise, the Instituto Nacional de Obras Sanitarias (INOS), created in 1943. This entity was a heavily centralized structure, in which the division responsible for water services to the capital city, the Acueducto Metropolitano (AZMC), had almost no autonomy. Projects for reform have succeeded one another over the past ten years, especially by means

---

1. For additional details, refer to:

Marcano E., La crisis del agua en Caracas, UCV, Caracas 1993.

Marcano E., Coing H., Meurant P., Infrastructura de servicios de agua, cloacas y alcantarillado en el Area Metropolitana de Caracas, UCV, 1984, vol. 5.

of internal deconcentration (1986), followed by the creation of regional enterprises, subsidiaries of a holding company (1989), whose intention was to become independent.

1989 marked the year of the election of Carlos Andrés Pérez as the nation's President; it also ushered in a new era, one towards liberalizing the economy and privatizing the public sector. Every major public service was concerned; telecommunications was the first to be restructured and privatized (through selling the enterprise CANTV). The sector of electricity services was next to experience the beginning of a reorganization and an initial wave of privatizations. In the area of public transportation, the creation of a national fund (FONTUR) helped pave the way for its restructuring. The international call for tender for Caracas's water services concession is thereby not an isolated case, but rather part of a more global-oriented project.[2]

Chronicle

1987: The government solicits the private company "Electricité de Caracas" (Caracas Electric Company), in charge of energy distribution for practically the entire metropolitan area, to be responsible for handling the collection of water service fees and household waste disposal fees. The company turns down the initial offer, considering it too risky.

1989: The government takes the offensive, and obliges all electricity companies to assume collection of fees for water and waste services.

1990: The situation of Caracas's water services is worsening, especially following the drought. The government asks Caracas Electric Company to take on responsibility for all water services throughout the capital city.

June 21, 1990: The President of INOS announces publicly that his organization has planned to grant concessions for the construction and operations of water production and conveyance facilities to foreign groups, while granting the concession for treatment and distribution to Caracas Electric Company.

July 9, 1990: The project is presented to a meeting of selected Cabinet members; the media proclaims: "The Ministers approved yesterday the awarding to Caracas Electric Company of the contract to operate the service at every phase, from water distribution all the way through customer billing." Start-up is planned for January 1991.[3]

---

2. See: Coing, H., La privatisation des services urbains, Vénézuela 1989-1993, mimeo 72 pages LATTS 1994.

3 . Comments provided by L.J. Diaz Zuloaga, representative of the Caracas Electric Company, during the public meeting organized by the FIV at the end of 1991, entitled: BCV, La privatizacion, un dialogo necessario, FIV 1991, 286 pages.

Chronicle

The FIV Bulletin presents the decision as a fait accompli: "Caracas Electric Company is responsible for the entire running of Acueducto Metropolitano".

1991 starts up with no major event. Shortly thereafter, the process once again picks up, but this time under a different format: an international call for tender, led by INOS and its appropriate oversight Ministry; the FIV, in charge of the privatization program, was not involved in the procedure.

July 1992: Five consortia announce their candidacy: Soraguas (SAUR, Aguas de Valencia, Viccler de Venezuela); Biwater-Thames; Compagnie Générale des Eaux, (OTV, Sogesur de Espana, Precomprimido de Venezuela); Aguas de Caracas (Electricidad de Caracas, Lyonnaise des Eaux-Dumez, Aguas de Barcelona, Anglian Water); and Canalven (Canal Isabel II, FOCSA de Espana).

August 8, 1992: The call for tender is officially nullified.

However, with respect to water services, the process went awry and eventually came to a halt. Why? To find a response, let's first take a glimpse at the story's chronicle.

As an initial step, between 1987 and 1990, the government considered entering into a management contract with a company selected in accordance with the principle of "intuitu personnae" (the selection of a corporate entity outside a competitive tender procedure), in this case being: Caracas Electric Company, a large private Venezuelan-held group[4], which planned on forming a specialized company in association with French partners. The Group then assumed responsibility for the entire workforce involved in the service's provision. A concessionary system was foreseen, provided one fundamental exception: the vast program to renew the water mains would be financed by a loan issued through the IBRD (International Bank of Reconstruction and Development), to be paid back out of the State's budget. Rates would be progressively adjusted, over a period of seven years, with a decreasing level of subsidy being allocated by the government.

---

4. Created in 1895, Caracas Electric Company produces and distributes electricity throughout the Caracas Metropolitan Area. It controls less than 10% of the nation's production, yet almost one-third of the distribution. At the time of the privatization of the telephone industry, it entered into this sector of activity, where it now holds 23% of the firm's capital. Its quoted stock market valuation in 1993 was 1.25 million US$, and its revenues reached 425 million US$. In 1993, the Spanish public corporation Endesa purchased 8% of the capital of Caracas Electric and signed an agreement with Banque Latino (part of the Capriles Group) to take control of the company.

As the negotiating process was coming to completion, the project suddenly hit an impasse. For what reason? Certain ministries feared a concentration of power by conceding water services to a company that had already built for itself a powerful position in the area of electricity and telephone services. Furthermore, a conflict ensued between Caracas Electric Company and the government: the latter cancelled the preferential rate of exchange being accorded up until then for the payment of private external debt. Caracas Electric Company fought with determination in order to retain this privilege, deemed so vital to the company, which was heavily indebted..., their efforts were nonetheless in vain.

The attempt to delegate the service had therefore met with an initial failure. In 1991, when the project had returned to the forefront in the form of an international call for tender, an intense round of negotiations was being held with the candidate consortia in order to draft the contract document as well as to outline the obligations incumbent upon the concessionaire. Each of the interested parties was supposed to propose a per-m^3 sales price, and the low bidder would then be declared the winner. At the same time, discussions were underway with local authorities on the creation of a "Mancommunidad", a sort of intermunicipal syndicate, that would perform the roles of both concession-granting authority and regulator. However, on the 7th of August, 1992, the date the bids were officially disclosed, the Mancommunidad had still not been created; two of the most concerned mayors would not attend the envelope-opening session and instead simply requested a copy of the final bid evaluation report. The message was clear that some crucial questions had gone unaddressed.

Moreover, the privatization commission within the National Assembly had announced three months prior its opposition to the concessionary project "on the grounds that it hadn't respected the rules stipulated both by the law of privatization and by the law governing the municipal system". From their perspective, trade unions were protesting against the favoritism being accorded one of the candidate consortia and against the conflicts of interest that concerned some of the negotiating team's leaders. [5]

The entire operation was poorly orchestrated. As opposed to what was transpiring in other sectors, no preliminary study on the restructuring of the water supply sector was actually carried out, nor

---

5. The sheer fact that the negotiation was conducted by the sector's oversight Ministry (Environment) and the heads of the public enterprise (INOS), as opposed to the Fondo de Inversiones de Venezuela (FIV), the organization in charge of the privatization program, raises some very pertinent queries.

was any definition of the new ground rules actually forwarded. It's not purely a coincidence then that water supply just so happens to be the one sector for which the World Bank has decided to break ranks with the approach adopted, and whose members have delivered in private their harshest criticisms. Everything that occurs is performed on the spur of the moment, without applying any kind of explicit strategy, and under a state of emergency.

Yet, the failure of these initiatives cannot be fully explained by this mere overlapping of conflicts. It does actually serve to highlight the entire set of problems, which affect laying the ground rules for the entire sector, thereby potentially hindering the application of any other model for restructuring this public service.

Financing the service

The new policy established in 1989 is clear in its guiding principle: the services themselves must provide their own financial equilibrium. Such a stance represents a complete change in course from the previous model, according to which the bulk of capital investment was being financed by budget allocations, and rates weren't even covering operating costs.

An initial attempt to introduce reform took shape in 1974, when the government decided to eliminate all operating subsidies and to require INOS to attain financial equilibrium for its operations (not including capital investments). Owing to inflation and in the absence of any rate adjustment mechanism, this equilibrium was in fact never reached, and the deficits only accumulated. This effort engendered a significant drop in the service rates being charged in real terms during the 1970's. Over the 1980's, with inflation running between 20% and 40% per year, the situation would take on dramatic proportions! From 1981 to 1988, the service rate remained unchanged while inflation soared to 348%! In 1988, operating costs alone reached 6.5 Bs/m^3, whereas the user was only paying 1.03 Bs/m^3 under the fixed rate, and 2.40 Bs/m^3 under a volume per-m^3 based rate.

In 1992, the average price per m^3 in Caracas was 8 Bs (0.08 US dollars). At the same time, the concession's set of specifications called for a maximum per-m^3 price of 36 Bs, that included covering operating costs, capital investment and network renewal; the candidate firms found this price ceiling too low. The limited scale of the programmed price increases lent a sufficient explanation by itself for the political difficulty encountered in implementing such a rate ceiling.

This difficulty was only accentuated by the new policy that also projected a reduction in cross-budget subsidies, between regions much like between categories of consumers, along with a closing of the gap between household service rates and industrial / commercial rates.

In addition, the promise of "rates that cover costs" was seriously discredited by a presumed ignorance of actual cost levels. It had become common knowledge that the public-sector enterprise was operated with a bloated staff size, and that its level of productivity was relatively poor. Any price increase was therefore difficult to justify, while along the same lines, high costs couldn't be easily defended either. For example, users were able to read in El Diario on July 5, 1993 that operating costs for the water treatment plant amounted to 300 million per year in personnel expenditures, whereas after "privatization" (through service management contract), the plant's total operating costs had been reduced to 70 million. The reputation of wastefulness and inefficiency typically attributed to public enterprises, in combination with a very low level of service, impeded any effort to raise rates. In much the same way, such a reputation also hindered the effort to collect outstanding bills. In Caracas, not even half of the water produced was actually billed, and only a minute fraction of the bills sent was ever collected (which serves to explain why the request was submitted in 1987 to tie payment for water services with that for electricity).

The main problem has resulted from a breakdown in the economic model on which the social equilibrium of the country had been founded prior to any redistribution. Subsidies for basic services corresponded to a redistribution of oil-related revenues; the social and political compromize in application at the time implied that services would be assured practically free of charge. Though the working class benefitted from huge State subsidies, the big winner in this system happened to be the middle class; the inequal access to public services would incite a massive redistribution of revenue in their favor.

This equilibrium was jeopardized by the economic crisis and a liberalization of the economy decided in 1989. The ensuing changes caused a dramatic drop in the real buying power of the working class; according to the Venezuelan Central Bank [6], the buying power of

---

6. In order to fully comprehend the setting, it is essential to grasp the contrast between an economy reentering a growth phase (an increase in GDP of 26% over a three-year period), a stagnant or slightly decreasing level of unemployment, coupled with a strong rate of inflation that acts as a stifling "tax" being levied on all wage earners. As a means of maintaining the buying power of a minimum-wage salary at 1984 levels, it would be necessary to raise the salary in 1993 to 19,000 Bs, in comparison with the real figure of 9,000 Bs.

a minimum wage earner decreased by 45% between March 1989 and July 1993. And yet, both inflation and the removal of price controls on basic goods (for example, milk and medecine) had a much stronger impact on the budgets of working class households than did the increase in the rates charged for public services [7]. However, these rate hikes just happened to symbolize the straw that broke the camel's back and served to assemble a united front, composed of both the middle and lower classes most heavily affected by the increases.

The government was actually hesitating between several means of financing public services. In the initial plan for delegating service to the Caracas Electricity Company (1989), the rate was slated to rise gradually over a seven-year period and didn't include the cost of the network's facilities renewal program. In the concession project (1990), the rate charged covered the total extent of costs. In 1993, following the failure of the tender procedure, the average price of water in Caracas (for a consumption level of 40 m^3/month) was set at 25 Bs, meaning significantly lower than the price established for the concession (equivalent to 50 Bs in 1993). In the meantime, the government had launched a "mega social project" of some 800 million dollars, devoted particularly to infrastructure facilities within working class districts; it had also introduced the notion of a socially-progressive service rate, whereby the amount of the water bill could not exceed 3% of the minimum wage for the target group. Ultimately, the government decreed in 1993 that water supply constituted a service of "basic necessity", and as such was to fall under the scope of application of consumer protection laws and to have its rates established by formal edict. Over a span of four years, the government had thereby successively or simultaneously relied upon very distinct models for the financing of public services.

It goes without saying that the previous model is most assuredly defunct: Venezuela will simply never again encounter the kind of financial situation that enabled the model's development in the first place. Nonetheless, no alternative model has yet to be defined and calibrated; depending on the nature of constraints and circumstances, the current tendency is to oscillate strongly between contradictory objectives. Herein lies the reason why the contract's rate clauses could be acceptable to residents while lacking credibility in the eyes of the firms bidding for the concession.

---

7. With the exception of the area of urban public transportation services, almost all major political crises over the past ten years have been ignited by increases in transportation fares.

The regulation of public services

The word "regulation" itself is new to Venezuelans, as it is to the rest of Latin America. Its roots are decidedly Anglo-Saxon, introduced via the World Bank and the Interamerican Bank. For example, the sector of electricity services underwent a restructuring program that included the separation of the functions of production, transmission and distribution, thereby engendering the break-up of monopolies along with the creation of a national regulatory authority. In the area of water services, the reference model has been more along the lines of a service delegation, and especially that of the concession. However, in order to assure its effective control, the creation of a special body called "agencia reguladora" has been planned (Privatizacion, n° 12, 1992).

Besides a mere change in vocabulary, a real redefinition of responsibilities and roles assumed by the various actors is actually taking place. New rules have come into effect that dictate the relationships between public authorities and service providers, as well as between these service operators and the users-residents themselves.

In the previous model, public-sector enterprises, acting in the capacity of instruments under public control, had been directly overseen by the Ministry responsible for the particular public service sector. In cases where private firms were conferred a public service, they would enter into either a service provision contract (for waste services), or a "permit" (public transportation) or a "license" (electricity); nonetheless, their obligations, the methods utilized for controlling results and their costs were all barely formalized. For both public-sector enterprises and private firms alike, the "reporting" obligation actually turned out to be scaled back to its most basic format. As a result, official explanations about costs, rates, the operating deficit or promises for improvement had lost all credibility [8]. This lack of confidence on the part of the people towards public service institutions had become one of the causes for the crisis they were experiencing.

The new policy implied a thorough transformation of the relationships with the service provision entity. The outset of this transformation was clearly visible when the FIV, assigned responsibility for the

---

8. The same mechanism serves to explain the difficulty in raising rates: the continual presence of corruption, reaching the very highest echelons, engendered the attitude that resources were being wasted. Why should employees, or families living on limited incomes, alone pay the consequences, through higher rates? Once again, we're confronted with a weakening of the State's legitimacy, whether it be more regulatory-driven or more market-oriented.

privatization effort, signed contracts with new regional water supply firms. These firms were required to attain certain objectives with respect to financial autonomy (reaching within a span of three years the "first-stage equilibrium"), service extension and productivity. In the Caracas water services concession project, the presence of a contract

---

The new set of service obligations

- continuity of service; equal treatment of all customers. INOS was not held accountable for service interruptions, nor for its strategy to share water shortages across the city's different zones. A wide disparity in customer treatment could be observed to the detriment of the residents of working class districts, where water sometimes would simply not arrive for hours or days, and even in some cases for weeks or months on end. It had become impossible to obtain information on the rationing plan and its applicable set of criteria. Caracas's outlying municipalities would complain of being sacrificed for the well-being of the capital city.

The new concessionaire is contractually obligated to treat all service subscribers equally. In case of rationing, therefore, it must announce its apportioning plan. For a service interruption exceeding 24 hours, or if the cut-off impacts more than 5% of all users (to be lowered to 1% by 1995), it must devise a special program to mitigate the effects of the service interruption. In the case of an unjustified interruption, service subscribers will be entitled to some form of compensation. In cases of water shortage, the resource should be allocated among the various distribution networks in a proportional manner depending on consumption volumes.

- illegal connections and incorporating new zones. Network extension programs in working class districts undertaken by INOS and other public-sector institutions were sporadic and lacked a single overreaching plan. As the district continued to grow, after installation of the network, new connections, performed either by INOS or by illegal means, would go unrecorded. The network could thus not be strengthened, and these consumers could not be billed. The service was deteriorating while the service's users were not paying.

The new concessionaire agreed to put the recordkeeping on hook-ups into order, within a contractually-stipulated time frame; yet, it must build beforehand the facilities that allow guaranteeing service quality.

- results-based obligations. INOS submitted an annual report to the Ministry overseeing its operations. No results-based obligations however were imposed, and it only furnished information on how its financial resources were being put to use. Furthermore, it only made mention of ongoing problems to announce that they'd soon be resolved, provided the new investment plan was financed. INOS was never held accountable to the municipalities, that did nonetheless act as concession-granting authorities.

The new concessionaire agrees to carry out a network extension program by specifying the coverage ratio, the rate of meter installation, the number of additional service subscribers per year, the rate of pipe replacement, along with a program for improving the level of service quality (see infrastructure description). It is also required to present an annual report on the results obtained as well as on service extension and quality to the Mancommunidad.

   - quality of service and customer relations. INOS didn't make use of any indication of service quality, and its customer relations activities were continually being criticized. On a daily basis, newspapers would print complaints about excessive response time and drawn-out repair schedules as well as pipe ruptures flooding out streets and leaving families without water. In addition, no one actually believed in the potability of the water being supplied by the network [9]; anyone who could do so either procured their drinking water straight from the source or equipped their homes with water filters.

   The new concessionaire must implement, within a month's time, an effective system for processing and responding to complaints, and for identifying and repairing flaws. Every year, it must inform Mancommunidad of the number of complaints received as well as of the time required for response and reparation. Furthermore, it must conduct two customer satisfaction surveys a year of service subscribers and publish their results. The contract includes annual objectives for improving the following array of service indicators: water quantity billed / quantity produced; % of meters in operation; number of complaints received per 100 subscribers; % of repairs completed in less than 48 hours (which must increase from 50% to 90%); number of complaints registered per 100 bills sent; number of hours of continuous service (in the very first year, the objective is set at 24 hours a day); maximum number of service interruptions in working class districts (from 72 hours the first year to 24 hours as of the fourth year); number of quality analysis results failing to meet acceptable water quality standards (from 10% in the first year to 0.5% in the fifth year); and the list goes on.

would serve to forward a definition of a set of completely revised obligations for the service operator.

This planned concessionary contract, while never signed, did nonetheless represent an effort to profoundly transform the relationships between the service provider, the public-sector bodies assigned to exercise control and the users. Could it have been applied? A document, contractually-binding though it may be, simply doesn't suffice on its own to transform a social relationship. The past experience with service delegation in the sector of wastes serves as a useful illustration. During the 1980's, the Report of the Contralorio General de la Republica - the equivalent of the General Accounting Office - repeated the same set of observations year in and year out: the level of service is very poor; those companies upon which waste collection was conferred were not being subjected to any controls. "The IMAU

---

9. In February 1994, the newly-appointed Minister of the Environment proclaimed, "Caracas's water is not drinkable," and announced that he would "seek the procurement of appropriate resources for renovating all water treatment facilities... so as to finally be able to tell the local authorities that they are actually consuming potable water" (El Diario de Caracas, 3/2/94).

(public-sector entity assigned to run the service) is lacking the basic information necessary for evaluating the achievement of the objectives set" (COPRE 1989). Moreover, the Report added: "The State nurtures its relationships with the private sector, within the framework of new management structures, showing promise in their own right, whereby both a concept and a strategy for autonomy / responsibility are applied to its own public enterprises: great autonomy coupled with a weak level of responsibility; the non-existence of any actual and effective set of objectives" (COPRE 1989).

Holding the service provider accountable for its management and its results to the concession-granting authority and to the user or resident involves a transformation in the very spirit of the notion of public service. The fact that on the day of the opening of the bids Mancommunidad, the concession grantor and regulatory authority, had yet to be created displays that this transformation of mentalities still had not taken place. No real consensus could be reached on the respective responsibilities of the various actors participating, and no management structure was capable of effectively overseeing the contract. Had the contract actually been signed, would the chances of reciprocally enforcing its clauses have been very strong? The model for delegating public services encompasses an entire political culture, which can't necessarily be developed overnight.

This attempt at redefining the relationships between actors could not withstand the 1992 tender failure. None of the clauses included in the concession proposal were in fact utilized by the public-sector service operator [10]; it's as if they weren't deemed pertinent for direct public management purposes. The basis required to apply the regulatory model was simply not present, nor for that matter was the basis to implement a public service delegation or a contract.

Decentralization

Up until the end of the 1980's, the model for water services management was an extremely centralized one: a national public-sector enterprise was assigned the scheduling, construction, facilities operations and management responsibility for both water and wastewater services throughout the nation's entire territory; financing was also national in scope. The situation constituted a paradox in that,

---

10. whereas in neighboring Colombia, the techniques utilized for controlling results, as stipulated by newly-enacted legislation governing urban services, are applied uniformly for all service providers, regardless of private vs. public, or national vs. local.

according to the Venezuelan Constitution, the service fell under municipal jurisdiction. The legal act that empowered INOS as the sole nationwide service operator was the granting of the concession by the municipalities themselves, even though there was no real relationship of concession-granting authority to concessionaire established with the operator. The municipal level accepted to leave in the enterprise's hands the actual responsibility for the service (and in so doing, the municipalities could still attribute service deficiencies to the enterprise); INOS exercised its role with complete independence and without being held accountable to the localities, which were supposedly granting the concessionary privileges.[11]

The policy outlined in 1989 was intended to reignite and accelerate the decentralization process through both political reform (State governors and mayors being elected by popular vote) and a massive transfer of authority to the local and regional levels. With respect to the topic under study herein, this policy got translated into a dismantling of INOS and the creation of regional public enterprises assigned management responsibility for water services. Yet, this transformation turned out to be more in appearance than in reality, for the enterprises only existed and exercised autonomously on paper.

When the national government decided to place service in the capital city under concession, the granting authority could be none other than the municipalities, wherein lies the impetus to establish among themselves a Mancommunidad, along with a technical body assigned to manage the concession. This configuration was not in place at the time the proposals were submitted, nor was anything further advanced two years hence. Besides, the municipalities hadn't even been included in the initial round of negotiations held with Caracas Electric Company, just as they hadn't with the five candidate consortia. Evidently, Venezuela's national authorities didn't consider the municipalities as the real concession-granting entity even though the planned system relied explicitly on this premise.

Confronted with decentralization, the national government's primary fear concerned rate-setting. Within the framework of the concessionary contract between INOS and the municipalities, the sole domain of authority that the municipalities had retained dealt precisely with rates. INOS (and/or the government) would propose

---

11. This scenario is not all that rare, since similar conditions can also be witnessed in Brazil within the sector of water services, as well as in France within electricity distribution.

rate adjustments, and the appropriate municipality held the right to reject them. What served to introduce a classical game of populism into the context was that the municipalities, in defending the population's interests, were placed in a position to reject proposed rate hikes without having to assume the consequences of this refusal, nor to seek alternative solutions. Herein entered into the picture the countless rate increase initiatives that would never come to fruition as well as the extended periods with no readjustment being applied. This action framework justifies the concerns expressed by the firms bidding for the concession.

The government thereby decided to strip the responsibility for water rates from the municipalities. Ironically, the government did so at a time when the decentralization process was being carried through, and when municipal autonomy was being reinforced. It would promulgate a decree (no. 2786 of 27 January 1993) declaring that "the services of water supply and wastewater collection and treatment (were truly services) of basic necessity to the public and covered the nation's entire territory"; this decree served to empower, by reference made to the Consumer Protection Law, the Ministry with the right to set prices. The second step then consisted of publishing the Resolution of 24 February 1993, which outlined the new rate system as well as the level of rates applicable to each of the nation's regions and cities.

In so doing, the government was attempting to circumvent the traditional opposition of municipalities to rate hikes. Yet, this effort created a most paradoxical and unstable situation since in raising rates, the government was applying a law that had actually been designed for quite the opposite purpose: preventing against excessive increases in the price of goods and services deemed of basic necessity. A law clearly emanating from concerns for social justice was being used to enforce a more liberal rationale. Rate setting would from then on rely upon ministerial decision and legal guidelines based on social criteria rather than on economic parameters. The message being sent out to the municipalities, to the firms and to the user was, in the least, an ambiguous one.

The entire privatization program was designed and implemented from a very centralized perspective; it was managed in such a way as to avoid any "political interference", both nationally and locally. The intention herein was to circumvent the political system and generate "faits accomplis" in order to outpace the States and the municipalities. Transferring responsibility and oversight of public services onto the municipal level was the aim, yet municipalities themselves, whose "populist" traditions raised fears, were generally mistrusted. This defiant relationship between central government authority and municipality served to hinder the development of new regulations and of a set of contractual guidelines defining relationships between the two actors.

However, municipalities found themselves in a quite uncomfortable situation, being left with a very low level of responsibility, of resources, of expertise and of organization. In order to insure electoral victory, elected officials needed to improve service efficiency and prove their capability of resolving problems.

Let's examine the Caracas experience. Following the failure of the concession attempt, the prospect of transferring service responsibility onto the municipal level did undergo certain changes. The central district (Libertador), for example, acknowledged its responsibilities and publicly committed itself to improving the service; to keep this promise, the mayor called upon both the human and technical resources held by the national enterprise.

The fact of having to assume oversight for the service in the presence of their electorate will perhaps incite change, yet such an outlook does indeed frighten some officials, cognizant of the immense difficulty they'll face in addressing the dissatisfaction of local residents. In the past, and in spite of the psuedo-concession run by INOS, municipalities held absolutely no responsibility; they would simply back the population's complaints and instill an operational approach towards responding to emergencies and seeking immediate solutions to service deficiencies. They exercised a short-run planning horizon, punctuated by recurring problems. Their intervention style upset INOS's natural tendency to favor remedial measures, and to function in a "jerky", rather than a smooth, fashion.

Today, since municipalities do enjoy an increased level of responsibility, they are becoming interested, above all else, in service operations; in response to the criticisms voiced by users, municipalities are calling upon the enterprise's technical staff to perform around the clock. Their obsession is clearly identifiable: to respond as quickly as possible to emergencies, and to instill the service with credibility in its day-to-day operations. Yet, devoid of both the technical and financial capacities necessary to cope with problems generated by the system's overall functioning, thereby implying more medium-term solutions, municipalities are finding themselves ill-equipped. The relationships between service provider and municipal staff are evolving nowadays towards a certain confusion of roles (a joint impetus to resolve more short-term difficulties) rather than towards a clarification of each actor's set of responsibilities.

"I'm being placed in the position of driving operations with a pedal-powered tractor," proclaimed A. Isturiz, Caracas's mayor, in equating the management tools at his disposal with a child's toy. Municipalities are being confronted with a most arduous assignment in exercising control over urban services that are managed either directly or contracted out; a climate of responding to emergencies makes it difficult to master the use of delegation and the redefinition of roles. The experience with waste services has demonstrated that a process of accelerated differentiation is currently taking place between those municipalities developing their own technical and political capacities to negotiate contracts and those remaining hostage to a climate of emergency and confusion in their roles with the service provider.

These transformations should rely upon a real strategy for change as opposed to mere decrees stipulating a transfer of responsibilities. It's only following the failure of the concession project that the problem was actually formulated: "responsibility for water services is in the course of being transferred to the municipal level in and around Caracas, in accordance with a three-year work schedule to commence at the beginning of 1993" (El Nacional, 21/6/93). As for Caracas, a completely different solution was eventually outined, whereby a multi-service municipal enterprise was created by the lead municipality.

The ("English") regulatory model strips all responsibility from the municipalities, much like the Venezuelan centralized model. The ("French") model of local public service delegation, in contrast, provides the municipal level with the bulk of decision-making authority; the ("German") model, based on the strength of its municipal enterprises, goes even further in this regard. The appropriate choice of model is open to discussion; it all depends on the objectives associated with the specific local context. The Caracas case illustrates well the necessity for the solutions retained to be consistent with one another; any model transformation implies a corresponding strategy to change the existing set of parameters. Venezuela's privatization program was basically carried out according to a bureaucratic process, enacted at the uppermost echelon of government, without any real supporting social agenda.

Conclusion

Venezuela in 1989 was a country on the brink of bankruptcy, whose economic, social and political model had become irrelevant. The privatization program undertaken for urban public services was just one aspect of an overall reform of both the State and the economy. Its goals were to achieve the financial equilibrium of each service area, to decentralize the decision-making process and to privatize management, either through the sale of assets or through a concession.

For the most part, States and localities were hesitant to accept their new sets of respective responsibilities and the revised ground rules. The private sector (at both the national and international levels) kept a cautious and suspicious stance. The population massively rejected the political party holding power. The reform had reached an impasse. Hence, an even more urgent need was felt to find a new model, since the State was bankrupt, thereby prohibiting any potential about-face.

There is a sharp contrast between this situation and what was happening during the same period in Argentina, where a tremendous and accelerated push towards privatization was under way, spearheaded by a government that succeeded in its re-election bid after having implemented the program.

Why then did the process launched in Venezuela run into hurdles? From the standpoint of the program's proponents, one of the major problems had to do with the delay engendered in defining a clear set of "ground rules". Despite the prolific output over this four-year time span, in terms of laws, decrees, regulations and new institutions, a real lack of definition could be noticed, thus straining relations between central government and municipalities, in much the same way as between public authorities and private enterprise. This absence of definition was manifested in assigning responsibilities, in splitting up work tasks, in the financing and rate-setting mechanisms, and finally in the regulatory instruments. To quote a World Bank staff member in reference to the area of water services: "Several key points related to the legal and regulatory framework are still unclear. This feature will certainly impact the credibility given the decentralization effort by local authorities as well as by the private sector." These "ground rules" are mandatory for the application of the revised model. Venezuela during the years 1989-1993 provides one more example of how the market cannot be created through simple decree alone; rather, it is a social construction and the result of a lengthy process.

Instituting a market context, or through reliance on a contract, as an alternative mechanism for regulation presumes, and paradoxically so, a rehabilitation of State authority. Withdrawing from direct service provision is not in itself sufficient; involvement is also required in restructuring entire sectors of the economy, in establishing the rules to replace the market within monopolistic environments, in thoroughly redefining the rules for a socially-equitable redistribution, etc. This undertaking supposes the existence of a new social compromise, a pact negotiated on the basis of newly-developed alliances. In Venezuela, this process has been triggered right as the government is coming apart!

This is undoubtedly what explains the difference between Venezuela and several other countries in the region, which have also experienced similar types of restructuring. The model of the State as an agent for development and of public services has always exhibited specific features in the case of Latin America, that Touraine referred to as the "national-populism". In Venezuela in particular, oil-related revenues have also instilled in this model its very own set of characteristics, which can be found within the financing and service provision model as well as within the management style of public enterprises, etc.

Hence, the process of destabilizing the model took on a special form; it was similar to what was occurring in neighboring countries by virtue of the outdated import substitution model, yet it was unique by its effects on Venezuela's revenue profile generated from the two successive oil booms of the 1970's. The drop in oil prices during the 1980's would serve to render the model's form completely disconnected and indefensible, up until the decline experienced under President Lusinchi. As of 1993, there still hadn't been any reconfiguration of the political system nor of the social alliances.

Rebuilding a management model of public services entails a good deal more than merely signing a service delegation contract. Basing our presentation herein around three themes, financing, regulation and decentralization, we have attempted to display how far-reaching this concessionary project was in impacting the vital workings of Venezuelan society, and the requirements for radical transformation in its application. No wonder then that a decree alone could not engender such a process.

The failure of the water services concession project was therefore a precursor to the overall failure of a political strategy. The removal of C.A. Perez from office prior to the end of his term, in addition to representing the end of a project to restructure Venezuelan society, signified the beginning of an era full of question marks. It left the country devoid of any public service management model, and even worse yet, of a definition of public service itself.

CHAPTER 7

Daniel Faudry

The concession of Buenos Aires' Water Supply and Waste Water Services (The largest water services concession in the world)

Buenos Aires' water services concession represents, in many respects, a symbolic operation for Latin America and for the entire planet as well. This project came to fruition over the past several years when privatizing public services, a key urban issue throughout the continent, was - and remains - a sharply-debated topic. Even before the issue actually came to the fore of public policy, the first significant operation had already involved one of the world's major capital cities. The Buenos Aires case is also both critical and paradoxical, since its service coverage ratio ranks among the lowest of the large Latin American metropolitan areas, following a time when it was the highest, even above that of the capital cities of the Old World.

While it is somewhat premature, only one and a half years after signing the contract [1], to draw definitive conclusions on the concessionaire's actions, generating lessons from the methodology implemented is nonetheless possible. These lessons are of tremendous interest given the difficulties encountered by other similar initiatives.

---

1. This text was written in November 1994.

The situation of Obras Sanitarias de la Nacion (O.S.N.) on the eve of the concession

An extremely low level of service. Of the eleven million population comprising greater Buenos Aires, nine million reside within concession's service area. Among this population base, only six million are actually connected to the water supply network. The remainder, along with those located outside the concessionary perimeter, rely on individual wells for their supply, which gives rise to a truly exceptional case for a city this size. Yet, the groundwater table is being drawn down, and groundwater quality continues to worsen, due primarily to the discharge of industrial and household waste; the sewer network only serves some five million residents. These summary figures don't necessarily highlight the strong level of spatial disparity, in that it's only the city of Buenos Aires - the Federal Capital - that's being entirely serviced by both networks. These service inequalities however don't coincide with social class stratification since some of the more affluent residential districts located at the outskirts do, in fact, lie within the non-serviced zones. In addition to these quantitative shortcomings, poor service quality also plays a part: water supply interruptions, summer shortages, turbid yet drinkable water, sewage overflows, long reparation times, etc. With respect to treating the effluent from households and industries connected to the sewer network, practically none was being performed, since the lone treatment facility had a capacity of 300,000 resident-equivalents per hour and, was barely operational at that. The greater Buenos Aires area is thus being subjected to a rate of water-related illnesses comparable to that of countries considerably less well-developed.

A disastrous economic and financial situation. Three primary causes can be identified to explain this current situation.

First of all, operating costs had swelled due to the bloated staff size, resulting from an overly customer-oriented management strategy as well as from the influence being exerted by the trade union, conditions far from being specific to Buenos Aires or to Argentina for that matter. Working conditions between the union and O.S.N. were running very smoothly, and had reached a point where a union-initiated workers' cooperative was contractually assigned to repair leaks in the street network and participated in awarding works contracts.

On the revenue side, bill collection efforts were particularly inadequate as only 75% to 80% of the amounts billed were actually being collected. This low rate was accounted for by companies and public-sector administrations not paying their bills and often for periods of several years at a stretch (within the concessionary contract, the State has mandated that these public-sector customers be required to pay). In 1994, a legal dispute was still being waged with the City of Quilmes, which receives water delivered in bulk supply and then oversees its distribution locally, for refusing to pay its bill. O.S.N.'s outstanding debt thereby rose to US$ 140 million, after deduction of US$ 40 million covered by the stipulated prescription, based on a total annual billing of US$ 290 million.

The percentage of unmetered water delivered was estimated at 43% in the preliminary tender specifications; this figure was extremely approximative since no meters had been installed to measure the outflow from water supply plants. It had become even less pertinent to distinguish, within this total, between losses experienced throughout the network and illegal hook-ups which, according to current estimates, could provide water to more than 500,000 residents. This figure is then to be summed with the leaks and wastage occurring at each of the use locations. Since billings were essentially based on a fixed-rate scale, the apparent level of household water consumption had reached 573 liters per resident per day on average within the serviced zone and up to 700 liters/resident/day inside the Federal Capital city, in contrast with 180 to 200 liters in Europe.

Faced with these serious deficiencies in the level of service, capital investment expenditures had been extremely low for several years: from a little over US$ 40 million in 1986 and 1987 (expressed in 1990 prices), which was already insufficient, they had fallen to US$ 19 million by 1990. A US$ 98-million loan, granted by the Interamerican Development Bank in 1990, went untapped up until 1994, due to a lack of matching national funds. One positive outcome of this experience: O.S.N. remained relatively debt-free, with an indebtedness reaching only US$ 30 million at the end of this period.

A deficient administration. Without intending to present an exhaustive list of system flaws, it's nonetheless worth noting that several of them are indeed detrimental. Those mentioned in the customer files were undoubtedly the most obvious and the most likely to bear economic consequences. Their actual significance only became apparent once the concessionary period had commenced; remedying these flaws came to represent one of Aguas Argentinas' top priorities. Capitalizing on the complexity of the rate structure being applied and in the absence of any updated information, a good deal of fraudulent activity was taking place. Examples encountered range from the typical scenario of formerly disused land that had been recently re-zoned for constructing high-rise towers to companies benefitting from residential use rates, all the way to those 30,000 so-called "libraries" exempted from paying for services.

This weakness in administrative authority may be attributed to both an inadequate facilities base (at the time Aguas Argentinas first took control, O.S.N. was only equipped with two microcomputers) and poor organizational structure. Heavy turnover in the executive staff, due to low income levels as well as to unbridled political interference, was also very much to blame. Thus, the feasibility study on privatization highlighted that "the accounting criteria employed by O.S.N. suggest correspondence with those being used in professional practice in Argentina, yet it's not possible to be absolutely sure of this fact or to definitively rule these figures as reasonable for a series of limitations" that have been fully listed.

The same study also rendered the diagnosis that in spite of a solid technical base, "the lack of specific objectives and of an identifiable corporate culture, combined with a management approach devoid of entrepreneurship will drive O.S.N. to failure". This assessment, that one might have suspected as being orchestrated from behind the scenes, nonetheless did match that issued by the Argentine Association of Sanitary Engineers, which portrayed O.S.N. in its 1986 publication as "un servicio publico al borde del colapso" (on the brink of collapse). In so doing, however, they were actually primarily incriminating the lack of State-budgeted capital investment; this judgement had no basis in fact, as would be later confirmed by the results obtained from the tender procedure.

A deep-rooted process of deterioration. From a structural standpoint, O.S.N.'s failure resulted from an overly-present technical orientation towards service provision, derived from its original purpose and applied to a context that had since been completely altered. Following the severe epidemics of 1867 and 1871 along with the various subsequent efforts to procrastinate taking action, the State finally seized hold of the situation and, in 1912, officially created O.S.N. as an "Obras" and not as a "Servicio". This distinction served to instill a more public hygiene and social calling into the culture of this service agency, which would leave an indelible imprint. It was to be the culture of a builder - as opposed to that of an operator - that would dominate, and the public works companies would be aware of this image. Both a model and a technical project were developed in tandem, founded on a dual resource availability: an abundant and easily-accessible resource (the Rio de la Plata River) on the one hand, and an equally-abundant State budget, prepared to finance capital investments without any expectation of return, on the other. The focus of a public hygiene and social-oriented system was reflected in the application of a fixed and redistributive rate structure (referred to as the "canilla libre" system). The 1941 project called for a rather generous level of service that would supply some six million residents by the year 1970, with volumes projected at over 500 liters a day. Such a program seemed plausible at that time for O.S.N., which, when operating at peak capacity, could serve nearly all of the Federal Capital's 2.4 million population, at a daily volume of 400 liters. The project's failure would essentially emanate from two sources: urban growth patterns that were both stronger and more dispersed than expected; and the incapacity of the national budget, under the pressure of an expanding public sector, to maintain water services at the same priority level as in the past. The search for solutions began as early as 1955 with a privatization project, followed by a status change of the service provider; then decentralization was attempted in 1962 and finally achieved in 1980. Despite this wide array of changes, O.S.N., because of its structural deficiencies, would still rely heavily upon State budget allocations; yet, the government was gradually cutting back on its commitment to compensate for the operating deficit. Due to a lack of financing available for carrying out capital investments and maintenance, the project's technical structure virtually broke down, bringing with it a deterioration in service quality along with the credibility of O.S.N.'s reputation.

The technical system. The water supply system has been developed around two water purification plants located along the Rio de la Plata River, serving as the origin for a network of 72 km. of "underground river" pipelines, ranging in diameter from 2.6 to 4.6 meters, making their way to the system's reservoirs and pump-lifting stations. A group of 214 wells supplement the overall supply conditions (this number was raised to 256 by Aguas Argentinas, as of the end of 1994). The conveyance network tends to be quite substantially oversized in comparison with total production capacity. Incidentally, this excess potential for conveyance would now appear as an advantage for extending the distribution network, which currently measures roughly 11,000 km. in length. Of the 1,100,000 service connections, 150,000 had been fitted with metering devices, half of which were inoperable at the time service was taken over.

The wastewater system counts roughly 800,000 service connections and a bit over 7,000 km. in sewers that lead, in almost all instances, to a drainage canal situated on the Rio de la Plata; the sole wastewater treatment plant operates with a mere capacity of 140,000 m^3/day.

Water resources. Thanks to an advantageous geographical location, on the banks of the Rio de la Plata River, Buenos Aires does not endure any major problems with respect to its water resources, either quantitatively or qualitatively. The river's strong flow rate also helps ensure the viability of a system devoid of any major wastewater treatment facilities. Swimming on the river's beaches has nonetheless been forbidden. The aquifers are becoming increasingly polluted; several wells supplying some of the network's outlying areas have had to be shut down, and others will soon follow as well.

The inevitable, yet problematic, privatization effort. Upon the failure of reform attempts, initiated as early as 1986 with the backing of the World Bank as part of its program to implement institutional reinforcement across Latin America, calling upon the private sector seemed to present the only viable option left for meeting the dual challenge at hand: instituting an efficiently-run organization and financing the enormity of the works required to improve water supply services; and, above all, developing a wastewater treatment system. This objective set of parameters also happened to coincide with the economic liberalization policies being adopted by the "social justice"-oriented government that undertook, in 1990, a vast privatization program. As such, this option was not an easy one to apply; the government was faced with at least three hurdles: a technical and economic assessment of both the service and the state of its facilities (uncertainty over costs coupled with economic production potential, thereby further complicating the choice of criteria in evaluating proposals); the inability to modify the rate structure over the immediate future; and, finally, the hostility expressed by the trade union towards any change in O.S.N.'s status, both out of protection for public service and out of fear of disappearing. This particular union wields considerable power; it manages a pension fund, a medical insurance fund and many other social services. It had been coexisting in perfect harmony with O.S.N., while holding a position of power. Nonetheless, the union was still quite aware of the degradation in service quality and recognized the need for radical changes; it had even come to terms with accepting a solution that would dispense certain obligations, provided a guarantee of the respect for public service along with the safeguard of its own existence. In order to assuage this ideological reluctance to privatize, the Privatization Committee devised an Employee Stock Participation Program, whereby 10% of the concessionary company's capital was reserved for the personnel.

The privatization process

The August 1989 Government Reform Act had declared the public sector in a "state of emergency" and listed the companies and public services that were to be privatized. It only foresaw an institutional restructuring for O.S.N., this restructuring was to be overseen by a three-party body grouping representatives of O.S.N. itself, the Municipality and the Province of Buenos Aires (since O.S.N.'s service territory had reached beyond the limits of the municipality alone), and not a privatization scheme. Without returning all the way back to 1955 when this topic was first brought up, exploratory talks had been held in 1988 with several firms (notably French) with the intention of implementing a partial privatization - either strictly for wastewater treatment and/or for certain specific geographical zones. However, this process never came to fruition. 1990 marked the end of the inflationary period and changed the outlook; this time the politicians' will was manifest. It was then possible to get private companies interested. To stress this strength in determination and the opening of the market, a promotional campaign was organized, consisting of seminars held in both New York and Brussels during 1991.

Once the principle of privatization had been acknowledged, its form still needed to be defined. A concessionary set-up had been retained over other formulae, such as a fixed-fee management contract, which would have kept the State actively involved in managing the service. Another potential option rejected concerned the sale of assets, which would have almost assuredly triggered a rate hike so as to recover the initial outlay, not to mention the angst raised by the symbolic value of such an act with respect to a vital and national service. The option of a concession thus seemed the most suitable in that the government was not necessarily accountable for the financial success of the operation. Furthermore, responsibility for the water supply and wastewater problems affecting the nation's capital, along with the sizable capital investments required, would be placed into the capable hands of an experienced company.

It was therefore decided, due to the economic considerations and time constraints involved in preparing the bidding competition, as well as to the subsequent efficiency in carrying out operations, to confer the service in full to a single concessionaire.

Following the October 1990 decree confirming the principle of the concession, a Technical Commission for the Privatization of O.S.N. was formally set up in April 1991. It included two representatives from each of the following institutions: the Undersecretary's Office of Public Works and Public Services (playing the lead role), a Joint Congressional Commission, the President's Planning Secretary's Office, O.S.N. and the professional trade unions. The Commission solicited the assistance of the British engineering consultancy Halcrow & Partners, Ltd. on the technical side of the program, while the

French firm of Paribas-Interbonos was called in to advise on the financial side. These two consultants were selected on the basis of a set of specifications administered by the World Bank, which had been involved from the very outset. It participated in the initial discussions held concerning the role of the private sector in providing water services, as well as in the choice of concessionary system; nonetheless, the World Bank did not conduct any feasibility study nor did it officially take part in the tender procedure. It was the consultants themselves that carried out the concession's feasibility study, drafted the tender specifications and, subsequently, assisted the Commission in evaluating the proposals received. It was stipulated that the financial consultant's professional fees (amounting to about US$ 2 million) already paid in advance by O.S.N., through a World Bank loan, would be reimbursed by the contract award winner.

Preparing the call for tender. The feasibility study was primarily geared to present the range of economically viable investment scenarios, given the likely improvements that could be assumed through a revised management approach; the study also closely examined potential bid selection criteria.

This examination focused both on the conventional set of criteria and on two other innovative ones: total revenue required and level of financing committed.

Among the conventional criteria entering into consideration, payment for the right to utilize existing facilities was ruled out straight away, in accordance with the government's firm belief that such a consideration doesn't exactly fit with the priority goal of improving and extending service. The criterion of a rate reduction was also dismissed by the consultant on the same grounds, since it could be assimilated into a facilities use fee that then would be passed on to the service's users. Expanding or accelerating a program of setting minimum investment levels wasn't favored either as an appropriate criterion, due to uncertainty over the economic potential, which could lead to generating proposals that were overly-risky and untenable or quite simply underestimated.

According to the mechanism of total revenue as preferred by the consultant Paribas-Interbonos, candidates would have been selected depending on the minimum revenue amount that they deemed necessary in order to fulfill the contract's specifications. Within such a system, the difference between real revenues and required revenues would have been deposited into a fund for complementary or anticipated investments, after deducting a percentage to be kept by the concessionaire so as to maintain an incentive-based orientation. The adoption of this criterion was recommended as being the most economically effective as well as the best-suited to meeting the concession grantor's objectives; furthermore, it was expected to allow the concession to carry on with its work while sorting out the billing system's potential and modifying the rate structure. This last feature was judged both very desirable and yet quite difficult to achieve with the other possible selection criteria.

The criterion of the financing amount to be committed by the bidder along with its associated costs was equally eliminated, since it implied setting a total revenue cap for all proposals submitted, thereby preventing against choosing the one that presented the best overall economic performance.

As a matter of fact, despite the consultant's advice, the criterion actually retained was the variation registered with respect to the existing rate, given that fund management problems would have certainly arisen with the criterion being recommended. The tender specifications did not indicate whether the expected rate variations should be higher or lower; however, the first versions that had been made public did foresee a reduction in rates, based on the strong potential to increase the level of revenues generated through a reorganization of customer records. The risk of an overly-daring bid, followed by the inevitable need for renegotiation, related to such a criterion was definitely not overlooked. In order to avoid this situation, the tender specifications purposely contained full details, including almost all of the contract clauses with, in particular, the financial guarantee requirements and the set of strict sanctions to be applied in case of failure to fulfill commitments.

Awarding the contract. The procedure that led to selecting the concessionaire emphasized transparency and consensus-building through calling on an iterative approach. Candidates could request certain clarifications or modifications of the May 1992 tender specifications, up until the publication of their final version, to be released two months prior to the submission deadline, which had been scheduled for September. Nonetheless, even before the initial specifications were released, informal contacts had already been established between the candidates and the Privatization Commission.

During the pre-qualification phase, five firms or consortia had been retained on the basis of their references, thus accounting for all the announced candidates, with the exception of an unfortunate bidder who was closed out of the competition because of missing the deadline by an hour. The Générale des Eaux company succeeded in winning pre-qualification on its own. It seems however that the company was unable thereafter to form a consortium since all potential Argentine partners had already become involved either in previous privatization programs or in other candidate consortia for the same concession bid. The Générale des Eaux company thereby teamed up with the other French consortium, and in fact only four bids were ultimately submitted.

A two-stage selection process was instituted: first, bids were judged on technical grounds, then on the basis of their financial criteria.

Both stages of this bid evaluation process made use of an original measure wherein the decision on the bid's technical merit, as well as the Commission's ultimate contract award, could be appealed within a period of five days following these rulings by any of the eliminated candidates. Nonetheless, a safeguard had been foreseen by requiring the appellant to deposit US$ 1.5 million as a guarantee, to be remitted only if the protest were upheld.

Following the elimination of the consortium headed by Canal Isabel II, whose proposal while most original was nonetheless judged unrealistic (another candidate, though benefitting from a solid reputation, was also nearly rejected), only three consortia remained in the competition:
- Aguas de Buenos Aires, consisting of Thames Water, Waste Management and three Argentine companies, Sideco Americana, Empresa Argentina de Cemento Armado and Lockwood y Cia., along with the financial backing of City Bank;
- North West Water Industry with, on the Argentine side Acindas and Loma Negra, supported mainly by Morgan Guaranty Trust; and
- Aguas Argentinas, which was awarded the concessionary contract (see section on the consortium's composition).

The three proposals, each in conformance with the tender specifications, and their markedly distinct financing strategies were all deemed realistic; thus, the concession was awarded based on the straightforward, stipulated criterion of service rate reduction ratio.

Aguas Argentinas won out by a hair, with a reduction coefficient of 0.731, ahead of Thames Water which came in at 0.739; both of these reduction levels apparently surpassed the Commission's expectations. North West Water could only muster a proposal of 0.895. The Franco-British competition, so eagerly anticipated on the part of the tender organizers so as to help insure the validity of the entire process, did actually come to pass.

Though the submission and the technical evaluation of the proposals both overshot their intended schedule to some extent, assessing the financing programs and awarding the contract were actually carried out within the matter of a few days. Such rapidity was encouraged not only to assuage the various pressures being exerted, but also to highlight the rigor and straightforwardness of the selection process. This approach was suitable due to the unequivocal nature of the selection criterion; furthermore, the possibility of a dual winner through a tie (which almost came about) had even been foreseen.

Setting up Aguas Argentinas and the Concession's first year of operation

The contract award was officially announced on December 20, 1992, and the signing was held April 28, 1993, a bit later than planned. This lag period was used for writing up the contract, conducting negotiations with the union and preparing for the official handing over of the facilities, which was to take place on May 1st of the following year.

The contract. The concession-granting authority is the Argentine national government, since the concern herein pertains to a State enterprise. Some participants however would have preferred the pertinent authority to be local or provincial in scope.

The function of the concession "is the extraction, purification up to drinking water standards, ... and the sale of water, along with the collection ... and the treatment of wastewater, including industrial effluent discharged into the sewer network". The service area delimited by the concession encompasses the Federal Capital (municipality of Buenos Aires) as well as the thirteen adjacent municipalities which had been within O.S.N.'s jurisdiction. The concession does not encompass the rainwater drainage system, except in Buenos Aires' historic city center, where one joint system collects both stormwater and wastewater.

The length of the concessionary period is thirty years. Upon completion of this term, with respect to the concession service area's projected population, all residents shall benefit from water supply services and at least 95% from the collection and secondary-level treatment of all effluent discharged. These objectives correspond with the schedule that appears as an appendix to the contract, which lays out subsequent service extensions within each individual municipality. This schedule also specifies, in addition to a set of results-based obligations (which include quantifiable objectives towards reducing the volume of unmetered water), means-based obligations in terms of the facilities to be overhauled or built. According to Aguas Argentinas' proposal, the total of the capital investments required amounts to US$ 4 billion, one-fourth of which is to be carried out over the first five years.

The winning consortium of the bidding competition thus became the concessionaire, a registered Argentine company composed of the following partnership split [2]:

- Lyonnaise des Eaux-Dumez............................25.3%
- Sociedad Commercial de La Plata 20.7%
- Sociedad General de Aguas de Barcelona........12.6%
- Meller...10.8%
- Banco de Galicia y Buenos Aires......................8.1%
- Générale des Eaux 8.0%
- Anglian Water PLC 4.5%
- Programme de Propriété Participative.............10.0%

Banco de Galicia is Argentina's leading merchant bank. The firm Sociedad Commercial de La Plata has traditionally concentrated its activities primarily in the areas of oil exploration and engineering, and has diversified into the sectors of communications and transportation ever since the wave of privatizations took hold in Argentina. Meller is an industrial group present in the textile and telephone markets.

The company's minimum level of capital had been set at US$ 120 million, to be raised within the first two years of concessionary operations, including a mandatory 50% as of the very first year.

Within the constitution of Aguas Argentinas, Lyonnaise des Eaux retains the special status of service operator, linked by agreement to the consortium entity which recognizes its position of control over the company's management. Moreover, this agreement serves to oblige Lyonnaise des Eaux to assure the transfer of its technical expertise and stipulates the remuneration of its assistance provided. The operator

---

2. Since this time, the International Finance Corporation has also entered into the consortium.

commits to holding 25% of the capital throughout the concession's duration, and the consortium's members taken as a whole must retain 51%, in conformance with the contract specifications.

The company benefitted from a financial allocation of US$ 200 million, equivalent to slightly more than 60% of the financing needs projected over the first three years, as called for in the specifications. This financing package was underwritten by two banking syndicates: the first, consisting of Crédit Lyonnais, BNP and Société Générale, for a total of US$ 112 million; and the second, Galicia Bank along with the Argentine subsidiaries of Deutsch Bank, Crédit Lyonnais, BNP and Société Générale, for an additional US$ 88 million. Furthermore, Aguas Argentinas took over the loan granted by the Interamerican Development Bank to O.S.N. for the development of water supply facilities to the service area's western zone.

With respect to setting rates, the contract doesn't contain any automatic rate revision formula. Rather, it foresees two types of revisions: ordinary, corresponding to modifications either in the service's objectives or in the capital investment financing plan; and extraordinary, in cases of cost variations exceeding 7%. The contract does stipulate that heavy water users be equipped with meters within a span of two years. For other use categories, a fixed-rate or a metered-rate system has been instituted depending on the equipment located inside the buildings or dwellings. Changing from a fixed rate to a metered rate could be requested by either the user or the operator, with the cost of the meter itself as well as its installation being picked up by the requesting party.

The voluntary severance plan. The contract's set of specifications provided the concessionaire with the capability of renegotiating the collective bargaining agreement and of implementing a voluntary severance plan for a maximum of 1,830 employees (out of a total workforce of 7,600). The Argentine national government had agreed to assume a financial charge associated with this plan of US$ 37 million. All of the candidate consortia had established contact with the labor union at the outset of the privatization process, fully aware that therein lied one key to the success of the future concession.

Very quickly thereafter, a frame agreement was signed. It served to set out the objectives and guiding principles of the company's operations and of human resources management in addition to specifying the respective roles, especially the union's non-interference in the management function. Prior to Aguas Argentinas assuming possession of the service, an intermediate accord was concluded in order to settle matters arising during the transition period; a new collective bargaining agreement was negotiated immediately afterwards. The essential points of this agreement are that any change in the wage scale or salary structure (for example, the simplification of the bonus system) would insure the same level of remuneration while, in exchange, the duration of the workday would increase from seven to eight hours. Finally, Aguas Argentinas acknowledged the right of the union to hold a seat on the Board of Directors, the seat that had been attributed to the Programme de Propriété Participative.

The voluntary severance plan was truly welcomed beyond any expectation, in that a total of 3,600 employees stepped up to volunteer and were actually all accepted (not without some subsequent regrets for a portion of them). The maximum limit was surpassed both out of respect for the union's request and in light of the fact that no selection criteria could be imposed, due to a lack of knowledge of the personnel. Aguas Argentinas absorbed the expenses generated beyond the Argentine government's commitment. The total cost of the operation reached some US$ 80 million. As a result, almost all of the upper-level management staff took their retirement. The current workforce of 4,000 strong, including new recruits from the local job market along with the arrival of about fifty "expatriates" coming from either Lyonnaise des Eaux or Aguas de Barcelona, thus remains noticeably below the 1997 target level.

The concession's first year. According to the strategic plan announced, the concession's first year encompasses the takeover of control from the previous operations.

The priority objective was, quite obviously, to upgrade the level of service, a clear demonstration of which was the continuity of water supply throughout the summer months, a feat that hadn't been accomplished for fifteen years. This result was achieved through restoring the capacity of the treatment plants and pumping stations, as well as through improving the network, particularly by overhauling facilities and significantly shortening the repair response time, which in fact fell from 180 hours to 46 hours on average.

Besides the emergency repair work that corresponded to this initial objective, the second most important task consisted of preparing the capital investment program, necessitating a more thorough understanding of the entire network. The proportion of unbilled water consumption could be estimated at between 25.9% and 40.4%, which represented a better result than the contractually-bound objective for this specific date. Yet, it should be pointed out that the objective had been established in a very approximative fashion since no reliable information existed on the state of the initial situation.

A third group of actions to be undertaken immediately pertained to the training efforts that involved more than 2,800 employees, for a total program duration of more than 50,000 hours. Concurrent to these efforts, a medium-term training program had also been devised.

From an economic perspective, the major project remaining to be completed was updating the service user files through aerial photographs, and supplemented by site visits. This operation sparked some tension with ETOSS over the method to be employed for evaluating the coefficient of construction quality within the overall rate formulation [3]. At the same time, a program for refurbishing or replacing meters had been initiated; its scope was less ambitious than that outlined in the contract since the state of the meters had deteriorated far below what had been foreseen. The results of these actions yielded an increased rate of billing, in conformance with the projections. Nonetheless, the revenues collected remained less than projected because the base level, derived from information provided by O.S.N., had been overestimated, and the slight modification in the rate structure didn't produce therefore the desired effects.

No service cutoff has of yet been imposed for unpaid bills, except on a trial basis so as to help implement internal management procedures. Service cutoffs do not pertain to zones of illegal water hook-ups, where the facilities, not being maintained by Aguas Argentinas, cannot be brought into conformance and where the users cannot be billed.

Regulatory environment

Though the concession was designed along the lines of the French model, its accompanying regulatory framework follows more the Anglo-American approach. The types of regulations to be applied were defined in the "Marco Regulatorio" as decreed by the President of the Republic on June 18, 1992. He formally approved the creation of a three-party entity, (composed of the Ministry of the Economy, Public Works and Public Services, the Municipality of Buenos Aires and the Province of Buenos Aires), called ETOSS - Ente Tripartito de Obras y Servicios

---

3. The rate formula employed includes the built land area, the size of the parcel, construction quality and the geographical zone, in addition to the category of user (residential, commercial, etc.).

Sanitarios-, which was empowered with autonomy as well as both a public and private legal status; "its purpose is to exercise policing powers in overseeing services provided in the areas of water supply and wastewater".

Regulation is thereby not being enforced through a direct face-to-face relationship with the concession-granting authority, in this case being the State. However, the State has been and will certainly continue to remain the primary actor. It actually holds majority status on the Board of Directors of the controlling body, by virtue of its responsibility for naming the mayor of Buenos Aires, a responsibility that had been assumed up until the application of the new constitution mandating open mayoral elections. Furthermore, the Argentine provinces are in fact relatively uninvolved with this control function, as none of the thirteen adjacent municipalities holds a seat on ETOSS. Due to its somewhat heterogeneous composition and the inevitable quest to strike a balance among the competing political party influences, as well as within its jointly-run directorate, ETOSS does not possess a strong political power base. This feature is further reinforced by the imposed annual rotation of the body's presidency. Such a lack of political strength may surface at the time of the negotiations invariably being held to specify priorities within the concessionary zone with respect to the service extension plan, which the contract document was obviously not able to detail explicitly.

Though politically weak, ETOSS is nonetheless administratively powerful. During its first two years of existence, this body benefitted from financial assistance provided by the World Bank in order to develop its level of technical competence. With a staff size of 72 and including its set of external specialist consultants, ETOSS has been allocated an annual operating budget of US$ 9.6 million, generated through a surtax of 2.67% of the amount being billed by Aguas Argentinas. It can be remarked that this budget is equivalent in size to that of O.F.W.A.T., which, to control the activities of 32 companies, employs only twice the number of personnel. In addition, the ETOSS staff is made up for the most part of former O.S.N. executives, who, while extremely competent in their respective fields and fully knowledgeable of how to run the "shop", tend to manage, or rather to request information, more from a manager's perspective (second nature to them) than from a control standpoint. They are also, quite naturally, somewhat displeased by the changes being observed in practices, which obviously strike them as a criticism of their efforts at the time they were "running the show".

The regulatory system thereby took a bureaucratic turn - over a period of one year, Aguas Argentinas was to receive on average two letters a day from the pertinent regulatory authorities. At times, this turn would also appear conflictual in nature, more with respect to the company's operating procedures than to its results or management strategies adopted, which have remained up until now uncontested. A significant rate increase (+13.5%) was thus granted in July 1994 in order to keep up with the overall rampant increases in prices, and in particular to compensate for the financial surcharges engendered by the capital investment program's acceleration. Moreover, Argentina is devoid of any experience in running this kind of institution, hence an explanation for its tendency to instill an inflexible system, out of fear of appearing overly lax.

The set of sanctions envisioned is rather strict and mainly concerns the interruption of both water supply and wastewater services. The severity of these sanctions could potentially give rise to litigation if the joint collection network within the historic city center district were to overflow. The concessionaire would in fact be exonerated from any responsibility should such an overflow be caused by rainwater alone, a difficult assessment to draw for a joint collection system. However, over the course of the concession's first full year of operations, only a few minor amendments and a mere additional expense in the tens of thousands of dollars at most were actually imposed. This fact should serve to illustrate the system's successful initial functioning and is one that warrants recognition in comparison with the US$ 4.5 million fine levied against EDENOR, the northern region's electricity services operator, during the same period.

Conclusions

The privatization program has undeniably succeeded inasmuch as the objectives defined in 1992 by the Argentine national government have been attained in accordance with the planned process. The care taken in both preparing and conducting the tender procedure has significantly contributed to this success. It goes without saying that any judgement passed at this point in time on the privatization program's results would be premature. For it can simply be noted that the results obtained upon one year of activity do correspond more or less with what had been projected. As far as service users are concerned, the reorganization of customer records, accompanied by clear-cut service improvements, seems to have been well-received up until now. The progress registered over this first year of operations has not, and paradoxically so, been made without creating any disadvantages, in that the population has grown ever more demanding. This feature has incited greater impatience on the part of residents within those zones still awaiting service connections, who had previously accepted their plight with resignation.

While the first year would tend to portray the future in favorable terms, several key issues do nonetheless merit attention.

The most critical of these is, without a doubt, the programming of capital investments, at least from the standpoint of the regulatory authority and the concessionaire. The uncertainty lies not in the availability of financing, but rather in the technical potential to build such major facilities in such a short period of time. It is not altogether clear whether the sector of public works in Argentina, seriously weakened by a long run of very low activity, has the capacity to meet these construction needs, in terms of both scheduling and quality.

From the concessionaire's perspective, these lofty expectations, heightened by the prospect of extending water supply networks to the outlying municipalities, risk compromising the optimization of the investment program. This endeavor had already proved difficult since it's one that must be performed without complete knowledge of the system's determinant variables, such as the unit consumption rates for different user categories. Complicating the task is the fact that these municipalities have not been contractually recognized as fully-vested partners. Negotiations are currently being held to confer facilities ownership for the service extension project, which would thereafter be operated by Aguas Argentinas, in accordance with a procedure previously implemented by O.S.N.

The internal economic risk run by the concession has however not been deemed the most important. It's the "country risk" that would appear more serious, in both macroeconomic terms (even though the currency exchange risk has obviously been addressed in the contract, a "dollar-based" system has still not been imposed) and institutional terms, less as a result of recent Argentinian history than of the possible difficulties raised during relations with ETOSS.

Nevertheless, this concession does play the role of a pilot project, as much for the country of Argentina, where other programs are being prepared utilizing the same model, as for all of Latin America.

BOX
Update of the situation from October 1994 through June 1995.

The period extending from October 1994 to June 1995 brought to the fore some highly critical elements of system reinforcement which enabled the company to undertake an economic and operational approach for insuring the viability of the service over both the medium and long-run perspectives. The key events occurring during this period meriting recognition are the following:

- November 1994 saw the finalization of a financing agreement with the International Finance Corporation (IFC), a subsidiary of the World Bank, for a total loan amount of US$ 172.5 million, along with the participation of the IFC into the capital of Aguas Argentinas at a level of 5%. These loans took effect as of April 1995, thereby allowing a restructuring of the company's financial orientation from a short-term time frame to a longer-term horizon, and as a result, serving to strengthen its balance sheet outlook.

- Successful initiatives were aimed at fostering an enhanced profitability profile for the company, primarily through consistent revenue increases thanks to the reorganization of its commercial management structure. The effect of this policy change produced a net result in 1995 of US$ 25 million, in relation to an annual turnover of roughly US$ 300 million. These financial ratios do remain somewhat modest in comparison with other water companies; the crucial management objective herein still consists of securing an adequate level of self-financing in order to enable the company to finance a portion of its capital investment programs. From his standpoint, the user is able to benefit from a service rate that has been, on average, 14% less than the going rate at the time the call for tender was held. This figure represents the outcome of more efficient bill collection efforts along with greater productivity.

- A dynamic capital investment program was launched to extend the network, with in particular the construction of 800 km. of water supply pipelines over a period of eight months, that accounted for some 80,000 service connections, thus an additional 300,000 residents hooked up to the system. By the end of the program's second year, Aguas Argentinas had already exceeded the contractually-specified service expansion objectives for both its water supply and wastewater activities.

- The development, during the program's second year, of a more balanced and more constructive relationship with ETOSS permitted finalizing some of the major definitions concerning rates - evolution of the metering system, infrastructure charges - as well as laying the groundwork for a structured, collaborative process towards updating the service provision master plans.

- Ongoing policies favoring an improvement in service quality for the user along with continuously upgraded water quality have proved their worth. Efforts undertaken have in fact been acknowledged by the users themselves since consumer surveys, conducted on a regular basis, have revealed an increasing proportion of service satisfaction, reaching upwards of 92% in the number of positive opinions recorded during May 1995.

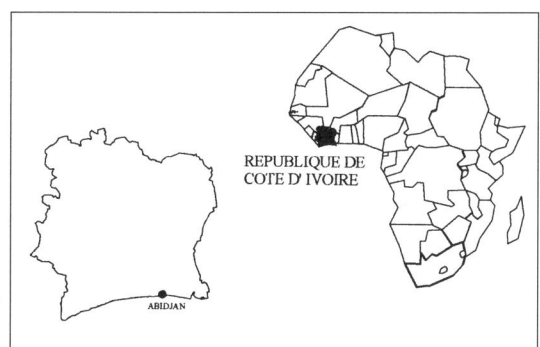

CHAPTER 8

Ivory Coast

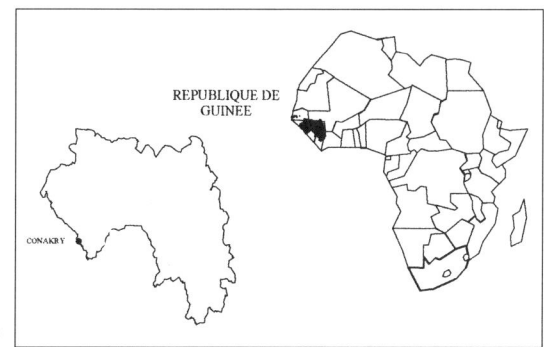

Guinea

Jean-Claude Lavigne

Two African Experiences

Coping with strong demographic growth rates and their consequences on cities constitutes one of the major challenges facing African nations today. This challenge looms even larger in capital cities and becomes more acute when, at the same time, the level of national economic output is held low. How is it possible then to provide basic urban services to a fast-growing population with relatively little income-generating potential? Herein lies the crucial task that developing countries the world over must confront.

In the aftermath of the independence movement, most of Africa's French-speaking countries had empowered public authorities with the responsibility of managing this set of problems. This assignment could be carried out through either newly-created State-run enterprises or organizations overseen by local authorities in charge of basic urban services: water supply, electricity, urban transport, etc. These entities didn't exactly post glorious successes, neither in terms of the quality of services provided nor from an economic performance standpoint. The costs shouldered by these public authorities were high and couldn't be absorbed any longer by national government budgets. The trend throughout Africa, over the past years, has been heading towards gradual government withdrawal from this domain in favor of service privatization and a restructuring of responsibilities.

Against this backdrop, the case studies presented herein on the Ivory Coast and Guinea are quite instructive; both cases also offer very contrasted situations, with respect to both the institutional approaches adopted and the evolution of their water supply networks.

Ivory Coast

At the time of its independence in 1960, the Ivory Coast comprised a total population of 3.5 million, of which Abidjan accounted for 177,000. Only a small number of urban residents had access to urban services, and the rural areas were essentially neglected. The existing institutional system, shaped after the French model, empowered the municipalities with the responsibility of administering this public service: drinking water was thus being directly distributed by municipal water departments.

In 1956, the local authorities of five of the nation's major cities (including Bouake, the second largest) opted to sign fixed-fee management contracts with a public-sector enterprise, called the EECI (Ivory Coast Electric Energy Company). A few months prior to the country's independence, in 1959, an international call for tender was held for the provision of water services to the city of Abidjan; the contract was awarded to SAUR (a French firm specialized in both urban and rural services provision), who then went on to sign concessionary contracts with five other municipalities and three management contracts. President Houphouet Boigny himself, along with his original conception of economic liberalism [1] and the reliance on Western capital, instigated the decision to entrust a private company with the provision of a part of the country's range of public services (Faure, 1981). This decision could also be explained by the selected company's special relationship enjoyed with the country's political leaders, in addition to its longstanding experience in the Ivory Coast.

---

1. see "Etat et bourgeoisie en Côte d'Ivoire" by Y.A. Faure and J.F. Menard, Karthala, 1981 (pages 24-30), and the declarations of the Third Congress of the PDCI-RDA in 1959, which gave rise to the very liberal investment code promulgated on September 3, 1959.

From 1959 to 1974, two principal actors thus shared the responsibility for water supply services: one was public, EECI, while the other private, SAUR, which would go on to become the water distribution company for the entire Ivory Coast (Sodeci), a private Ivory Coast-registered company. This represented a first for the African continent south of the Sahara, but in fact no real competition did actually exist between the two companies, as each one was responsible for covering a specifically-delimited service territory.

This initial period was also the time for major network improvements, especially in Abidjan, where pipes were being installed more rationally, treatment facilities were being constructed and storage reservoirs were being created, etc. At this stage, the combination of certain technical factors and technology transfer had become essential, since SAUR/Sodeci sought to demonstrate its level of expertise and thereby gain credibility.

The necessary capital investments were being financed by the City of Abidjan (except for the wells which were being financed by Sodeci) through taxes or borrowing. The Ivory Coast had thus procured the means, along with a strong reputation, to easily generate external financing, a feature which yielded a very favorable context for Sodeci's expansion.

The company was also exerting substantial efforts to achieve economic profitability: a program for installing meters more systematically, exercising control, closely tracking billing records (computerization would be introduced in 1967), developing prompt customer response service, and more. From a total of 3,947 service subscribers in Abidjan in 1960, this number had climbed to 29,907 by 1972, resulting in a water consumption of 27 million cubic meters and a staff size of 405. Sodeci began recording profit margins right from the outset of its activities, and in doing so enabled rapid development and the transition into a modern company.

In 1968, Sodeci decided to reserve a portion of its increase in capital to Ivory Coast-owned capital. This operation turned out to be a huge success, which served to demonstrate the company's good reputation and strengthened its position with respect to the Ivory Coast's economic operators and political actors.

Though Abidjan was in fact benefitting in priority from the initiatives undertaken by Sodeci, the company was nonetheless expanding its services to Bouake in 1966 as well, by taking over the EECI concession, and then again to Grand Bassam, Bonoua and Adiake. By 1972, Sodeci had registered some 4,000 subscribers located outside of Abidjan.

The growth years

In 1973, the National Water Supply Program was created; until that time, this public service sector had received secondary priority behind electrification or the road network. In order to overcome this lag, an extensive seven-year program was launched to provide water to the nation's major towns down to the size of county seats (about 200 in all), to create around seven thousand water fountains throughout the rural areas, to initiate a program of installing water pumps, to build twenty-four dams and forty-two fully-integrated treatment plants, and the list goes on. This plan was intended to insure an excellent nationwide distribution of drinking water in accordance with the principles of social equity and national cohesion; it was also supposed to improve the living conditions of all Ivory Coast residents, and in so doing act as a showcase for the success of government economic policy. In addition, this program had a social policy dimension: small-scale users could benefit from subsidized service connections.

The National Water Supply Program also presented a detailed expression of the State's rate-setting philosophy. The Ivory Coast government had already decided that the sales price of water would be identical throughout the country, which naturally implied a rate equalization among the nation's various regions (much to the detriment of Abidjan). This ambitious plan was to be self-financed with no involvement of government budget allocations.

Three key actors [2] were responsible for implementing the National Program:

i) Sodeci was in charge of managing and operating all water service facilities in the Ivory Coast, including maintenance. This was applicable for rural areas as well;

ii) The Ministry of Economy and Finance was responsible for procuring financing; it created the National Water Services Fund for the purpose of contracting loans and channeling the State's share of revenues generated from service payments collected by Sodeci. This revenue was then used to cover debt service on loans earmarked for the water supply sector (115 billion CFA); and

iii) The Ministry overseeing the execution of the Plan, acting through the Independent Water Supply Services, was assigned all capital investments and water supply construction works, thereby assuming responsibility for the State's property. This assignment would be taken

---

2. Also created was FOREXI, a State-held company, which then became private and independent, to be assigned the drilling of wells by the use of hand pumps. This company plays only a marginal role.

over in 1977 by the Ministry of Public Works and Planning when the Division of Water Services was created. It's this department that defines the technical options available for the network's development, and which would become at times a source of problems due to erroneous estimations of demographic growth trends, hence inappropriate sizing of the network in comparison with actual water consumption levels.

On the 24th of June, 1974, Sodeci was granted a fifteen-year leasing contract by the Plan's oversight Ministry; this contract would cover the nation's entire territory with the exception of the city of Abidjan, which depended upon a concessionary contract whose status was to be redefined in conformance with the terms outlined in the National Water Supply Program. Sodeci took over the thirty centers managed by EECI and incorporated the component of this company's staff specialized in electricity service provision. This evolution was related to two considerations: the strong performance being realized by Sodeci, and the political will to pursue privatization in order to withdraw the State from water service operations, while nonetheless maintaining some level of control.

The sales price of water was being defined solely by the government on the basis of Sodeci's operating accounts and in line with government objectives, laid out in terms of projections, on potable water consumption. Sodeci was being remunerated for its activities performed both in distributing water and in collecting, on behalf of the State, the share of revenue that gets channeled into the National Water Services Fund.

Sodeci was decentralized to insure coverage of the nation's entire territory and then underwent a thorough reorganization. A training program was instituted for its 564 employees, Ivory Coast nationals for 70%. 1973 was thus the year for a revamped organizational structure to fully exercise its monopoly status and to attain the goals outlined by the National Plan. Coordination between private company objectives and national government agenda had become absolutely essential.

From 1973 to 1980, Sodeci fulfilled its obligations within the framework of the National Water Services Plan in keeping pace with the financing being procured by the Ivory Coast government. During this period, major new works had to be undertaken as a complement to the company's primary activity: water distribution. It then became very involved in the country's large cities located in the interior, and benefitted from major urban renewal projects occurring in Abidjan as well as from the construction of large property developments in the capital city. In 1977, narrower legislation was passed with regard to building permits making it mandatory to connect every building to a water supply network. In 1978, the publication of the National Master Plan for Regional Development provided the opportunity to introduce a policy based on priorities, even though Yamoussoukro -the nation's capital- had become the country's largest center for public investment.

In 1975, the total population of the Ivory Coast reached 6.7 million, with 922,800 in Abidjan. In 1980, Abidjan, then accounting for more than 1.4 million residents, was being subjected to a tremendous growth rate due to the economically prosperous times and political stability. Sodeci, which five years earlier was serving 57,100 subscribers, would see its customer rolls rise in number to 130,500 (with 75,600 in Abidjan alone) by 1980. The company employed a workforce of 1,558, with 1,326 being Ivory Coast nationals. It was providing service directly to about 50% of Abidjan's population and sold 72 million cubic meters of potable water. An increasingly greater number of small-scale individual users, favored by the government's policy on public services, were requesting hook-ups. The average annual water consumption per subscriber had dropped to 553 cubic meters by 1980.

Abidjan's fast-paced development had exposed a whole new set of problems specific to major metropolitan areas within developing countries experiencing accelerated levels of growth. At the end of the 1970's, zones of haphazard housing development were cropping up very quickly; 10% of Abidjan's land area was soon dedicated to such developments. These zones had few facilities and were often being built up illegally without any deeds held for the property; they were unsanitary districts where running water was extremely rare. Water merchants did operate in these zones, but shortages were common and water was still expensive for potential customers. Residents of these areas lived on very limited sources of fixed income and were not eligible for service connections, nor could they afford the sales price of water consumption, which was billed on a quarterly basis. Even within planned subdivisions, many of the lots were not hooked up to the supply network (despite the applicable legislation), and, as a result, a good number of illegal operations to divert drinking water (as well as electricity) were being conducted.

To insure the supply of drinking water, Sodeci had to take these problems into account. It would seek to exercise control over water merchants through specific billing procedures, yet also did acknowledge their unique social utility. The company supplied the water for public fountains, installed by the State and located in very densely-populated (and often illegally) urbanized areas. However, this approach has often incited extremely high water consumption levels and considerable wastefulness in addition to maintenance problems, thus giving rise to heavy costs being borne by the local authorities.

For social policy reasons, small-scale users were connected free of charge to the network in 1976; the connection's ascribed cost was reimbursed to Sodeci by the National Water Services Fund. This policy engendered an increase in the number of low-income service subscribers, but at the same time created new constraints for the distribution company, especially in the form of a substantial management cost in relation to the volume of water being consumed.[3]

This period between 1973 and 1980 was one of very rapid development for Sodeci, yet it was also one marking the company's transformation into a "model Ivory Coast company". An Ivory Coast national was appointed to the post of Managing Director in 1978. An organizational structure, based on participative management by objective, was introduced; a true decentralization of all departments was implemented in order to instill the workforce with an added sense of responsibility as well as to improve company performance. A push towards computerization applied to all departments. The employee training policy became intensified with the creation in 1978 of the Water Professionals Center, which enabled better adapting personnel qualifications to company needs while raising overall skill levels. This Center is also open to staff members from other African water companies. This policy has made it possible to strengthen - albeit gradually - the number of Ivory Coast nationals among the company's executive ranks just as it has to introduce long-term modernization into company operations.

In 1978, Sodeci began trading its shares on the Abidjan Stock Exchange, a move which enabled raising the rate of the company's Ivory Coast-owned capital to over 50%. 400,000 shares currently exist, corresponding to a registered capital of two billion CFA.[4]

---

3. This problem is even more serious with respect to rural water services, yet innovative solutions that rely upon a strong level of public participation have been envisioned.

4. The share is currently being quoted at 11,000 CFA; the price has been relatively stable over the past few years. Capitalization has thus reached a level of 4.4 billion CFA, equivalent to US$ 8 million. The Ivory Coast government holds 3% of the capital, and the personnel holds another 5% (by means of a joint investment fund); the ratio of Ivory Coast-held capital was 53% in 1994.

A backdrop of economic crisis

The years 1981-1987 saw the opening of a new phase marked by the country's economic crisis that would culminate, towards the end of this period, with the Ivory Coast's declaration of its inability to pay back its external debt. The shortage of capital that hadn't been experienced in the past had become acute. Few new water supply networks were being installed within cities located in the interior (despite the quantity of needs assessment studies conducted in 1980-81). Water volumes sold increased but only very gradually; in Abidjan, sales would even drop because of a slowdown in urban expansion and an industrial downturn. One fact serves to highlight the magnitude of this crisis: a development tax, that contributes to the Development Fund, was added to the water bills in order to subsidize small-scale users, since the National Water Services Fund was in fact short of the resources necessary to absorb the full costs of small-diameter service connection installations.

Sodeci has sought to improve its level of economic performance through progress made in the management techniques employed, in more sharply defining the objectives to be achieved and the budget constraints to be respected, as well as through a decentralization of its computing facilities. It is also attempting to diversify activities by developing a presence in the market for wastewater services (a market offering rather poor profit potential however) and in pipe construction/installation work.

In 1985, Sodeci was serving some 170,000 subscribers and was distributing 92.5 million cubic meters of potable water, 85% of which was being billed. A workforce of 1,633 (composed of 89% Ivory Coast nationals) were involved in operating the service.

On December 31, 1987, Sodeci was awarded a twenty-year concession covering all Ivory Coast water supply networks [5] - with the exception of wells and pump-operated water extraction sites serving rural areas [6]- by the national government's Water Division (acting as concession-granting authority on behalf of the State). This contract

---

5. The term is, in fact, an improper one in that new construction work (including subsidized service connections) is being carried out through a service development fund, whose revenues don't legally belong to Sodeci but rather are ascribed to these projects. Herein lies one original feature of the Ivory Coast case study.

6. which reports to the Water Division.

was signed just a few months prior to the expiration of the previous one. Entering into this new situation reflected the difficulties being encountered during the previous stage, and in particular the lack of coordination between capital investment and operations, as well as the excellent results being recorded by Sodeci.

In its role as concessionaire, Sodeci has fully assumed, within this revised institutional configuration, responsibility for drinking water production and distribution, in addition to service management, facilities maintenance and small-scale network extension projects. These works have been carried out with the funding provided by the Development Fund upon the approval of the concession-granting authority. The company is remunerated at the outcome of negotiations held with the granting authority, in accordance with a schedule of computations and revision procedures outlined in the contract, taking into account its operating expenses.

The Water Division, owner of the supply network [7] on behalf of the Ivory Coast government, is in charge of monitoring compliance with regulations along with pilot projects; it also exercises control over water quality and the management function in addition to monitoring service operations being performed by the concessionaire. Moreover, it negotiates the price of water sold to users and grants approvals for all construction projects falling under its direct supervision. Supervising the execution of works is a function that has been transferred to the "Major Projects Control Division" (DCGTx), an agency reporting directly to the Office of the President of the Republic.[8] The nation's President himself would actually be the individual most involved in renegotiating Sodeci's contract, thereby putting an end to the extremely preferential relationships enjoyed by the company with the ministerial-level departments that had been overseeing the water supply sector.

The DCGTx had been created in order to rationalize public-sector spending; however, it had become, because of its director and his team of foreign experts, an agency that merely overlapped the ministries and sought to impose its views on all problems arising. During contract renegotiations held with Sodeci, the DCGTx would obtain a water rate reduction not only on the grounds of social equity (battling

---

7. The municipalities are too politically weak and devoid of resources to hold authority over network operations.

8. This agency has recently been integrated into the services reporting directly to the Prime Minister's Office.

against both the economic downturn and wage cuts through lowering household consumption expenditures) but also to facilitate, in the eyes of the Ivory Coast public, the contract's evolution. In addition, this rate decrease would help Sodeci's parent group (the Bouygues Group) to expand into the electricity services sector.

The DCGTx performs analyses of Sodeci's cost allocations as well as furnishes information to the Water Division for negotiations concerning sales prices and the remuneration of both the State and the private distribution company. It also oversees the tender procedures for all major construction work to be carried out on the supply network. The DCGTx actually intervenes as a third party in the process, positioned somewhere between the Ministry of Public Works and Sodeci, acting to prevent a sort of symbiosis from occurring that would overly-bind both partners in addition to inciting an improved price structure from the user's standpoint. The role of the DCGTx has nonetheless become less important since the new government regime strengthened the authority of the Water Division along with its span of control over Sodeci's activities.

A restructuring of the water supply sector is taking place in light of the creation of the National Water Fund (which consolidates funds earmarked for wastewater services with those slated for water supply). This fund is responsible for covering the debt related to both the water supply and wastewater networks as well as collecting water service taxes (through the intermediary of Sodeci) and drainage taxes (included in property taxes). This National Water Fund is managed by the "Caisse Autonome d'Amortissement" (Independently-Managed Investment Depreciation Fund) within the Finance Ministry.

This new phase would be carried out against the backdrop of troubled economic times and during a period of political changes (the introduction of multi-party politics). A noticeable deterioration in living conditions is presently being experienced in Abidjan, where the population continues to grow despite rampant unemployment. The city of Abidjan counted more than two million inhabitants (out of the country's 12.5 million population) in 1990; many live most precariously. The current crisis is afflicting the whole nation, particularly the agricultural regions whose products are losing considerable value on the international market.

Since 1987, beyond the difficulty being encountered in raising public-sector financing, this sector's economy has also had to take into account the attitudes expressed by users, who have been witnessing an erosion in their buying power and have been consuming less while not respecting payment conditions. Sodeci has endured the economic crisis conditions that have afflicted the Ivory Coast; in so doing, it has been obliged to stabilize its staff size (see table of economic indicators).

90% of Sodeci's service subscribers could be categorized as economically disadvantaged and consume very low volumes of water (with the national average being 322 cubic meters per year in comparison with 886 cubic meters in 1973). The company must take stock of this situation. The Ivory Coast government, in conjunction with Sodeci, has implemented a socially-equitable rate structure; the effort was made to avoid encouraging wastefulness. Nonetheless, for a good portion of Ivory Coast's residents, water still seems like a rather expensive commodity and they feel constrained either to cancel their service subscriptions or to no longer pay their bills. In order to be connected to the network, a deposit of 18,780 CFA (including 16,500 as an advance on subsequent water consumption) is required should the new subscriber's residence be located within twelve meters from the supply network; this figure would obviously increase the further one gets from the network. Such a cost is not especially high in itself, yet it does represent a half-month's minimum wage in areas where many residents are unemployed. In addition, one must be in a position to save regularly in order to pay the water bill every three months, once again a difficult proposition for a substantial percentage of the population.

The most critical problem, within periods of economic crises, consists of establishing a balance in the State's social policy and control and management functions with the private water distribution company's ability to maintain service quality. This problem necessitates the ongoing cooperation between service partners as well as the willingness on the part of public authorities to let the private company carry on with its work independently, while at the same time insuring that the service needs of all categories of residents have been met equitably. The tension created, due to a cumulation of the consequences spawned by the CFA currency devaluation in January 1994, has led to reconsidering the components of the price structure of water.

The State first accepted to modulate its share of service revenues, and then in 1994, introduced a "Value Added Tax" to be maintained by the water services sector. The current rate [9] therefore includes a small component for the National Water Fund, a portion for the development fund, another portion earmarked for the remuneration

---

9. see Appendices for the service rate applicable on March 2, 1995.

of services provided by Sodeci and, finally, the V.A.T. A wide differential however does still exist between the price paid by small-scale users and that being applied to heavier water users. The State is nonetheless obliged to place higher priority emphasis on controlling its water consumption as well as on paying all its overdue bills, which amount to about twenty-three billion CFA, a sum weighing mightily on Sodeci's operations. [10]

In light of the budgetary constraints felt by Ivory Coast residents along with those of the State, Sodeci must look to earn its profit margin through greater management efficiency: reducing water losses (unbilled water produced) and illegal siphoning (uncontrolled service hook-ups), improving controls and meter-reading, and opening new connections (or transactions to maintain service subscribers with irregular payment records). The billing rate reached 86% in 1993, while the bill collection rate for private customers was registered at 97% the same year. This outstanding performance demonstrates a high level of rigor in applying coercive measures (quick meter removal [11] for customers failing to pay, reconnection tax). Good results can also be attributed to the networked computing system, which makes controls easier to administer, in addition to the development of a local-based customer service policy thanks to the decentralization of all company departments (technical, management, etc.).

Profit margins can also be maintained with the help of innovative approaches, such as the Yacoli public fountains, well-suited to very low-income users. These water sources, which have enabled eliminating the free public fountains as well as intensifying the pursuit of illegal water merchants, have served to generate employment: a fountain operator, with a standard subscription has been vested with the authority to sell water as an independent agent in twenty-five-liter units (at a price of 10 CFA). This system of privatizing the resale of water does meet the needs of society's poorest class, yet has still not become widespread due to the size of the outlay required (one million CFA per fountain station, which should also be upgraded in order to take account of social trends).

---

10. The State's overdue payments amounted to 1,138 days in 1993, which generated financial charges for Sodeci that were then passed on to the user. 30% of Sodeci's activity relies on government administrations. Herein lies a potential vulnerability even if Sodeci can manipulate the National Water Fund's service fee and the V.A.T. remittance.

11. Yet, at the same time, Sodeci is obliged to make greater concessions in order to keep customers experiencing temporary difficulties.

Personnel management is also determinant in controlling financial margins; Sodeci had to adapt its workforce to its activity base. It did so by imposing productivity criteria (three hundred meter readings a day per meter reader, eight service connections a day per plumber), yet it further sought to motivate staff through awarding bonuses, practicing merit-based promotions and instilling a corporate culture (complete with fringe benefits and a strong emphasis on employee training programs). The decentralization of company departments has facilitated the optimization of staff size, while additionally serving to cut costs. A policy of introducing greater numbers of women into customer-contact positions at Sodeci also warrants recognition.

Sodeci realized a turnover in 1993 of 19.8 billion CFA, 62.5% of which emanated from water sales (wastewater services comprised only about 5% of their activity). The company's profit ratio runs at 4% of turnover.

The Sodeci experience has come to represent a model for the rest of Africa, a model that's since been championed by the Water Professionals Center as well as by the African Water Distributors Union, in which Sodeci plays a key role, by virtue of the efforts undertaken by its President. The mobility of personnel has also proved to be a powerful means for disseminating this experience throughout all of Africa (for example, to Guinea). Sodeci portrays both a model of technological modernity (in water distribution and computerized management techniques) and an economic model (in its profitability and its rates of bill collection).

The keys to success can be identified in the gradual, yet constant, progression towards attaining a nearly-exclusive Ivory Coast-nationality workforce (and increasing the share of locally-held capital). This push was inspired by the charisma exuded on the part of the company's President, who was able to maintain his organization's independence with respect to the State while at the same time nurturing excellent relationships with the government. Also vital to the promotion of this newly-privatized system has been the strong will manifested by Ivory Coast's political leadership (and especially in the person of President Houphouet Boigny). A more dynamic working attitude exhibited among the ranks of company personnel has, in addition to these relational elements, been fostered by the professional training policy adopted as well as by the corporate culture instilled.

Sodeci's strength also pertains to the precision management methods and computerization introduced, which have enabled pursuing both a major decentralization strategy, accompanied by the transfer of responsibilities, and a serious control effort to crack down on fraud. The company has demonstrated highly-innovative behavior in terms of utilizing its computing systems for service provision, and hopes to sell these capacities in this field across their African region.

The weak points exhibited by Sodeci concern its outstanding debt held by the State as well as its relationship with users, who don't fully comprehend the company's function and who consider the price of water too expensive. In order for the monopoly not to be poorly perceived, Sodeci has had to develop a strong communications policy, which is very actively being implemented at the present time. The limitations inherent in the development fund could also, over the long run, give rise to another system weakness in that network renewal does depend on this fund.

The institutional organization of the water services sector also presents a certain number of weaknesses. The relationship existing between private company and pertinent ministerial departments does not automatically lead to realizing the collective optimum if nothing serves to stimulate the administration to take the concerns of users into account. The narrowed span of DCGTx's authority, at the behest of the government, has bestowed upon the private company much greater autonomy, which could engender a divergence of interest, and thereby to the detriment of users.

Sodeci: principal economic indicators

1993:

turnover:	19.8 billion FCFA (US$ 78 million)
profit:	4% of turnover
water production:	102.8 million cubic meters
water volume billed:	88.6 million cubic meters
number of subscribers:	275,150
number of employees:	1,327

1990:

water production:	99.5 million cubic meters
water volume billed:	85.6 million cubic meters
number of subscribers:	201,200
number of employees:	1,326

1985:

water production:	92.5 million cubic meters
water volume billed:	78.6 million cubic meters
number of subscribers:	170,000
number of employees:	1,633

Seeg: principal economic indicators	
1993:	
turnover:	7.6 billion GNF (US$ 13.3 million)
profit:	2.5% of turnover
water production:	26 million cubic meters
water volume billed:	12.8 million cubic meters
number of subscribers:	19,000
number of employees:	400

Guinea

The evolution taking place in Guinea presents significant differences with respect to that of the Ivory Coast, primarily because of the economic measures implemented at the time of its independence. This country had opted for a Socialist system, with the major share of economic responsibility being held by the public sector within a most constrained and centralized planning framework. Urban services were run by public enterprises, which had taken over from private companies. The Compagnie Africaine de Service Public, whose mission had been to deliver water, was nationalized in 1961. This "all-public" system collapsed in 1984, and a new government, espousing an alternative economic philosophy, came to power. The International Monetary Fund and the World Bank were thereby called upon to assist the country in revitalizing its economy; efforts were concentrated on developing a structural adjustment plan as well as thoroughly revamping the entire Guinean economy, which still remains to be accomplished.

The involvement of international organizations arose at a critical point in time for the Guinean economy. A complete economic restructuring was needed, while at the same time meeting the needs of a large and rapidly-growing population base (six million residents in 1985, 2.8% annual growth rate) located particularly within the more urbanized zones. Also necessary was a change in the economic and social ground rules, which had been implemented through the January 1987 revised capital investment guidelines, and then complemented in 1992 by the adoption of a code governing all forms of economic activity. This updated orientation looked favorably upon private-sector initiative and guaranteed the transfer of profit. Mentalities, in particular those of former administration members, however are evolving rather slowly; the social environment is only being transformed very gradually, inasmuch as highly positive economic performances have still not been registered.

The institutional framework

Water supply services primarily concerned those sectors that the World Bank had targeted for restructuring, as the service had proved inefficient and onerous for the budget. Costs could not be clearly identified as the State's overall budget had already incorporated them, thereby leading to a void in responsibility. Water was in short supply in Conakry and its quality fell below standards of adequacy. Shortages were also recorded within the cities located in the interior of the country even though resources there are plentiful and relatively easily accessible. The World Bank had already participated in a water supply network improvement program at Conakry (First Conakry Water Supply and Sanitation Project, 1976-1985), yet it had not yielded very positive results due to institutional problems along with the poor performance displayed by the institution assigned oversight for this sector at the time.

The World Bank (acting through the AID agency) proposed investing, in conjunction with other development banks (the African Development Bank, the CFD and, later on, the European Development Bank), one hundred million US dollars in the sector, with the intention that the structures and methods utilized to distribute drinking water be modified. From this standpoint, it had commissioned a very thorough study of the situation prior to its commitment; the consultant had suggested updated structures as well as the service's privatization, which had been up until that point provided by the Société Nationale de Distribution des Eaux de Guinée - "DEG" - (Guinea National Water Distribution Company). This company constituted an entire division within the Ministry of Natural Resources and the Environment. The DEG's executive staff was involved with the proposals being forwarded by the World Bank expert on site, a feature which served to facilitate the new system's implementation. It was necessary to start from scratch since at the end of the previous government's reign, pratically everything had been destroyed.

The revised institutional framework, acceptable to the Bank and approved by the Guinean authorities in 1986, proposed the creation of an independent water services company. Called the Société Nationale des Eaux de Guinée - "Soneg" [12] - (Guinean National Water Company), it was to be wholly-owned however by the State. The Secretary of Energy was responsible for the regulation and

---

12. It's with respect to this point that the Guinean model can be distinguished from that of the Ivory Coast. Comparisons between the two models have been carried out and presented in World Bank documents authored by T.A. Triche and A. Locussol.

overall control of this public service sector, yet did not have the right to intervene directly in network operations. A joint public/private company, the Société d'Exploitation des Eaux de Guinée - "Seeg" - (Water Services Company of Guinea) was assigned operations responsibility for the entire network. The nature of the service provided by Seeg on behalf of Soneg had been established by an operations contract that insured a service monopoly. In addition, the institutional format was intended to enable the sector to self-finance its operations so as not to exert undue pressure on the State's budget.

The development of institutional guidelines along with the formulation of contracts aimed at forging partnerships both preceded the 1988 international call for tender that was launched following a pre-qualification process. The winning bid was selected on the basis of the price required to distribute water over a ten-year period. The French companies SAUR and Compagnie Générale des Eaux would, in submitting a joint bid, be awarded the contract [13], which helped strengthen the collective experience applied and especially helped to reduce the risks run within a most uncertain context.

These two firms, in conjunction with the Guinean government, created on April 19, 1989 the Seeg, a Guinean-certified public limited company posting a registered capital of GNF 1.3 billion, divided among 130,000 shares, which could only be transferred upon agreement of the partners. The private-sector participants would hold 51% of Seeg's capital; however, all major decisions taken by the Board of Directors would require a 75% vote, a condition which allowed the Guinean government to retain a strong level of control over this public service area. According to the applicable statutes, the company's Managing Director must be appointed by the majority shareholder, and the President of the Board of Directors by the oversight Ministry. The company holds contractual guarantees with respect to the ease of not only importing necessary materials and equipment but also transferring profits earned. Seeg has entered into a technical assistance contract with SAUR and Générale des Eaux for conducting studies (such as automated cartography), providing financial assistance (generating cash flow) and performing specific appraisals. Firms called in to carry out these services are to be remunerated on the basis of 2% of Seeg's income level as well as a percentage on the operations undertaken with their purchasing groups.

---

13. Only two consortia actually submitted proposals; the others deemed the situation too risky.

The State (through the intermediary of the department assigned responsibility for water services) exercises oversight of the operations of both companies. It sets out the service area's general policy and planning guidelines, makes all legal and contract-related decisions, grants approval of water use rates within the scope of a three-year master plan and is also a shareholder. The Minister of Natural Resources and Energy is responsible for approving and monitoring the capital investment program, Soneg's level of performance in addition to the company's Board decisions regarding rate structures and loans.

Soneg fulfills the missions of the facilities owner. It identifies water supply needs, carries out network development studies, procures financing, puts construction projects out to bid, contracts out the building of infrastructure facilities, all the while acting in the capacity of the owner of a utility network for which it must assure the functions of maintenance and service extension. It supervises Seeg's activities in conformance with a set of contractually-defined procedures [14], which have not always been well-received by the water distribution company's directors, who have been pushing for greater autonomy. It's this constant tension that constitutes one of the mechanisms enabling, according to the institutional model chosen, both partners to be incited towards attaining a social optimum.

Soneg is in charge of managing World Bank monies - that are officially granted by the Guinean government, the actual borrower - and must submit to the government its project proposals for necessary approvals in cases of major capital investments. It also maintains responsibility for Guinea's debt service in the water supply sector. Its staff, reduced to a total of forty-three members, is composed in part of former DEG employees. Personnel management and smaller investment decisions [15] represent those areas wherein its level of autonomy remains greatest. The World Bank has financed a portion of the technical assistance required for becoming operational, especially in terms of defining its relationships and responsibilities with respect to Seeg and its funding sources. Soneg is committed to balancing its accounts without reaping any profit whatsoever; the price of water which it sets upon negotiation, to be applied and collected by Seeg, is based on this accounting restriction.

---

14. and may utilize for penalty-incentive purposes a guarantee fund of US$ 400,000 that Seeg was required to deposit in a Guinean bank.

15. For major investments, Soneg is responsible for conveying the decision to the National Contracts Commission and transmitting the ruling to the funding organizations for their approval. The entire procedure takes quite a long time.

Seeg operates the network conferred it by Soneg in accordance with a ten-year leasing agreement, whose economic-related clauses can be revised in respecting the procedural guidelines [16]. It maintains and refurbishes the installations and facilities in order to insure providing a quality service, connects individual service subscribers to the network, delivers water and collects service fees. Fees collected go towards remunerating the service rendered as well as towards covering distribution costs; they also pay for operations and investments (including charges on the loans underwritten to finance these investments) carried out on the part of the facilities owner.

Guineans were not used to paying for water services; they didn't practice a system of service subscriptions nor utilize water meters. Transition measures therefore had to be foreseen so that the partners could be remunerated, that the costs and investments could be covered, and that the users could be prepared for this new expense. After having required the application of a more realistic price for water consumed, the World Bank accepted paying out over a ten-year period, yet with a degressive participation beyond the fourth year, a subsidy so that costs should not be borne too heavily and too suddenly by the user. The service cost being billed the user has thus gradually risen and will reach a point of covering actual costs around the year 1998. In fact, the Bank is only subsidizing the share of the operator's rate in foreign currency. This measure has enabled Seeg to procure the currency it needs without having to raise capital through the bidding system set up in Guinea. The Guinean government has been subsidizing, also in a degressive fashion, the portion of debt service that Soneg must assume and that is passed on to users.

The World Bank got especially involved in Guinea's situation in order to facilitate the transformation of this particular service, and in so doing to create a model for other public service sectors [17]. This multi-faceted role being played by the Bank constitutes one of the originalities associated with the Guinean experience and relies upon the close cooperation developed between DEG managers and World Bank staff. Besides its actions of supporting capital investment, providing technical assistance to Soneg and subsidizing some operating costs, the World Bank has also financed a program to retrain personnel formerly with the DEG who couldn't be placed within the new organizational structure.

---

16. This rate revision is automatic with increases in the volume of water sold, with rises in certain components used to derive the cost price index, etc.

17. The electricity sector corresponds, in part, to the model describing the water services sector (with, in addition, certain common partners).

Nearly a hundred and twenty employees were enrolled in this program, preparing them to participate within a cooperative action framework and to perform as subcontractors for infrastructure projects related to the water services program. The World Bank loan was accorded under favorable terms on a thirty-year reimbursement period.

Service implementation

After having been awarded the contract, Seeg began operations against a backdrop of severe water shortage, with a network in a poor state of repair. To facilitate start-up conditions, Soneg contracted a component of the most urgent network overhaul and extension work to Seeg, yet contract award procedures, as stipulated in the loan agreement, slowed tremendously these projects. Seeg initiated a drinking water purification program and undertook evaluating the state of the network, executing the works, installing meters, billing customers on a regular basis, and so on.

Within this initial start-up phase (from 1988 to 1993), Seeg encountered two types of problems: internal, in creating a real company that utilizes criteria of efficiency, and external, in dealing with users.

At the beginning, Seeg called upon French expatriates, former DEG staff and new recruits. Providing training for this workforce of three hundred and twelve members presented a key priority; in particular by applying Saur/Sodeci operating procedures and computing systems. Beyond technical domains, training was also focused on instilling a new frame of mind: that of a company spirit, very different from the mentality held by civil service employees. This orientation was difficult to introduce, and conflicts of coexistence would sometimes arise with the expatriate personnel or with the company's newly-imposed code of conduct (regarding theft, punctuality, etc.). Over this entire period, human resources management problems, coupled with problems pertaining to the company's transition, took on critical importance and comprised one axis of development within each of the procedures being formulated to privatize a formerly public-run service. The Managing Director's level of competence, acquired with Sodeci, was crucial at the outset of the company's existence.

In this phase, users had no experience whatsoever in managing their water use economically. It was necessary to explain the qualities of drinking water, how to avoid wasting water, the notion of a distribution cost, etc. Information campaigns were undertaken; convincing residents to give up diverting water illegally and to pay regularly for service did nonetheless prove rather fruitless, especially considering that water appeared as an expensive commodity and one engendering higher costs. It had become necessary at times to call upon the army to remove illegal network hook-ups or to enforce service connection cutoffs in case of non-payment. The lack of a water use policing authority represents a major obstacle to the privatization effort [18] in that an absence of rules tends to impede the application of an effective bill collection policy.

In order to serve its customer base, Seeg requires a densely-laid out network; however, Soneg has proceeded quite slowly given its set of operating rules. Friction between the two companies started to appear, with each one foisting off responsibility on the other for, notably, overhaul of the network left by DEG, the lack of coordination [19], the arduous assessment of maintenance needs or even of the need to replace certain components of the network, etc. Working in unison would nonetheless remain the strongest characteristic depicting their relationship, and the network would ultimately operate at full capacity by the end of 1993. At that time, the network was even operating with a excess capacity. It's really only since then that the "Guinean system" could truly be exhibited.

The city of Conakry is not alone in receiving water supply service, yet the cities located in the interior of the country are slower in getting set up because of the absence of electricity. At the present time, eighteen cities are receiving service and ten others are on the verge of initiating operations.

Since 1993, the system has entered into its new phase, which nonetheless still constitutes a start-up phase. Seeg produced 26 million cubic meters of water in 1993, 86% of which went to Conakry, but only billed 12.8 million cubic meters. The billing rate is quite low, especially in Conakry. In 1993, Seeg registered 13,580 subscribers in Conakry and 5,455 in the interior cities. Billing for 72% of these subscribers is based on meter readings (thus on consumption). The rate of bill collection among private subscribers is at 77%, while public-sector administrations are taking longer and longer to pay [20].

---

18. This situation should soon change, as a new piece of legislation is slated to be introduced in the near future.

19. Seeg nonetheless retains the right to a technical verification prior to the reception of all new network components, thereby reducing the risk of stirring conflict.

20. This situation should improve with the inclusion of expenses to be settled by the State into the Finance Law.

Seeg's turnover amounts to 7.6 billion GNF and its profit margin is running at 2.5%. The company employs a staff of four hundred, including eight French expatriates.

Bill collection is made difficult not only by the economic hardships facing the Guinean population, but also by the behavioral resistance to paying for services; Seeg prefers organizing informational campaigns rather than systematically cutting off service. Nonetheless, 4,800 connections had actually been cut as of the end of June 1994. The "learning" period for users is still ongoing, yet Seeg does have to improve its operating ratios in order to be credible in Soneg's eyes. In particular, it needs to reduce the quantity of water that goes unpaid.

Furthermore, Seeg must increase the number of service subscribers both in the country's interior cities and in Conakry. Two operations are currently aimed in this direction: the "15,000 subsidized connections" operation launched in February 1994, and the municipal fountains project. For a sum of 60,000 GNF [21], any resident can be conected if his dwelling lies within thirty meters of the network; as a result, 650 new subscribers were connected, which represents a relatively small number. Seeg has also proposed setting up, at the municipal level, public fountain operators to sell fountain water (which would no longer be at the expense of municipalities) to users on behalf of Seeg itself; however, this project has been slow in getting off the ground.

Seeg has also been seeking to implement the decentralization of its workforce as well as its computing systems so as to be nearer its customer base, to better monitor consumer trends and to further develop the network. This mission's success has relied, to a great extent, upon a solid training program strengthened by the creation of a training center and the allocation of a sizable budget. Employee motivation has been on the rise, thus favoring internal promotion in addition to social benefits. This upward motivational trend constitutes a key element in achieving optimal performance both in the realization of company objectives and in the gradual "pro-Guinea" influence being exerted upon the company's executive management staff.

The Guinean experience and its success depend upon an extremely fragile system balance, wherein each of the system's four partners (State, Soneg, Seeg and users) must act in cognizance of the others. Should one of the partners default, the whole system would break down. If Soneg, for example, were late in its network extension schedule or could

---

21. plus an additional guarantee of 27,200 GNF. The cost of a service connection represents roughly one month's legal minimum wage.

not furnish water meters, or if it set rates too high, Seeg would then be penalized in its distribution activities (and thus in its remuneration) due to an insufficient number of service connections when faced with an apparently strong level of demand [22]. If the State were to delay in setting up a water policing authority or in paying its debt, Seeg would not be able to provide service. If users weren't practicing greater discipline in their water use patterns and didn't earn adequate incomes (since the effort being asked of them is significant), the network couldn't be developed any further. Finally, if Seeg were to operate too slowly or too inefficiently, Soneg's funding sources would be curtailed.

The risks of system failure are thus numerous despite the precision written into contractual obligations, and Seeg would like to obtain a margin of flexibility in the form of direct management responsibility over a service development fund [23]. The Guinean system would therefore appear to be naturally evolving, based on the cumulative experience gained, towards assigning greater authority upon the distribution company; neither the State nor Soneg however, for reasons of public interest, wish to have their power to exercise control and to impose constraints taken away.

The strengths of Guinea's experience lie in the independence, as affirmed by the nation's political leadership, of the distribution company - and of a portion of the facilities owner as well - with respect to the political arena. Seeg's technical and management expertise (in relation with its foreign partners) also account for the successes realized. The company should nonetheless upgrade its overall performance in the area of bill collection.

The weak points of the experience consist of the users' behavioral tendencies as well as their capacity to pay in a period of economic difficulties. Once the subsidies granted for reducing costs have run out, will the actual cost be bearable for a maximum number of potential users? Another weakness has to do with the institutional setting itself and, in particular, the perception of the contract held by each of its two principal parties: Soneg, respecting the bounds imposed by the contract and nothing but the contract, and Seeg, preferring an interpretation yielding greater freedom. Though institutional relationships have been clearly defined, they are still capable

---

22. 7,500 requests for subsidized service hook-ups, yet only 650 could be satisfied.

23. as carried out for the operation "15,000 subsidized connections", for which Soneg had provided a pipe section 60 km. in length to be used in accordance with the needs being expressed, as detected by Seeg.

of isolating partners, and becoming causes of system delays or inciting friction that could hinder network extension projects, one of the top priorities on the social policy agenda.

A comparison of the two experiences presented in this chapter reveals the importance of a water services policing authority in addition to improving user awareness as two preliminaries to any privatization program. It also highlights the necessity to adapt utility networks to the economically-troubled times and to the precarious conditions affecting a very large number of urban residents, through reliance on means such as public fountains and water supply merchants. The convergence of the State's interests with those held by the private sector still remains an awkward feature in countries where the notion of public interest has not been fully distinguished from that of political interest. This is particularly so given the relative youth of some of these countries, especially in Africa. The management capabilities and skill levels displayed by administrations seem inadequate in promoting quality in the provision of urban services; moreover, privatizing the distribution of water has enabled battling against inefficiency and, in so doing, improving the quality of life in urban areas. Taking into account the range of social-policy objectives does nonetheless require the close cooperation between State and private partners, a cooperation that's both clearly-outlined and yet remains flexible.

APPENDICES

IVORY COAST

fixed rate for consumption volumes of less than 15 m^3:
        159 FCFA including 0 for the State and 0 for system development

household rate 75 m^3:	230	5	22
normal rate 210 m3:	368	20	145
full rate	424	50	171

rate effective March 2, 1995, inclusive of V.A.T.
1 FCFA = 0.01 French francs

Breakdown of functions within the water services sector in the Ivory Coast

Functions	Roles	Actors
1. Defining the public service sector's policy 2. Water resources management 3. Developing the legislative and regulatory framework 4. Setting rates and the price of water 5. Facilities management (upgrading, depreciation and debt service) 6. Scheduling new capital investments and procuring financing 7. Monitoring the quality of the service provided and of the water supplied 8. Fulfilling project owner's role for all renovation work, extension and connections	Strategy for the sector and resource management	METT Water Division
9. Facility operations and maintenance 10. Renewal of infrastructure and operating equipment 11. Control of water quality as well as service quality 12. Customer billing 13. Bill collection 14. User awareness programs and customer relations 15. Assessment and motivation behind investments aimed at facilities renewal, extensions and subsidized service connections	Technical and commercial management	SODECI

Source: TECHWARE-AQUANET, "Institutional reform of the urban water supply sub-sector", June 1994 for the Republic of Senegal

GUINEA

subsidized rate: volumes less than 20 m³: 680 GNF including 435 for Soneg
special rate, volumes less than 60 m³: 850   605
heavy-use rate: 925   680

rate effective August 1, 1994
1 GNF = 0.0055 French francs = roughly 0.5 FCFA after devaluation

Breakdown of functions within the water services sector in Guinea

Functions within the water sector	Roles	Actors
1. Defining the public service sector's policy	Strategy	State
2. Water resources management adopted	for the sector	
3. Legislative and regulatory framework		
4. Rate setting system		
5. Debt service management	Management of	
6. Scheduling new capital investments and procuring financing	Resources used to implement strategy	SONEG
7. Replacement of primary installations	for the sector	
8. Works design		
9. Works execution		
10. Facility operations and maintenance		
11. Depreciation of operating equipment	Commercial	
12. Replacement of small-scale equipment	management	SEEG
13. Customer billing	for the sector	
14. Bill collection		
15. Customer relations		
16. Public service mission	undefined	

Source: TECHWARE-AQUANET, "Institutional reform of the urban water supply sub-sector", June 1994 for the Republic of Senegal

Institutional framework in the Ivory Coast

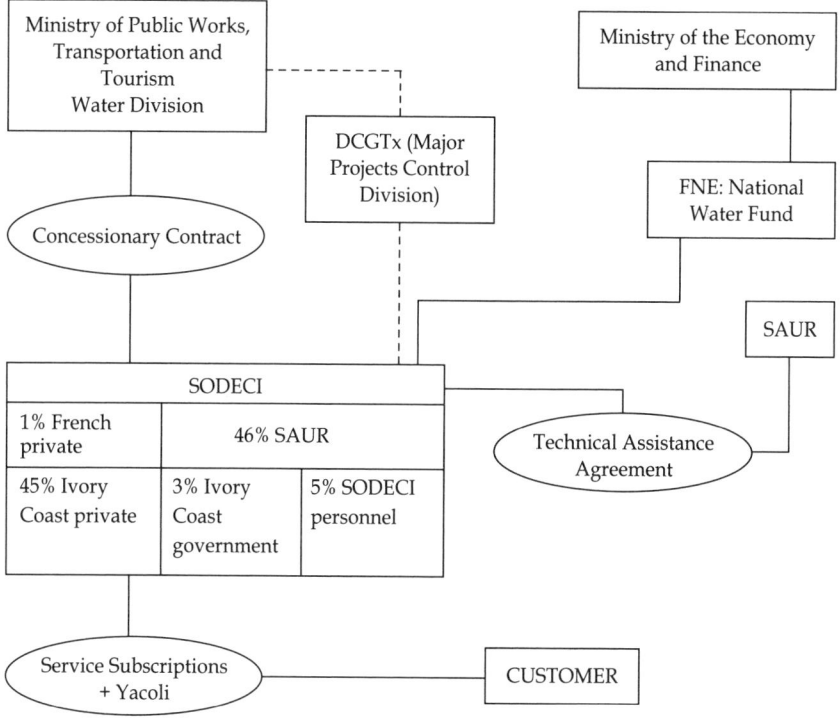

Institutional framework in Guinea

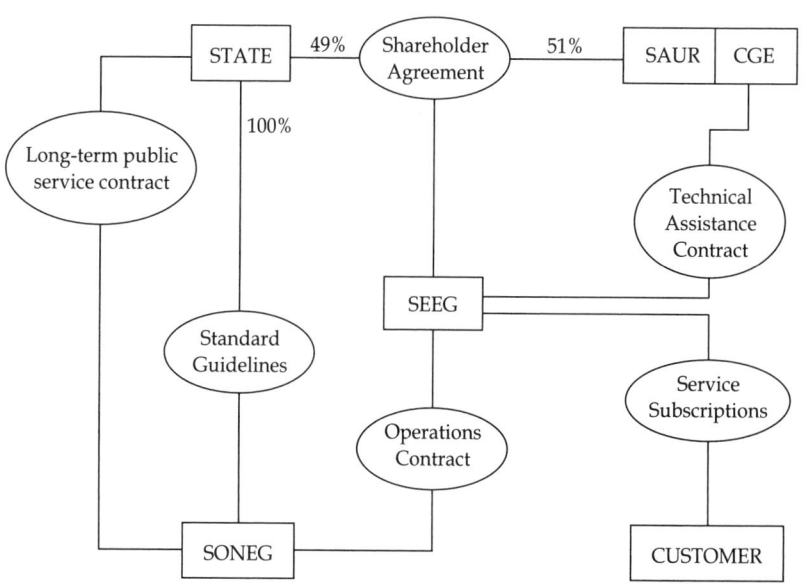

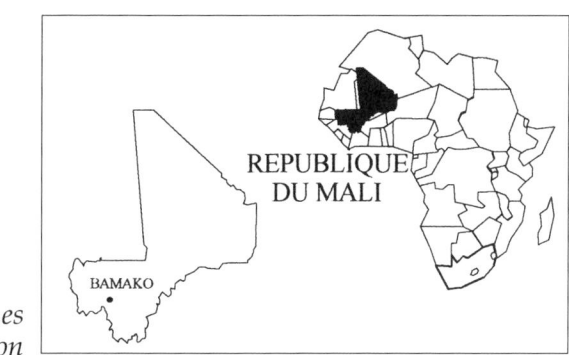

CHAPTER 9

Hugues
Le Masson

Village Water Supply in Mali

The history of the works carried out by a Catholic missionary for the village water supply to the villages of this Sahelian country explains why the principles applicable to the distribution of water in urban environments pertain to rural areas as well. Ownership of water and its sources must remain in the hands of local authorities; however, resource management assuring water delivery to the local population must be conferred to the private sector.

This example also serves to demonstrate that individual initiative, along with the level of support it raises through calling upon private charity organizations, such as the "Sahel Aqua Viva Foundation", constitutes a fundamental factor in development progress. The efforts of these organizations tend sometimes to be forgotten by the public-sector development assistance institutions. Just like the mouse in the fairy tale, these institutions are sometimes able to garner the accolades intended for someone else. "An elephant and a mouse are walking in a plain, chatting away. The mouse then turns towards the elephant: 'Don't you think that, you and me, we're kicking up a lot of dust'."

Mali

Mali, one of Africa's largest countries (1.2 million km² in land area, double that of France), is located towards the western part of the continent. It belongs to the "Sahel" States and borders countries that, generally speaking, are as impoverished: Mauritania and Algeria to the north, Niger and Burkina Faso to the east, the Ivory Coast to the south, Guinea and Senegal to the west. Three distinct climatic zones, and therefore different precipitation profiles, characterize the country's geography. To the north, the Sahara Desert comprises over half of the nation's territory; rainfall there amounts to less than 50 mm of water per year. The center of the country, called the "Sahelian Zone", receives less than 600 mm of rainfall per year; it covers a quarter of the total land area and contains a well-renowned city, Timbuktu. The south, with over 600 mm of annual rainfall, has a climate that actually allows rainwater-dependent cultivation; this area is referred to as the "Sudanese Zone", whose capital city Bamako lies at a distance of 1,200 kilometers from Dakar and 1,300 from Abidjan.

Mali relies, first and foremost, on its agricultural activities, yet its lands are poor in quality and rainfall is unevenly distributed throughout the year. The dry season extends from to May October, during which no rainfall is present, while all the year's rains are concentrated in the rainy season, lasting from June to September. The sun's rays, shining brightly over the vast majority of the year, are strong and hot; at the end of the dry season, the temperature can easily reach 45°C. The country does nonetheless possess a rich geographical resource in the Niger River, which flows over Mali soil for a total distance of 1,700 kilometers. Its presence gives rise to fishing activities, transportation means and, on its banks, cultivation requiring changing water levels; furthermore, it supplies neighboring residents with a continual source of water.

The same cannot be said a mere few kilometers away however; water supply to villages out of the river's immediate vicinity is provided from the ponds remaining after the previous winter's rains. The droughts, that have ravaged the Sahel region ever since the 1970's, have only served to heighten the severity of this problem. The availability of water sources represents a vital issue for those villages located away from the Niger River.

Mali's ten million inhabitants reside, for the most part, within the "Sudanese Zone". They are primarily peasants, divided into sixteen distinct ethnic groupings (and thus speaking sixteen different languages). The Bambaras, the largest of the ethnic groups, grow millet and cotton;

the Bozos are fishermen and live off the river; the Peuls raise livestock, and so on. Strongly attached to their local customs, these peoples would only emigrate to the city out of necessity or when the rural areas no longer afforded a minimum number of now universally-recognized commodities. Among these, of course, would be water supply.

A "missionary-developer"

Born in 1924, Bernard Verspieren became a Catholic missionary following studies in the field of agronomics. Assigned to Mali in 1950, he would go on to devote twenty years of his life to evangelizing populations of the San region, located 400 kilometers to the northeast of Bamako, at the border of the Sahelian and Sudanese zones. The droughts of the 1970's focused his attention on a new priority: in order to keep the peasants on their land, they needed water; in order to keep the villages alive, it was necessary to save the women from exhausting themselves by collecting unhealthy water from ponds at times located quite far away.

Yet, the question nonetheless remains where to find water in a country with no rainfall. Underground water must be extracted through the use of wells or bore-holes fitted with appropriate pumps. 1975 saw the creation of the "Mali Aqua Viva Project" for the construction of bore-holes intended to serve the villages of the San region.

Twenty years later, the list of accomplishments is indeed an impressive one: over 3,000 bore-holes supplying water to a million residents, or 10% of the nation's population, the highest concentration in the world of photovoltaic solar pumps for extracting water. In addition, these achievements includes health centers, a model farm, a hospital, a testing center for renewable energy production, the development of solar-powered irrigation systems, the creation of centers for the disabled, and the list goes on.

The focal point of this project lies at Teriya Bugu ("The Friendship Hut"), a farm created on the banks of the Bani River (the Niger River's main tributary), located between Segou and San. It's where one might meet up with Bernard Verspieren when he's not out beating the path in Mali or the world over in pursuit of the financing necessary to running these various operations: 100 million US$ were thus raised in the span of twenty years by this man alone, capable of pronouncing the right words to rally the public around his cause. Three-fourths of this sum was in fact contributed by individuals, companies and associations, while the remainder came from public assistance loans earmarked for the well-drilling program.

As a conclusion to this presentation on Bernard Verspieren, the words of Lamine Samaké, chief of the village of N'Woro whose territory encompasses the site of Teriya Bugu, would seem especially pertinent; these comments have been extracted from a report written February 8-10, 1988 that recounts the history of Teriya Bugu:

"I've attempted, dear readers, to chronicle twenty years of life experiences with my cherished friend, Patron and Father.

- Our tireless gardener,
- Our unforgettable well digger,
- The fervent protector of our trees,
- The loyal friend of our animals and birds,
- The relentless enemy of brush fires,
- The intolerant enemy of laziness and lethargy, and finally
- The resolute ally of the poor, the tired, the hungry.

History of the "Mali Aqua Viva Project"

Launched in 1975, with the support of the Catholic church, this project's initial objective consisted of completing, within a period of four years' time, 400 bore-holes to supply water to villages located away from the river. In order to reach this objective, it was decided to utilize two drilling equipments called "well-bottom drilling hammer" (see below).

The first one, financed by former West Germany's "Misereor", came to Mali towards the end of 1975, and the second, financed by the Dutch charity organization Cebemo, arrived at the beginning of 1978. Responsibility for both was assumed entirely by local Malian teams whose level of productivity matched Western companies: 82 wells drilled during the 1975/76 campaign, 100 during 1976/77, 123 in 1977/78 and 165 in 1978/79.

As of October 1, 1979, after thirty-four months of effective work carried out, the Mali Aqua Viva Project had thereby completed a total of 470 bore-holes at an average depth of 60 meters (reaching up to 130 meters). This feat was achieved thanks to the work of Verspieren's team, along with all those - individuals, companies, associations - who, whether in France, elsewhere in Europe or in North America, rallied to support this endeavor.

Once the objective had been reached, the charity organizations actively backing the project withdrew in favor of letting the Mali Government assume the lead role in its financing. Ultimately, it fell upon the "Caisse Centrale de Coopération Economique" - CCCE-, a French public-sector financial institution assigned the mission of assisting in the development of African countries, to continue to fund the project.

This turn of events gave rise to some significant impacts. The actions undertaken by the Mali Aqua Viva project teams, having demonstrated their competence, had to be extended into something more durable through the provision of repair shops, warehouses for storing equipment, offices, hangars along with the loan packages necessary for pursuing their efforts. A "water services base" was built on a nearly four-hectare site in San. Control of both the construction and the equipment for some 1,000 additional wells enabled insuring the project's operations during half a dozen annual campaigns. Lastly, a flexible administrative and accounting system was implemented in order to facilitate managing a company financed through both private and public borrowing, donations and business loans.

The specifics of the events that have affected Mali Aqua Viva since that time will not be dealt with herein. It should nonetheless be highlighted that the project's primary financial backer had gradually imposed a more administrative and bureaucratic type of structural model that, while feasible in Western nations, was difficult to apply to a country like Mali. This funding organization decided in 1991 not to renew its support for the project so as to eliminate any potential dependence on these external "subscription" monies. The question remained however where to turn for procuring the financial resources that Mali itself couldn't come up with.

From 1992 on, with no other means than charity for financing the working teams imposed by the French administration, Mali Aqua Viva found only one solution left: start from scratch by associating, into a kind of workers' cooperative, all the agents required to carry out its mission of equipping the villages of the region with groundwater extraction facilities. This could have been performed by the all-Malian team that had assumed responsibility for the project; the team proved capable of building strong bonds with a wide array of charitable organizations, local authorities, various associations, French as well as from other countries. The financial resources enabling the extension of the program to equip villages had thus been assembled. Here's how the number of 470 wells drilled as of October 1, 1979 had grown:

- to 802 on October 1, 1981,
- to 1,800 on October 1, 1987,
- to 3,400 on October 1, 1995.

Why opt for pump-equipped borings over conventional wells?

To the lay person, the difference between a conventional well and a pump-equipped boring site may not be readily apparent; their distinction, provided in the box below, should be of some help.

To recap:
Conventional well = no pump = no maintenance = continual operations, yet resulting in high costs, water pollution and the risk of draining the well.

Bore-holes = pump-equipped = maintenance assured = haphazard operations, yet more economical, generating low levels of water pollution and no risk of draining.

In light of the advantages, most notably financial in nature, presented by pump-equipped bore-holes, the Mali Aqua Viva Project opted for this technique over conventional wells. Nonetheless, two types of problems arose with this choice:
- selecting the appropriate well-drilling machinery for executing the works, and
- procuring the adequate set of pumps and scheduling their maintenance in order to avoid any long-term equipment down time.

The pumps. The choice of a well pump is a delicate one in that striking a balance is not always easy between the various constraints, which pertain to well-drilling, energy sources, maintenance programs, to name the three primary factors.

In light of these selection criteria, along with the criterion of price (highest price doesn't always translate into most costly solution), Mali Aqua Viva was led to retain for low flow rates (95% of the well sites) the Vergnet pedal-powered pumps, and for the heavy flows (well installations capable of delivering a flow of over 10 m^3/hour) the photovoltaic solar-powered pumps.

The Vergnet pump, invented during the mid-1970's, is based on the notion that a light, easy-to-disassemble pump was preferable to one that's more robust, yet difficult to disassemble. Its unique operating technique (inflating a gold beater's skin acting as a piston by means of hydraulic transmission) is renowned among specialists. For the lay person, it should suffice to understand that two men, working without any special equipment, are able to remove the pump from the well. Maintenance should therefore proceed smoothly.

BOX 1
Wells vs. bore-holes for groundwater

In order to draw groundwater, it's first necessary to dig a hole in the earth at a sufficient depth to reach the level of the groundwater table. Two techniques are used to accomplish this:

Conventional wells with large diameters (one-meter minimum): the extraction of water is performed by a bucket tied to the end of a piece of rope. Maintenance is quite straightforward; this type of installation may last a long time without undergoing any maintenance whatsoever. Yet, certain disadvantages do persist: potential draining of the well at the end of the dry season; often difficult and dangerous well-drilling conditions; high costs (reaching up to five times the cost of a boring installation); water pollution caused by the means of extraction employed.

Pump-equipped bore-holes sites with small diameters (maximum 30 cm.): the extraction of water is performed by means of a pump (pedal-powered, hand-powered or motor-activated). Its construction is rather simple (when in possession of the drilling equipment adapted to the particular type of ground), and the corresponding cost remains less than that for drilling conventional, manually-operated wells. Pollution is limited, and drawing water with a pump is far easier than with a bucket tied to a rope. However, this type of installation loses its usefulness whenever the pump is down; its maintenance thus takes on vital importance. Daily maintenance is required for combustion motors; fuel supply is thereby essential. Maintenance measures must be foreseen for the inevitable mechanical failures; one staff position must be devoted to eventual reparations, and a stock of spare parts must also be held.

Well-drilling machinery. The choice of boring installations on the part of Mali Aqua Viva was facilitated by the development, during the 1970's, of the technology called the "well-bottom drilling hammer", which enabled building facilities economically in hard ground. The technique employed made use of specific "drilling work sites", at a unit value of approximately 700,000 US$, including a core drilling machine, a compressor, a cistern, the accessory equipment (drilling shanks, tubing, a welding station, etc.) as well as the trucks used for transportation. Such a work site operates with a crew of around ten workers.

No further discussion will be provided herein on the drilling technique utilized; suffice it to say that it is now well-mastered and no longer poses any problems.

This pump, at a unit cost of roughly 2,000 US$, is installed at practically all of Mali Aqua Viva's well sites. For a family of ten, the pump's monthly operating cost comes to an estimated 1 to 2 US$, which represents a price for water at around 40 cents per m^3. These prices are extremely reasonable; the purchase of the bucket and piece of rope needed for a conventional well would result in higher cost prices. The simplicity of maintaining this type of pump might lead to concluding that the wells drilled in the region of San are all in perfect working order. An assessment of the conditions required for an effective maintenance program should help illustrate this point.

BOX 2
The "well-bottom drilling hammer"

This method consists of perforating the ground with the help of a boring bit placed at the extremity of a train of drill shanks, activated by a strong flow of high-pressure
compressed air. The technique, derived from the use of the jackhammers on the
streets of our cities, allows advancing quickly in hard ground: a boring depth of
60 meters can be drilled in the span of two days (in comparison with three to four
months for a similarly-sized conventional well opening), at an average cost of
5,000 US$.

The "well-bottom hammer" method is well-suited to the San region. The hard
ground (Bandiagara sandstone) encountered, after five to ten meters of ground cover,
could necessitate the installation of temporary tubing. Drilling in the sandstone
is straightforward enough; these rocks present partially-sealed cracks across their
faces and thus prevent against sliding. The excavated material is evacuated to the
surface by means of compressed air, and drilling is halted at the appearance of water.

The groundwater, stored in the sandstone's cracks, originates from the infiltration
of rainwater; it's therefore not at all a fossil-based water and is renewable. As a result,
the volume of the reservoir is practically unlimited for water extracted from very
dispersed well sites.

The final operation consists of "fitting out" the bore-holes:
- installation of permanent tubing; a perforated plastic tube is used to prevent
against any rock slide that could make it impossible to recover the pump in case
of malfunction;
- construction of a "well head"; the ring-shaped space located between the
well opening and the upper part of the tubing is cemented in order to avoid the
infiltration of polluted water. It's also advisable to lay concrete paving on the surface,
thereby eliminating the possibility of any slime accumulating collecting around the
well head; and
- installation of the pump.

The photovoltaic solar-powered pumps are dream-like working tools
for a country like Mali, where the sun constitutes the people's most
evenly-shared source of richness; these pumps consume energy
that's both abundant and free of charge. Here's why, despite the high
capital outlay, the resultant per-m^3 cost price of water also turns out
to be in the range of 40 cents. The premise behind their functioning
is simple: in shining on the silicium panels, the sun generates the electricity
that's supplied to an electric motor; an average amount of sunshine
yields seven to eight hours of full-scale operations.

On the technical side, the difficulty lies in producing electrical
current. However, the cost of the panels is still too expensive to envision
installations in the tens of kilowatts in power; the power of the
photovoltaic solar-powered pumps will thus remain relatively low.

BOX 3
Factors influencing the choice of pump

- Well-drilling: Mali Aqua Viva deemed the well site to be operating in a productive fashion if it was capable of generating a flow of at least 1 m^3/hr (1,000 liters an hour); this flow rate enables supplying from 300 to 400 residents. Another key data element would be the water level at which pumping should be performed. Just because a well may be 60 meters deep doesn't necessarily mean that water should be extracted at that particular depth; within a well, the water stabilizes at the "level of the groundwater table" (15 meters in the region of San). Herein lies the reason why the project was able to adopt the use of lightweight pumps, thereby easy to disassemble.

- The energy source: In order to raise the water from below the surface of the ground, energy is required. This could take the form of the physical force being exerted by the users themselves; since the instantaneous energy supplied by an individual (and most likely a woman at that) is rather weak, the human-powered pumps shall only be utilized for low-output wells. This energy could also be provided by gas or diesel-powered pumps; these combustion motor pumps, more economical for the heavy flows, are not used by Mali Aqua Viva. Also of potential interest is the category of renewable-energy pumps (wind turbines or solar-powered). It's this category, which began appearing on the market at the time the project was being launched, that was retained and made Mali Aqua Viva one of the world's pioneers in the field.

- Maintenance: a pump that's down means that the capital investment in the well can't be recovered. Nonetheless, there mustn't be any misconception: all pumps break down at one point or another. Since a solidly-built pump is costly and tricky to repair, it might be preferable to opt for a pump that's lighter, less expensive and easy to repair, even though it's also one that does experience greater down time. The maintenance program applied must therefore be adapted to the particular pump selected.

Motors that run on the electricity generated should also be better developed. By serving as a testing center for a variety of equipment (submersible pumps for well water extraction, surface pumps for irrigation, solar generators for dwelling units), Mali Aqua Viva has significantly contributed to the progress made in this field.

The pumps currently in use for the wells cost about 30,000 US$ a piece (including solar panels); they are each capable of supplying 60 to 80 m^3 of water per average day of sunlight. Such a volume would serve the water supply needs of major villages, of several herds of livestock (in assuming 40 liters per head of cattle per day) and of the irrigation of small vegetable gardens. The zone encompassed by the Mali Aqua Viva project counts more than 100 such installations, representing the world's strongest concentration.

The pumps destined for irrigation purposes make use of permanent water courses. As a consequence, their solar panels have been mounted above the floodwater level, with the pump being assembled on a raft. The pump's power ranges from 1,500 watts to 5 kilowatts, at a total cost of somewhere between 20,000 and 60,000 US$. They are increasingly found along the banks of the Bani River, where their presence has stimulated the creation of orchards on land that had heretofore laid fallow.

These observations could lead to the conclusion that solar-powered pumping represents the path of the future. Such an interpretation must nonetheless be qualified. Solar capabilities within the Mali Aqua Viva project were developed through the input of young engineers assigned to complete their military service obligation at Teriya Bugu. These unique conditions demonstrate why it becomes difficult to fully draw all the pertinent lessons from this experience. It is especially problematic to ascertain when and how the local population will be in a position to assume responsibility for facility maintenance and renewal that does remain, after all, quite costly: a 50-watt solar panel costs roughly 600 US$. Such a substantial expenditure also helps explain the presence of new behavioral forms in societies that, to European eyes, would tend to appear dormant. For protection against animals roaming wild, the solar panels have always been fenced in; fifteen years ago, wire fences would be stolen since peasants considered them valuable in comparison with the more common thorny-brush protection. Nowadays, the wire fence is left in favor of stealing the panel itself, which serves to illuminate a light bulb or run a television set.

These new types of behavior encountered may lead to reconsidering the development of solar energy financed by external sources; it would be necessary to determine whether operating conditions could incite behavioral modification.

Lessons to be drawn from this experience

Projects financed by public-sector funding organizations (World Bank, European Community, bilateral institutions) as well as by Non-Governmental Organizations (NGOs) often display similar characteristics: their local-based field representative spends anywhere from two to five years maximum on a given project. Mali Aqua Viva functions quite differently. This project, comparable in size to major international ventures, has been driven for twenty years by the same team, Father Verspieren and his Malian colleagues. Why is this so? Because this missionary has simply dedicated his life to the people of Mali.

Such continuity of service obviously presents certain advantages: after twenty years of activity carried out in the same place, one is in a position, by virtue of the experience gained, to correct past mistakes and to improve one's approach through successive trial and error. With time, it also becomes possible to comprehend why the technique employed, vital as it may be, is not entirely sufficient to change the behavior acquired over the course of many generations. Fully understanding what motivates people takes on primary importance, thereby necessitating the ability to listen to others. It's an ability that's not at all foreign to men like Father Verspieren, who's been in the same region for forty-five years ; whereas, how can the same be said of the experts dashing through these countries on short-term assignments?

Herein lies the richness of the history of Mali Aqua Viva; in conveying the various initiatives undertaken, in understanding the reasons behind the failures encountered, one lesson worthy of widespread attention becomes abundantly clear: **"in both the rural areas and the cities alike, even though water is a public good, its management must nonetheless be entrusted to the private sector."**

"Learning by trial-and-error." At the outset of the project, it was clear that the maintenance of the pumps would be the key to its success or failure. At the time, the need to train repairmen, and to equip them with a toolbox and a motor scooter in order to respond to the village's requests, was deemed crucial. As the Vergnet pump was unknown to locals, the initial training effort was conducted by specialists called on from France. The result proved to be very mediocre. A few years hence, responsibility for training was placed in the hands of a group of Malians themselves who mastered the use of the pump. The success of this approach was immediate. Why such a difference? In all likelihood, the answer lies in the attitude of the apprentice repairmen with respect to their instructor. In simplistic terms, for the former training context, it could be inferred that the apprentice was convinced of his inability to comprehend "the white man's magic", while in the latter, he was sure of being as intelligent as his compatriot instructor. And twenty years later, in the region of San, everyone, or almost everyone, is able to disassemble and repair a Vergnet pump.

Once the repair teams had been trained, spare parts then had to be made available to them. Since the pumps were all foreign-built, it was necessary to request the manufacturer to set up a network to sell individual parts. Such a request would normally be accommodated provided a sizable enough market existed; or, put otherwise, if, within a market still rather limited, the level of competition were to be kept low. This reasoning has not always been grasped by project funding organizations. Their concern for promoting national industries, coupled with their intention to utilize technically-advanced products (or inexpensive ones), has often led them to condition their financial participation on the acquisition of equipment being supplied by their own countries. Unfortunately, this concern is not consistently accompanied by appropriate consideration being paid to whether, once the initial investment has been made, the suppliers would undertake the efforts necessary to assure maintenance of their products. Creating a network for the purpose of supplying spare parts represents an expensive venture; those rejecting the proposition on the grounds of an insufficient market can thus be easily understood. Should it really come as that much of a surprise then that certain water supply projects for rural areas don't succeed when their maintenance is not assured, because of the impossibility for local workmen to access the spare parts required in repairing mechanical malfunctions.

The solution adopted by Mali Aqua Viva consisted of relying upon the "Compagnie Malienne de Développement Textile" - CMDT (Malian Textile Development Corporation); this company, with stores located throughout the region, entered into an agreement with Vergnet to sell spare parts to the local repair crews who would then invoice the villages for parts as well as labor.

Final point to be settled: paying the repairmen. Who, within the village, should be held responsible? And with what money? Initially, it had been envisioned to require "village ownership of the pump" through a purchasing procedure. From a practical perspective, drilling the well had been contingent upon the prior acquisition of a pump; it had also been hoped that the financial outlay up front would incite the villages to decide to pursue the effort so as to recover their investment. Given that the result didn't exactly meet expectations, charging for the repair services was thereby deemed essential. The village received assistance in planning a maintenance budget and in setting up a fund capable of paying expenses.

In light of the moderate success enjoyed with this final initiative, the next step was taken, whereby the village was advised on how to go about organizing the collection of funds destined for maintenance purposes. This provided the occasion for creating a "Management Committee" whose presence would influence the completion of the works; this committee must determine where to drill the well, how to operate it, etc. Once again, this approach was a semi-success (or a semi-failure as the case may be).

From these various initiatives that didn't exactly yield any crowning successes, Bernard Verspieren wound up drawing three conclusions. Firstly, facilities given to a local community will inevitably experience a relatively short life span, owing to the fact that since no one really has a stake in their ongoing operations, there's no incentive to repair the mechanical failures arising. The "Management Committee" thus doesn't represent a viable solution. This attitude is further confirmed by the more recent incidents occurring with respect to the solar pumps: residents were finding that stealing solar panels was more profitable and less tiring than working to produce pump-drawn water.

Secondly, facilities assigned to an individual would insure a longer working life. An individual tends to pay more attention to the machinery that's under his control due to a more profit-driven mindset. Yet, entrusting certain individuals with heavy pieces of equipment (especially solar pumps) provokes jealousy, particularly if the recipient earns money in exchange for the work performed. His envious neighbors could be driven to break (or steal) this valuable production tool.

Here's why, as a third conclusion, Bernard Verspieren and his team esteem that this vital machinery (wells and pumps) should be transfered to the local community in order to avoid stirring any jealousy. However, so as to provide for greater service durability, operations of the equipment must be conferred upon individuals. He also considered that it was necessary to eliminate abuses on the part of the recipients of this reserved property. Such a guarantee could be obtained through a "contract" established by the community, defining the rights and obligations of the entrusted party; this approach is not all that far from the notion of a "public service concession".

The concept portrayed herein might appear novel for the countries of the Sahel region in Africa; in fact, it is nothing of the sort. This very same principle has been applied for a good number of years to the public water fountains serving the outlying districts of the city of Ouagadougou (Burkina Faso). These fountains have been entrusted to individuals who purchase water from the National Water and Wastewater Office and sell it at a set price. No abuse can therefore be perpetrated. The issue of public hygiene is also being adequately addressed: the water merchant, earning his profit on water drawn from the tap, has every interest in insuring good operating conditions and preventing against leaks.

What are the other lessons to be drawn from this experience?

"Appropriate financing for the facilities (wells and pumps)." Some observers feel that the guarantee of equipment durability would be more simply obtained through a financial participation on the part of the beneficiaries themselves. It has been witnessed that such an approach proves insufficient and that a private management scheme is, first and foremost, required. While this participation may be foreseen for new facilities within villages already equipped, it cannot be so easily imposed in the case of a village's initial capital investment. Why would the village residents spend their money on a piece of equipment that seems superfluous to them when the nearby pond provides the same amenity free of charge? The village's first acquisition of equipment should therefore, in all likelihood, continue to rely entirely on external financing sources.

Exactly who should finance what? Except for truly outstanding cases, the pump-equipped installation would appear preferable, at present, over more conventional wells. Yet, it requires a cumbersome technical and administrative set-up, which remains relatively inaccessible to African companies; well-drilling thus would most likely be reserved exclusively for foreign firms. The Mali Aqua Viva project however is the exception to this rule: its ability to survive over a ten-year period as a conventional well-drilling company was thanks in large part to the public-sector financial assistance it had been accorded. From the day these subsidies were cut off, the project was forced to turn back to the more artisan-styled methods that prevailed at the time of its creation.

However, one must go even further: the public institutional aid will serve to finance well-drilling as a priority. All the European and American actors would certainly come away satisfied: the financial organizations through allocating sizable loan packages, hence ensuring conformance with their administrative procedural guidelines; the well-drilling companies and equipment suppliers through winning additional contracts. But what kind of durability will be attained for projects that are often carried out without any heavy participation from the local population?

In contrast, the limited resources associated with decentralized cooperation (whether public or private) will not attract the drilling firms. This cooperation will tend to favor wells constructed by the local workforce within villages designated and recognized by donators (local community authorities, associations), and, in so doing, will foster the organization of joint support efforts among villages as well as with towns in foreign countries. Though less promising from a technical standpoint, this approach could encourage long-term prospects through public participation and through the mutual discoveries that this participation implies.

"A collective actor." These observations lead to the assessment that in Africa, official public subsidies are not very compatible with projects that incite public participation and technical progress. The example of Mali Aqua Viva offers a response to this dilemma. And here's how.

Across our industrially-developed countries, a village's wells or boring sites represent publicly-owned facilities under local authority control; these authorities are responsible for procuring financing and selecting contractors to manage the corresponding works programs. Since this arrangement is virtually incomprehensible in developing countries, the normal procedure would be to entrust national governments with the responsibilities that are commonly assumed, in our countries, at the local or regional levels. What might the long-term viability be for those governments increasingly helpless when confronted with the challenges of the day? Quite poor, in all likelihood. But then, where should one turn to provide rural populations with access to technical progress.

The Mali Aqua Viva project shows us the way by virtue of its capacity to rally together a disparate group of actors; the project enabled an efficiently-run company to benefit from the assistance of both decentralized cooperation and institutional cooperation, while serving to mobilize local populations.

Why have Misereor, Cebemo, the Caisse Centrale de Cooperation Economique, local and regional authorities, NGOs, and today Belgian or Austrian cooperation institutions, all accepted to support Mali Aqua Viva? The most plausible reason would be that the project is, above all else, an African company responding to the motivations inherent in an African company. Dedicated to serving the public interest, Mali Aqua Viva's well-drilling activities were not primarily intended to reap huge profits or to increase turnover. The Mali Aqua Viva experience also serves to illustrate that, in Africa, a company can:
  - compensate for the State's shortcomings,
  - be motivated by concerns other than those of our Western companies, and
  - be managed in harmony with local customs and traditions.

Unable to grasp this feature, the institutional cooperative efforts sought to transpose our Western behavioral models on this African entity. Such a strategy nearly killed the venture. The institutional actors also didn't comprehend that, in reality, they weren't necessarily financing a well-drilling operation but rather directly contributing to equipping villages to provide services. Therein raises the question of their capability to cope with the major problem facing countries so poor: that of their populations. Yet, are we in a position, from our vantage points in Western capitals, to take care of the Mali population? The appropriate response is not all that obvious for cities within industrialized nations, with too much money, too many technicians and too much power for a mission that can only really be conducted on site.

Getting back to the Mali Aqua Viva project, which was driven for a long time by a few individuals, which acted as a collective actor by coordinating the efficiency of private enterprise, international financing sources along with the mobilization of the local population. The operation has been held together by the balance achieved among these three forces; nonetheless, this delicate balance could break down should one of these poles be transformed. Here's why actions carried out in a country like Mali must remain cognizant of the observation that: without an "active" actor, all forms of assistance lose their effectiveness.

"Wastewater service." The preceding discussion has strictly concerned the area of water supply. Yet, wastewater service also raises some highly critical issues. At some point in the future, it will become a dire necessity to develop the appropriate set of techniques for wastewater treatment, and to determine its proper financing. As in the case of water supply, it would appear essential that the initial facility investments be carried out by the appropriate external funding organizations. The facility maintenance issue would next come to the fore. Capitalizing on the experience provided with water supply, privatizing the wastewater management function, by conferring it upon the water supply "concessionaire", would appear a vital first step. Maintenance of the public toilets, or even of the entire wastewater network, to be assured by designated individuals, would be financed by a price increase in well water sold and would be overseen, as for any public service delegation, by the pertinent organizing authority, meaning at the village level.

CHAPTER 10

Eric Baye [1]

Experimenting with the privatization of water services in Indonesia - from Surabaya to Djakarta

Following the trend set by its neighbors, the large Malayan archipelago has been experiencing high growth rates in real GDP (6.4% in 1992 and 6.5% in 1993), which the supply in infrastructure has difficulty accommodating. Neither the public sector's budgeting capacity, nor Indonesia's financial system nor the level of national expertise in the field is able, at the present time, to adequately insure meeting the demand for public facilities. Public funding from international sources is not sufficient either [2]. The debt-service ratio (32.1% in 1992) is one of the highest in the entire Asian-Pacific region; any further reliance by the authorities upon major lending schemes would thereby constitute an extremely dangerous move. Against such a backdrop, public authorities have been striving to include [3] private capital in

1. The author would like to sincerely express his gratitude to the representatives from Indonesia's central authorities and from Pam Jaya who provided their input and made available to us the working documents used in this chapter.

2. Approximately five billion dollars a year including: one billion from the World Bank, one billion from the Asian Development Bank and another billion from the Japanese OECF. French assistance represents one of the primary other sources benefitting Indonesia.

public infrastructure programs (telecommunications, toll roads, energy); Indonesian groups have been actively participating in these programs.

The Indonesian government is committed to developing a legal framework suited to this newly-adopted policy. Such is the case for Regulation 1990-4, promulgated by the Ministry of the Interior, concerning the procedures for conducting cooperative ventures between local public-sector enterprises and third parties, or the recent Presidential decree 1994-20, which facilitates the access of foreign capital into activities aimed at serving the public interest (Article N° 5, in particular). These regulatory measures were, in part, the result of a specific assessment program undertaken by the Indonesian government that already dates back a few years. At the request of three national ministries (Public Works, Interior and Finance) along with the National Planning Agency (Bappenas), both the American Agency for International Development (USAID) and the Indonesian Office for the Development of Private Enterprise have financed and directed, ever since 1990, a detailed examination of the conditions necessary to accommodate private sector participation and public/private partnership in the field of urban infrastructure management. The WASH projects were designed especially for the sector of water supply, while PURSE currently covers all aspects of urban services. Though the issue raised herein does not necessarily pertain to the private sector seeking to appropriate the means of production, the two techniques mentioned above for involving the private sector will nonetheless be used as references whenever the term privatization is employed.

Assessment of current conditions

In light of the population growth projected for Indonesia's urban areas (52 million in 1990, 79 million in 2000, and 152 million in 2025), coupled with a lack of appropriate technical expertise and facilities provision, the sector of water services appears at the forefront of the privatization issue. This policy orientation has resulted from a political will expressed at the very highest levels of government, then pursued to a great extent by the Ministries of the Interior and of Public Works, and subsequently shared among a good number of mayors (Walikota) and governors. Yet, at the same time, the theme of privatization also tends to trigger an outpouring of enthusiasm and

---

3. Until the opposite can be demonstrated, the Indonesian approach does not correspond to an ideological choice aimed at placing all public services in the hands of the private sector.

initiatives often deemed too hasty, especially by the World Bank. In addition to long lists of privatization projects (twenty-three at current count in the area of water services alone) are many letters of intention (MOU) signed between private companies and public authorities; however, no real stipulation is made in these proposals of any regulatory or legal framework, and a satisfactory level of coordination among the various administrative agencies involved is still lacking.

In 1994, out of a national population of 190 million, 34.8 million Indonesians were serviced by one form of water supply network or another (5.5 million actual connections, including public fountains). The 35% coverage ratio in urban areas is less than that being experienced in many other Asian countries; only 20% of all urban dwellers are directly connected to the water supply network. Along the same lines, the population greatly depends on the use of individual wells and drilling sites (with wells reaching depths of 40 meters in Djakarta), operated for the most part illegally (80% of those already hooked up to the water supply network also have access to their own wells or individual water sources). In addition, residents can rely upon mobile water vendors. Nationwide, water consumption is primarily accounted for by households and government offices (75% to 80% of the total).

How does this natural resource match up against projected needs? According to the World Bank, 100 billion dollars worth of investment would be required to properly equip the whole country! Yet, on the basis of the 6th National Plan (Repelita 6), the government will only be able to come up with 35% of the total expenditure amount (1.38 billion dollars) over the period 1994-2000. This plan's objectives call for lowering the rate of physical losses in larger cities to 25% and that in other urban municipalities to 30%; it also sets out to increase the country's total production capacity to 2.6 million m^3/day, to serve an additional 22 million population, and to improve the efficiency of netwok operators. In comparison with the level of projected needs by the year 2000, 14.7 million m^3/day (corresponding to an increased demand of 3.9 million m^3/day in the larger metropolitan areas), the production capacity to be realized from public-sector initiatives alone should reach 8.7 million m^3/day. Public authorities are hoping to compensate for this difference through private-sector participation.

Rather than delegate an entire network to a single private operator, Indonesians prefer conceiving a privatization scheme broken down into components (treatment plants, sub-sections of networks, urban districts, etc.); such an approach does tend to be more convenient, at least for the larger metropolitan areas. In fact, the size of planned projects typically remains greater than 50 million dollars; this threshold figure was assumed in 1990 to represent the minimum amount likely to attract the international investment community. The nation's private financial resources, modest in scale, should then be allocated to aiding the development of more remote areas, as illustrated in the case of Bali.[2]

Public authorities are well aware that their policy choices are quite ambitious. This is, among other reasons, why they seek to stress that their objective is not, at least over the short and medium run, to concentrate all of their financial efforts on bringing water treatment up to standards of potability. The country's more urgent preoccupation does not lie herein. Rather, the key issue revolves around providing the greatest number of residents possible access to clear water (air berish), which may not necessarily be potable (air minum), suited to the most widespread industrial and domestic uses.

Water services operators in urban areas

Responsibility for managing water services is currently conferred upon various entities, depending on whether the facilities are under construction, in start-up mode or in the phase of normal "operations".

- The construction phase is being run by the Projek Air Minum, or PAM, formerly under the supervision of the Ministry of Public Works and now overseen by the provincial government, or Kotamadya, and by major cities which have since been granted greater autonomy.
- During the distribution start-up phase, the network is operated by a BPAM (Badan Pengeloaan Air Minum), an agency placed under the direct supervision of either the Ministry of Public Works or the local authorities.
- Following a certain period of time, the facilities are then transferred back to the local authorities. Water distribution is then provided by a PDAM (Perusahan Daerah Air Minum), a local or regional company that, in theory, should be able to carry out operations without any subsidies. The PDAM remain under the authority of either provincial governments or the nation's prefectures (Kabupaten).

Public-sector operators function according to the principle of covering their operating costs by the output of the network under their control, while undertaking the social-oriented mission of supplying water at a good price. In reality, operators are not very aware of their actual profitability threshold. In 1991, the coverage of total cost by water sales revenue generated was estimated at 70% [2]. These municipal enterprises are normally required to turn over, whenever they serve more than 50% of the population (in accordance with the July 1985 official procedural instruction), 55% of the profits earned through operations to the municipality overseeing their activities. Nonetheless, the Asian Development Bank did make the observation in 1990 that the system had become subjected to some blatant exceptions in its prescribed procedures, as firms operating at a deficit were being taxed [3].

In a country like Indonesia, central government authorities have historically played a fundamental role in local public affairs. Water services management falls primarily under the responsibility of four national ministries: Public Works, Finance, Interior and the Bureau of Mines. This list should also include the National Planning Agency, the Ministry of Health, as well as the Office of Foreign Investments (BKPM).

1) The Ministry of Public Works, through its Division devoted to serving the population's needs - the Cipta Karya [4], is the primary authority in charge of developing urban water distribution networks and treatment plants throughout the country. Their range of competence spans the areas of control and technical assistance (especially by virtue of BPAM), as well as a financial support (State subsidies in favor of local authorities towards raising the level of capital investment). The Ministry also coordinates formulating the statement of investment needs and defines the guiding premises behind the national policy on urban public service facilities.

2) The Ministry of Finance is responsible for sectoral allocations, which are then attributed to the local authorities by the Ministry of Public Works. Finance Ministry staff negotiates with the local authorities the share of international loans that are to be earmarked for them, along with the amount of State subsidies deemed necessary for those in the most dire need.

3) The Ministry of the Interior, Dalam Negeri [5], establishes the framework for setting water rates and defines the accounting rules imposed on local authorities and their corresponding enterprises; it also

---

4. Up until 1993, a specific division for water services, called the DAB, did exist within the Cipta Karya.

5. The currently-applicable rating system is the outcome of a 1984 decree, promulgated jointly by the Ministry of Public Works and the Ministry of the Interior. It is based on a set of cost ratio coefficients (total production costs / distribution costs in relation to the total consumption quantity), varying according to the category of consumers. A rating grid exists for small and medium-sized municipalities, while a different one applies to larger cities. The Indonesian system, founded out of concern for social justice, will not go as far as implementing a nationwide cost equalization, and furthermore doesn't exclude geographical disparities in the price of water.

oversees the application of laws designed for the local level (recourse to private financing, subcontracting and delegation, personnel, etc.). In line with the decentralization policies pursued since 1990, only local projects exceeding a capital investment amount of 10 million roupies (5 million dollars) require approval from the Ministry; the provincial governor's approval would suffice for projects sized below this figure.

4) The approval granted by the National Planning Agency, the Bappenas, is mandatory in order to initiate any substantial project. Its role is to verify that the project respects the orientations laid out in the successive five-year plans, which have served as a veritable keystone to the nation's development policy ever since its independence.

5) The Dinas Pertambang Daerah, within the Bureau of Mines and Energy, is assigned to monitor water pumping activities for all aquifer sources; it's also the authority that grants drilling permits.

6) The Ministry of Health defines and controls the standards for measuring the potability of water.

7) The foreign investment bureau (BKPM), reporting directly to the President's Office, must sanction every capital investment project (site location, job creation for Indonesian workers, land ownership and building permit approvals, etc.).

The complexity of the decision-making process engenders a broad multiplication of the hindrances and obstacles to actually seeing the process through to completion.

Indonesia has been gradually pursuing, ever since the mid-1970's, the path of conferring responsibility upon its local level decision-makers: a difficult task in a country where any guideline established by the Ministry of the Interior has traditionally been perceived as a decree. With respect to the area of water supply, all investment decisions, project management and day-to-day operations have been, from that point forward, placed under the full control of local authorities. For a system accustomed to more centralized policy-making, this reform has served to highlight new difficulties: how to perform the necessary transfer of technical information from the Cipta Karya's departments, which are not centralized (three regional divisions have been in place since January 1994), to the localities? How to tie international negotiations on infrastructure financing conducted by the ministries with procuring agreements from the beneficiary municipalities to pay back these loans? As decentralization becomes interpreted as a limitation in the span of oversight exercised by both the Ministries of Public Works and of the Interior, it tends to lead to tension and misunderstanding, to the detriment of the pace at which projects can be developed and then managed.

Despite the context of disappointment and slowed pace that's been observed at various levels, foreign water distribution operators have been cautiously, yet actively, participating in this evolution towards privatization. The French and English are at the forefront, yet so are the Australians and soon perhaps even the Americans. Officially taking a more reserved stance, foreign firms pursue their action with discretion: this feature is substantiated by the ties established with Indonesian indutrial groups and the numerous, according to administration officials, investment proposals being submitted. As a result, foreign concerns have been able to obtain feedback directly from their Indonesian contacts and to better grasp the local institutional environment. Urban growth and development has been so strong, the trend towards generating a solid, financially-solvent middle class appears so irreversible, and the potential for operating the utility networks they've installed so vast that the major foreign operators must actively monitor the market. Their primary preoccupation is thereby not to be drawn into making a mistake by signing, under pressure exerted by the competition alone, a poorly-structured contract.

Along with the competition among potential foreign operators is the fact that entering into partnership with an Indonesian firm is a prerequisite for assuming the operations of a utility network. They must act quickly to identify an influential and powerful local partner. The largest Indonesian industrial groups are all waiting in the wings. Already active within other public service areas, these groups expect to benefit from the privatization of water services; other experiences (Bogor in the area of waste, Djakarta in the area of toll roads, etc.) have displayed their capability of getting involved with new activities through incorporating the reliance on foreign expertise.

Privatization as viewed from the past tense: Downstream from Bali to Surabaya

Against this backdrop, each party reflects upon the perspectives of privatizing Djakarta's water services, whose network of distribution mains does happen to be the country's most extensively developed. Today's critical debate focuses on two main experiences: Bali and Surabaya [6], with the former fueling the zeal of the thurifiers of

---

6. For the experiences in Bali and Surabaya, the data presented herein have been essentially extracted from an Indonesian government report (March 1994) co-authored by USAID within the scope of the PURSE program (4).

privatization thrusting themselves headfirst, while the latter exhibiting the prudence characteristic of those who adopt a "wait and see" posture.

In Nusa Dua and Kuta, in the southern part of the enchanting island of Bali, a joint venture was established in 1990 between the local water services department of Badung (accounting for 45% of the capital) and three Indonesian companies. This venture is linked to the municipal enterprise through a contract spanning several years that pertains both to the distribution of water to upper-income residential and tourist districts and to the construction works (network extension, participation in a reservoir project, development of pumping and treatment facilities for Tukad Ayung River water, etc.). Two investment phases were planned: the first from 1991 to 1993, and the second from 1993 to 1995, with each corresponding to a capital investment of around 15 billion roupies (6.86 million dollars).

Bali's success story would nonetheless appear far too specific to serve as a reference frame for other large-scale privatization schemes set in urban areas. It is unique in the type of customer base targeted (98% collection rate on water bills) and in the absence of any serious technical problems encountered (rate of pipe leakage estimated at 20%). These conditions make Bali an atypical case, one that's not very representative of Indonesia's larger cities.

The situation is quite different when it comes to the experience at Surabaya, the nation's second largest city (2.8 million population).

Surabaya's PAM (total production capacity: 388,800 m^3/day and 166,250 connections) has been involved with the private sector since 1985 for services performed such as meter reading and billing. In light of the demand trends observed, the Indonesian government has gradually accepted to enter into a "Build Operate and Transfer" (B.O.T.) contract in order to insure water supply throughout the city within reasonable financial conditions in terms of the public budget. The project involved pumping more than 5 m^3/second of water from the sources at Umbulan, located to the south of the metropolitan area; the water would then be conveyed, by means of a 62-km. long pipeline connected to the Wonocolo Reservoir. The initial calls for tender proposals were launched in 1988. The Bromo consortium was selected: it grouped Northwest Water International, Mac Donald Project Development, two Indonesian companies (PT Duta Comfact and Costain/Mowlem Umbulan Joint Venture) as well as the First National Bank in the capacity of financial consultant. However, the negotiating process came to a halt, hence the creation of a second consortium in 1992, bringing together Northwest Water International, the consulting practice of Mott Mac Donald, PT Duta Comfact, Transfield, Bakrie and the Bank of America (London office) as financial consultant. In both cases, financial guarantees were provided by the British Export Credit Guarantees (ECGD) public agency.

This second proposal entailed a 15-year B.O.T. contract, worth 180 million dollars in investment, 55% of which would consist of foreign capital. An administrative entity would be created in order to coordinate the various local PAM motivated by the project; this entity would also serve to represent the local PAM within a joint venture that included the private consortium. Nonetheless, this entity could not procure guarantees for expenditure overages in the form of a "take or pay contract" with the public operator, nor could it obtain the assurance of a free reign to increase the price of water at will (the cost of water transported all the way to Surabaya was estimated at 600 roupies/m^3, whereas tap water is billed by PAM at a floor price of 400 roupies/m^3).

The consortium was also unable to procure financial guarantees from the Indonesian government (the formal commitments made in favor of non-residents serving to add further pressure on the amount of the external debt) [7]. Ultimately, the negotiations were suspended in June 1993.

Informed of this impasse as early on as 1992, the National Planning Agency decided to entrust a foreign private operator with conducting an analysis of the points of contention between the two parties, in order to devise a series of proposals that would infuse new momentum into the negotiations. The company Lysa, a subsidiary of the Lyonnaise des Eaux-Dumez group, was chosen to carry out the audit [5]. This effort would wind up shedding light on the misunderstandings existing between private partners and Indonesian authorities on the very concept of concession, as well as on the principle of sharing risk responsibility (acts of God, inability of the concessionaire to honor its commitments, etc.). The consulting firm also drew up some guidelines of its own for improving the definition of terms appearing in the concessionary contract (January 1993); however, these recommendations fell short of enabling the successful completion of the negotiating process.

A study of the Umbulan experience goes beyond merely highlighting the pitfalls resulting from the misunderstandings between private and

---

7. A proposal was submitted to the consortium to accept as a financial guarantee the operating surplus generated by the Surabaya PAM, the project's primary management contractor and one of the nation's most profitable; the proposal was not retained.

public partners over the nature of the contract. Disagreements arising among Indonesian administrative authorities also contributed to hindering the process. The Ministry of Public Works, acting as the government's primary representative during the negotiations, was blamed for having excessively sped up the process, in bypassing any real level of consultation with the other authorities concerned. Initially, the Ministry could choose between two options capable of meeting Surabaya's needs: developing a treatment plant in conjunction with the World Bank (already heavily involved in financing water supply projects in the capital city of Java East), or relying on a concession to convey water emanating from the Umbulan site. The slow pace of the negotiating efforts engaged with the World Bank has spurred the Ministry to pressure local authorities to negotiate directly with the B.O.T. candidates on their own. As this approach placed the Ministry of the Interior in an uncomfortable posture with respect to policy shifts, it would not go on to display, during the ensuing period, a very inspiring cooperative spirit.

The Indonesian authorities are currently attempting to draw lessons from the Bali and Umbulan experiences, with the former being deemed encouraging while the latter having exposed difficulties that were unexpected or underestimated at the outset. Yet, the emotions and interest stirred by this all-important issue of privatizing Djakarta's water supply system could lead to neglecting the full extent of the instruction gleaned from previous experiences.

Privatization as viewed from an ongoing perspective: The case of Djakarta

With a population of 8.4 million covering a land area of 650 km^2, Djakarta is included in the group of Asian metropolises where the world's wealth and its dire poverty are juxtaposed: the boastful and brazen Jalan Sudirman, and the upscale districts of the Menteng nonetheless cannot gloss over the image of impoverishment in many kampungs, even though the average standard of living in the capital city is higher than that for the remainder of the country. Djakarta's demographic growth rate is truly phenomenal, in that a population of 12 million has been forecasted for the year 2005, and this despite the strong development being experienced by three of the capital's satellite cities: Bogor to the south, Tangerang to the west, and Bekasi to the east [8].

The city of Djakarta is run by its own local government (DKI), under the leadership of a city governor, who remains independent from the

8. JABOTABEK (13 million residents in 1990) designates the administrative jurisdiction encompassing Djakarta and its outlying urban areas.

authority of the Java West Provincial Governor's Office. The DKI is responsible for overseeing the country's largest and best structured water treatment and distribution company, called Pam Jaya (meaning "the main PAM").

A network subject to overhaul and extension. The Pam Jaya, a municipal enterprise founded some seventy years ago, counts about 380,000 subscribers, and thereby services 44% of Djakarta's total population and a land area of 213 km². Service subscribers consist primarily of households, public administrations and small and medium-sized firms; major industries, concentrated towards the west of Java, are often located outisde of Djakarta proper. Water supply originates from four principal sources: underground aquifers, water drawn from the Krukut River (then purified by the country's oldest major plant, built by Degrémont), Citarum River water from the East (the Jatiluhur Dam connected to the capital by the West Tarum Canal) and Cisadane River water to the Southwest, for which pumping and treatment facilities are located on the territory of the Tangerang Prefecture, under the jurisdiction of the Java West Province. This city's water services department has entered into a contract with Pam Jaya for the sale of 2,800 liters/second. PAM is responsible for running a total of twelve treatment plants, whose combined production capacity attains 18 m³/second.

The state of the network warrants special concern: its physical loss rate approaches the 45% mark; the press has even recently announced a figure of 60%. The network's initial components were put into place by the Dutch in the 1920's. However, many of the galvanized steel conduits laid twenty to thirty years ago have reacted poorly to the corrosiveness of the subsoil. As a result of pipe porosity, the poor quality of water (exhibiting low stability even after purification) renders it impotable. The commerce for mineral water, which sells at 500 roupies (25 cents) for a quantity of twenty liters, is thus a flourishing one.

In 1985, the capital's 15-year master plan for water supply divided the city into six zones. On the basis of this territorial split, both of the major programs of network overhaul currently underway have been developed: the World Bank program (total investment: 150 million dollars) within Zones 1, 2, 4 and 5, and that of the Japanese Development Fund OECF (70 million dollars worth) across Zones 3 and 6.

Inspired by the urban dwellers of other third world nations, Djakarta residents draw a significant amount of water directly from the aquifers on their own, due to the inadequate capacity of the network or to the cost of the water delivered: a cubic meter of water drawn from a well would cost a household about 175 roupies, while the same quantity of water purchased from PAM runs in the neighborhood of 1,200 roupies [9]. This extensive presence of wells is the outcome of a village mentality towards economic rationale and behavioral custom, and serves to thwart any policy favoring the profitability of PAM operations. Given the city's population growth rates, the volume of water being depleted from the aquifers greatly surpasses their capacity for replenishment; as in the case of Mexico City, the ground beneath Djakarta is subsiding, and especially disturbing is the increasing saline content of the aquifers. While in the past limited to more coastal regions, the encroachment of salinity is now progressing towards the southern part of the country. Up until the present time, public authority control over individual well drilling has remained relatively ineffective; a year ago, the responsibility for control (granting of licenses, measurement of water extracted) was stripped from PAM by the governor and placed in the hands of Dinas Pertambang Daerah. Yet, according to PAM, the chances of an about face on this decision cannot be altogether discarded.

Mixed calls for privatization. The structural economic conditions under which the company is operating are certainly not ideal. While the rate of outstanding bills and illegal connections has stayed within the realm of reasonable (5% to 10% of plant outflow), the rate of physical losses (45%) does constitute a major detriment to the efficient management of the entire system. Besides, the workforce (a staff of 2,790) is oversized in comparison with the dimension of the network. Despite these drawbacks, PAM must still pay back all operating surpluses to the municipal government.

For both the public authorities and PAM top management, the critical question is to know how to cope with the explosion of demand for new connections (600,000 forecasted by the year 2000), an indication of the pursuit for material comfort on the part of an increasing middle class. For those backing the more liberal economic theses, an increased participation by the private sector in the area of water distribution would better serve the public interest, by allowing stepping in for PAM, which at times fell short in terms of efficiency and resources.

Whatever the arguments espoused, few managers have actually declared their outright hostility to a policy of privatization. However,

---

9. Many water service subscribers also possess individual wells. A recent law has thereby authorized PAM to bill subscribers an additional 5 m3 monthly, whatever their actual consumption of well water.

the planned scheduling and control of the process have been the cause of relatively unpublicized conflicts between the concerned parties. The privatization of Djakarta's water supply network, while still in a state of limbo, thus already has a history behind it. Once again, the Ministry of Public Works has played a vital, if not controversial, role.

On the basis of the territorial split forwarded in the 1985 Water Master Plan, the Ministry of Public Works' year 2000 project calls for conferring upon the private sector operating responsibility for each zone under the format of a contract signed with PAM. The contractual stipulations are to be established in relation to the specific problem areas of each prescribed zone. In Zones 1 and 2, the private operator would be assigned the priority task of reducing the rate of the network's physical losses to 20%. For the pair of zones 3 and 6 along with the pair 4 and 5, it has been proposed to contract out to private operators the task of utilizing the surplus capacity from the treatment plants (Buaran I and II for the first pair and Cisadane for the second pair), along with all corresponding network extensions. Within such an overall configuration, the coherence of the whole program would be assured through the use of interzonal reservoirs, which would allow for making adjustments between surpluses and needs across the various zones. Other capital outlays could be conferred upon the private sector, such as projects related to the Cakung plant or to the conveyance of Jatiluhur Dam water (see infrastructure description). In all, the Ministry of Public Works has evaluated the cost of all projects requiring financing in Djakarta at more than one billion dollars.

Pam Jaya is not necessarily opposed to this outlook, provided it not be completely stripped of its technical and financial oversight authority. At the Ministry of Public Works, the mood tends to be one of reassurance, as PAM should maintain its status of operator. Nonetheless, it is regrettable that the municipal enterprise has expressed its reticence to cooperate in the development of this project.

Another project has been submitted to the Ministry of Public Works by the English group Thames Water, designed to supply the capital city through utilizing an underground piping system (three 2.5-meter diameter pipes, providing a total flow capacity of 20 m^3/second) connected to the Jatiluhur Dam. Such a scheme would solve the problems associated with pollution that currently adversely impacts water being conveyed via the Tarum Canal. The cost of the project has been estimated at 800 million dollars, with the operation being planned as a 20-year B.O.T. contract, associating Thames with an Indonesian company.

A second component, 300 million dollars worth of capital investment, is aimed at installing an underground circular drainage canal in Djakarta (at a depth of 40 meters) in order to adequately deliver water generated from all of the city's six treatment plants.

The reaction of PAM to these proposals has been somewhat reserved. It feels that these projects would force upping the price, currently set at 1,200 roupies/m^3 for households, to a level of 2,000 roupies/m^3. Such a prospect is simply not acceptable for a company that has just agreed with the World Bank to raise its price by 30%, on a triennial basis.

Whatever shape the privatization schemes took, PAM's critical stake is, in all likelihood, not to let itself be outdistanced by initiatives sponsored by the central authorities, control for which would remain out of PAM's hands. Such an outlook could incite the company to accept splitting "its" service territory in favor of private joint ventures being granted the water distribution rights to serve districts that were apparently more "profitable (affluent residential or business districts). A drift in policy orientation of this kind is not altogether impossible, as previous experiences in Bali or projects in Balikpapan, Medan, Bandung or Semarang illustrate [10]. According to other central government authorities, this risk, weak as it may be, is not just a theoretical one [2].

PAM therefore did not stay an inactive participant. In 1993, its director officially declared his support for the privatization initiative, and spurred by the momentum of this declaration, the company went on to sign five letters of intention with private firms.

These weak intentions didn't leave the World Bank entirely unaffected. While favorable to the notion of privatization, it doubted the adequacy of Indonesia's legal-institutional framework to effectively guide the efforts towards privatization in an expeditious manner.

Generally speaking, the Indonesian situation lends the impression that the World Bank was overwhelmed by the enthusiasm displayed on the part of certain local authorities and by the wide array of strategies adopted by private Indonesian groups. The same would apply to the Asian Development Bank, even though recent initiatives

---

10. A micro-zone where the major public-sector group Pertamina delivers water to residences and to factories.

launched (seminars, technical assistance, visits organized for representatives of the International Finance Corporation) demonstrate the willingness of both of these orgnizations to participate more actively in the movement towards privatizing Indonesia's water services. The third major financing organization, the Japanese OECF, tends to shy away from all proposals in the field of urban services management, ever so cautious of being tagged as "interfering" in domestic affairs. For its part, the Indonesian government doesn't intend to be submitted to any external pressure whatsoever, and even at times reacts irritably to the International Reconstruction and Development Bank's calls to exercise prudence.

And what about the private operators?

They are not yet ready to enter into untested contracts with the sole aim of increasing their market share. The Umbulan experience has decisively proved the opposite and, in spite of the quantity of signed letters of intention, PAM has estimated that the number of responses corresponding to its calls upon the private sector has remained low. This prudence, real as it may be, on the part of foreign groups is obviously not incompatible with the kinds of discussions and agreements they've entered into with major Indonesian groups, whose interests are probably somewhat biased with respect to public authority decisions and the infighting among government agencies.

Conclusions

The dynamic nature of an Indonesian-styled privatization could be placed undoubtedly against a backdrop of a rather propitious general economic climate: growth, emergence of a viable middle class, formation of a powerful private sector, etc. Nonetheless, sufficiency is still apparently lacking in the domain of legal and regulatory tools, and in a clearly-defined breakdown of responsibilities among the various institutions involved. Among the most serious obstacles to implementing a smooth privatization system would be the risk of misunderstandings and conflicts between authorities, and incompetence encountered at the local level.

However, waiting indefinitely for the ideal set of preconditions to be met before involving the private sector in Indonesian urban water services management is not altogether possible either. The majority of actors concerned are ready to react or take the initiative; evidence does suggest that some are seeking to jump-start matters, while others prefer taking the lead so as to avoid having their position usurped. For the debate's main protagonists, the risk at hand is having to renounce their responsibilities if they're not capable of mastering the process at an early enough stage. This risk includes: a diminished level of technical responsibility for public operators, a weakened influence exerted by international organizations, an increased number of joint agreements between service providers (to the detriment of competition), the disappearance of the role of intermediary between private investors and public operators as carried out by the technical ministries.

Following the failure at Umbulan, Indonesia's dynamic position with respect to the water privatization effort would appear to many as being stifled; a good number of presentations held before the appropriate authorities tend to fuel this "skepticism". Yet, the old adage of hiding the forest through the trees takes on much credence in this case. Many arguments forwarded by the skeptics might not be taken into serious consideration when compared with the long-term economic stakes at hand and with the risk, for private companies, of not seizing every opportunity available to gain a competitive edge in the marketplace. In other terms, it would seem unimaginable to protect the future of the water supply sector from those transactions affecting related sectors, where private firms have their own interests in mind as well: tourism, real estate development, other urban services. It also hasn't been mentioned that on the eve of President Suharto's departure, the problems pertaining to his succession are not interfering with the more technically and institutionally-based discussions.

And the user? Excluding price increases, which are relatively low considering the number of service subscribers, users are still in a position of low risk with the oncoming of privatization; many will gain a service connection and hence access to "clear water", as public monies are simply not able to cope with the level of expenditure necessary. At any rate, tomorrow's user will risk being indirectly solicited by powerful private operators who will be in a position to exercise the requisite pressure over public authorities so that the prickly issue of individual wells can be settled once and for all.

Main sources

[1] Ministry of Public Works. "Water Supply ans Waste Services Sector Paper, Indonesia". World Infrastructure Forum, Jakarta, October 1994.

[2] Private Sector Participation in Urban Water Supply, Issues for Investment in Indonesia. "Volume 1 : A Strategic Framework for Increasing Private Sector in Urban Water Supply in Indonesia; Summary of Principal Findings, Implications, Next Steps". Prepared for the USAID Mission to Indonesia under the WASH Task n°186, 1991, 32p.

[3] Asian Development Bank. "Water Supply and Sanitation Sector Study of Indonesia". May 1990, 132p.

[4] PURSE Project (Co-sponsored by the USAID/IOPED and the Purse Steering Committee). "Describtion of Existing Private Sector Participation Projects and Public Private Partnership Project in Indonesia and an Analysis of the Lessons Learned From These Projects. Purse Project Workplan Task 2.02, Preliminary Draft, March 1994.

[5] Lyonnaise des Eaux Services Associés-LYSA. "Independant Expert review of Proposals for the Development of Umbulan Spring and Other Bulk Water Sources for Kotamdya Surabaya and nearby Urban Areas". National Development Planning Agency, Final Report, Phase II, January 1993.

[6] Pam Jaya. "70 Tahun", Pam Jaya, Jaya Raya, 118p.

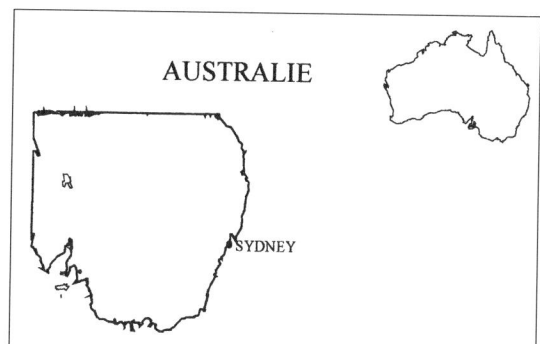

CHAPTER 11

AUSTRALIE

SYDNEY

Jack Moss

A contract for the production of drinking water for sydney boot bulk water supply contract-prospect

In the year 2000 the Olympic games will be held in Sydney. These will make this city of the great continent of the southern hemisphere, that the explorers of the XVIII sought for so long, the centre of the world for a few weeks. The visitors and the television viewers, will remember afterwards a few faces, a few performances, a few images. However in order for the festival to be complete, and that everything passes off successfully, the city has had to make considerable investments in a number of aspects of its public infrastructure. The production and distribution of water is one of these. The story that follows tells of the socio-economic process that enabled a private operator to be associated with the public authorities under the form of a BOT contract.

A BOT contract is much more difficult to bring to fruition than is generally recognised. In the early stages the complexity and fragility of such projects is frequently underestimated. As a result, there are probably more examples of failed attempts than there are of successes.

The Sydney Drinking Water Programme is an excellent example of the use of BOT/BOOT contracts in a monopoly public service - water supply. It can be used to illustrate a wide range of the benefits and mechanisms of such contracts. This paper limits itself principally to the process of establishing such contracts in a context of a complicated interplay of economic, political, environmental, and institutional factors. It will attempt to draw some conclusions that it is hoped will be useful for people embarking on a project of this kind elsewhere.

Background

It is essential to outline the contex of the projects to enable a proper understanding of the discussion that follows.

Geography. Sydney is the economic capital of Australia, and the State Capital of New South Wales. It is a city of approaching 4 million people on the scenic eastern coast of the continent. It is a young city, which sprawls over a large tract of land in a basin confined by modest mountain ranges to the west, north and south. These mountain areas are beautiful, and still largely covered with native bush vegetation. The whole area is subject to a very comfortable climate. Precipitation is very erratic with no rain for several years at a time. In this very delicate ecosystem, the interplay between man and nature has frequently worked to nature's disadvantage. This fact is now recognised by many Sydneysiders who are very alert to environmental issues.

From the establishment of the original colony to the present day, water has played a determinant role in Sydney's development. The majority of the water is harvested in the mountains to the south and west of the city in protected catchments. The water is stored in large dams in these mountains. The target is to maintain 7 years stock to secure the supply against the maximum predicted drought. From the mountain storages, the majority of the water is conveyed to the Prospect reservoir, and from there through an extensive pipe network to distribution reservoirs in the supply zones.

The water supply is operated by the Sydney Water Board, which is a public body depending directly on the State Government of New South Wales. This organisation has gradually expanded as the city has grown, incorporating over time a number of previously municipal or sub-regional organisations, so that it now extends to cover the whole of the Sydney, Illawarra & Blue Mountains region.

The Water quality Problem. During the 1980's the Water Board began to face a compounding of several problems in parallel. For two separate reasons, it was increasingly faced by a quality problem. The water from the storages was distributed untreated except for disinfection with chlorine. Over a long period there had been a gradual build up of natural deposits affecting the quality of the water in the catchments and storages, and a further problem due to the urban encroachment around the Prospect reservoir. As a result of the very extensive nature of the network (20,000 kms), there were also increasing problems of a further degradation of water quality within the distribution system due to the accumulation of natural deposits. These problems were growing steadily at the same time as the standards required for water were being tightened.

There was also a quantity problem to be considered. The City was continuing to grow at a rate of about 2% a year, and with the high level of per capita consumption, new water resources would be required for the beginning of the next millennium. The new sources identified, would be both extremely expensive and very hard to realise in the face of environmental concerns. Action to address these problems was becoming necessary on an increasingly urgent time span.

A Strategy for solving the problem. A programme was set up, called the "Clean Water Programme". Under this a three element strategy was defined. The elements were a) to provide filtration for all the water put into supply to complement the disinfection. b) rehabilitate the network to reduce the bacteriological re-growth problems, and c) introduce demand management to postpone the need for new resources.

To meet the first of these objectives it was decided to construct filtration plants at a number of sites. Of these plants, four would account for 95% of the water to be supplied. The most important was to be at Prospect, which is the hub of the system, and accounts for 85% of the volume. The other plants were to be at MacArthur to supply a new growth area in the south-west, Woronora to supplement supplies to part of the south of the city, and Avon to supply the industrial town and steelworks of Woolangong.

The second objective was to be met by a programme of network cleaning and improvement. The difficulty being to determine the value of cleaning the network before improved quality water was available. The third objective was to be met by a radical programme of tariff modification, incorporating user pays principles for the first time.

The estimates for the cost of this programme were around 2 billion $Aus. A figure that had to be viewed in the context of another requirement for a 6 billion $Aus programme to address urban pollution problems.

Economic and Political context. This heavy investment programme had to be met at a time when the Australian economy as a whole was in a very depressed state. Infrastructure investment in other sectors was also needed, and the New South Wales government was attempting a policy of tight economic management.

It looked very unlikely that the Water Board would be able to finance these two investment programmes from its own resources, and that the State would not be able to do so either.

It is probably true to say that Australia as a whole has too many layers of politics for the size of its population and nature of its settlement, (Federal, State & Local Government). The visibility of political action is also very apparent, and this has an important impact on the management of state owned enterprises such as the Water Board, which suffer from being easy "political footballs".

The N.S.W. Government of the day, was a minority government, depending on collaboration from several independent members to enable it to act. Two of the key elements of its mandate were its stand against corruption (it had set up an organisation called The Independent Commission Against Corruption ICAC) and the anti-pollution programme to clean the Sydney beaches.

Its tight economic management programme was rapidly to become unpopular. The ICAC was showing many signs of being an overkill solution to the problem it was set up to avoid, and creating new problems in its own right. The population was becoming impatient to see the results of the clean beaches project for which it was paying a special levy to the Water Board.

At the end of the 80's and the beginning of the 90's, the environmental movement was perhaps at the height of its popularity. It was, and still is particularly powerful in Australia. Environmental groups have a great deal of interest directly and indirectly in the activities of the Water Board, and their existence and behaviour played an important role in the story.

Politically, the Water Board was unpopular, because it was perceived as being inefficient, undemocratic, and the cause of the beach pollution problem. It is interesting to note that the water quality problem was largely unnoticed by the population, and the Board's management were afraid that they were "sitting on a time bomb" as far as this issue was concerned. They were equally concerned that the real issues of pollution were much more extensive than the beach problem alone, and that this issue could also explode politically at any moment. Privatisation and Private Sector Involvement were very much on the agenda as means of easing the State's economic problems, and in addition for "ideological" reasons.

The Plan

In the context outlined above, and after consultation with the private sector, the Water Board identified that the construction of the 4 new water filtration plants could be approached on the basis of BOT type contracts. It saw the possibility to convert the part of the Clean Water Programme relating to the treatment plants to this new procedure. This basic decision was taken in early 1991, and supported by the New South Wales Government.

The decision was based on four principles. Firstly there were identifiable economic benefits arising from the private sector financing of the projects and a more rapid realisation of the infrastructure. Secondly the Board saw an opportunity to benefit from the transfer of technology not available in Australia. Thirdly it saw the opportunity of introducing competition over both the short term and the long term, by setting up comparison between each of the four plants. Finally there was an opportunity to introduce greater clarity and responsibility into a government owned operating unit.

The Board established a task force within the Water Quality Programme team to manage the process of developing the project and conducting a competitive bid. This team was very professionally run, and took a positive but careful approach to the new challenge that it had been set.

To achieve the above objectives the task force developed a strategy which encompassed the following activities :
* Commission pilot studies and concept designs for all the plants which could be the starting point for plant design.
* Ensure that the private sector on an international basis had an opportunity to establish effective consortia, thus offering the best potential partners and creating strong competition
* Identify and transfer as much information as available to the consortia (Raw water quality, demand etc..)
* Carry out environmental impact assessment for the plants and the overall strategy for the double objective of defending the proposals in the face of anticipated objections from pressure groups and of securing the necessary approvals to enable the plants to proceed as quickly after contract formation as possible
* Manage the process of securing all necessary approvals in parallel with the bidding, to keep the overall period as short as possible. These

approvals included the EIS, planning permission, and approval by the Federal Treasury

* Develop a selection procedure that would enable it to choose and justify its choice of private sector partner

* Develop adequate documentation to support each stage of the process

* Conduct its selection procedure and choose a partner for each plant.

* Complete detailed negotiations for each plant and sign a contract for each one.

* Develop a relationship during the process that would be the basis of a partnership of mutual interest in the projects for the 25 years of the operational phase that had been chosen

* Ensure that public and political accountability was maintained at all stages.

Underlining all these points are at least one of the four guiding principles. To provide clear factual information to assist the quality of the final result. To ensure that the "rules of the game" are clear and fair. To ensure and demonstrate accountability. To foster a long term partnership relationship between the Board and the chosen consortia for the 25 year period of the contracts.

The Outcome

Contracts Let and Not Let. The period that intervened between early 1991 and late 1993, was a hectic but stimulating one for all involved. Many challenges had to be faced and difficulties overcome. A preferred tenderer was selected for each of the 4 plants and in September 1993 contracts were signed for two of the plants, MacArthur and Prospect. The fact that the process is not easy, and that the risks are high was proved by the fact that the plants at Avon and Woranora, have not been able to achieve a successful conclusion, at the time.

It is not appropriate to comment on the projects in which the writer's group was not involved, but useful to look at the project in which we are involved in a little detail.

Prospect - The Largest Water BOOT to date. The contract for Prospect is probably the single largest Build Own Operate Transfer contract in the water industry to date. The contract involving A\$200 million in investment gives Australian Water Services the responsibility to build, own and operate the Prospect Water Filtration Plant for 25 years, providing up to 3 million m^3/day (ultimately 4,200 million m3/day) of drinking water in bulk to the Board. The treated water must achieve a specified standard to meet the Australian National Health and Medical Research Council guidelines for drinking water at the customers' taps. The Sydney Water Board will pay a tariff for this clean water which includes an availability charge and a charge per megalitre of drinking water accepted.

Australian Water Services is a consortium comprising two Australian companies Lend Lease Corporation and P&O Australia and Lyonnaise des Eaux from France. The three sponsors each have complimentary business skills, which enabled them to assemble a strong core team of their own staff. This team was completed by a careful selection of Bankers, Engineers, lawyers and other specialists from both Australia and internationally. The care in creating this team is a major key to the venture's success.

The Process

Tentative First Steps. No real precedents for this type of project existed in Australia, and certainly none in the water sector. Indeed there were

---

BOX1,
A Procedure Defined.

The following steps were undertaken :
- Public advertisement of the intention to call for expressions of interest (Early Warning). This was done to give the private sector sufficient time to compose potential consortia.
- Discussion of the draft of the Expression of Interest document with interested parties.
- Formal advertisement of call for Expression of Interest and issue of document.
- Submission of Expression of Interest by 17 Consortia.
- Elimination of some consortia, demands for written clarification of detailed points from 10 remainder.
- Formal presentation by limited selection of 7 consortia to Board's Executive Directors and the Project Team.
- Final selection and publication of short listed 5consortia Prospect being so much bigger that the other projects, the Board stipulated that a consortium retained for Prospect would not be considered for any of the other plants.
- Issue and discussion of the draft commercial principles document with the short listed groups.
- Issue and discussion of the draft tender documents and Water Treatment Agreement (Contract) with the short listed groups.
- Issue of Formal Tender and conduct of the tender process.
- Receipt of bids, bid evaluation & clarification meetings with bidders.
- Selection and announcement of "Preferred Developer" for each plant.
- Final negotiations leading to contract formation and completion of "approvals".

very few examples anywhere in the world. The Board and Government officials therefore had much thinking and development work to do. In addition to the conventional recourse to consultants, they involved a number of the private sector companies, already active and interested in the field, in informal discussions. They also undertook a number of study tours visiting in particular France, the USA and Britain.

From this approach, they were able in a fairly short period to define a procedure that has proved itself in practice. It has enabled two of the contracts to be concluded and defended in the face of repeated attacks in Parliament and elsewhere.

Rules and Documentation Auditable for Every Step. As indicated above, the project team predicted that there would be much interest and opposition to the concept from many quarters, and therefore set out to ensure that its actions were always conducted correctly. Numerous challenges had to be faced both during the process and subsequently. The policy largely paid off, although a major reason why Woranora and Avon have not been let yet is a challenge to the EIS procedure.

It is of interest to note that the maximum of open consultation was conducted with the private sector. This enabled a constructive interchange of ideas to take place during formative periods. In contrast, at all times when the competitive process was being used, there was only formal contact, following a very clear procedure, for the purpose of clarification . Whilst this was obviously essential, both sides found it a stultifying and frustrating constraint.

How do you Evaluate? In this process, and with a long term contract as the objective, the question of evaluating the competing consortia and their various solutions presents a major challenge. It is evident that price alone is a totally inadequate criterium of choice. The procedure that was adopted in Sydney, using a two stage approach is recommended as being the only way to meet this challenge.

The first stage enabled the Board to reduce the contenders to a list any of which they felt confident could do the job. The main criteria at this stage included: commercial strengths and competence, ability to deliver the infrastructure, ability to operate the plants, approach to a long term contract, financial and corporate structuring, technical strength, management and quality issues.

The second stage, (Competitive tender) was to examine the detailed technical solution in relation to the tariff offered and to determine the best value for money proposal. It was also necessary for the Board to be sure that the anticipated cost savings were realised in practice. The tender also created a defendable benchmark for the negotiation phase.

Both stages needed to be very thorough, and were in every way complimentary. Had this procedure not been used, the process would have become unmanageable and prohibitively expensive. The first stage was viewed as being equally important as the second. It would also have been completely unrealistic to imagine that the process could have been concluded at the end of the bid process without detailed final negotiations.

The Final Negotiation. The final negotiation was a long and complicated process, which essentially comprised three phases.

- The first phase was the clarification and selection of the various options offered in the bid. Of necessity the Board's team had to challenge a number of aspects of the offer, and as a result this was the only stage of the process that approached being a conflictual relationship between the parties.

- The second stage involved the refining of the preferred option, and the negotiation of the contractual terms. This required not only the head contract, but also all the related agreements in respect of financing and construction. In all some 40 different inter-related agreements needed to be finalised.

- The third stage was the work that was largely undertaken jointly of securing the various approvals that were needed.

The negotiation procedure took a period of 10 months, but in no way was it time wasted. Considerable refinement and additional benefits were derived for the client, and very importantly it materially developed the spirit of co-operation and partnership towards meeting the common objectives of a long-term contract.

The Contract.

The principal characteristics of the head contract (Water Filtration Agreement WFA) is that it is an agreement for the acquisition of services. It is an advanced, sophisticated form of services contract. In general terms the water treatment company contracts to filter and treat the Board's water and to ensure :

(i) that the available capacity of the plant will not be less than the warranted capacity

(ii) to supply all of the Sydney Water Board's needs for clean bulk water up to the warranted capacity per day, of the plant

(iii) that clean bulk water will satisfy the water quality criteria.

The Water Filtration Agreement essentially followed the Commercial Principles Document prepared prior to the request for tender which outlined the projects, the anticipated allocation of risks, project delivery requirements, operational requirements and contractual requirements. The actual contract is made up of 3 components.

The agreement recognises that a project structured on a B.O.O.T. basis requires the assumption of substantial commercial risk by the water treatment company. Nevertheless, the most efficient risk profile for the project is one which allocates the commercial, financial and other risks inherent in the project to those parties best able to assess and manage them.

Risks Responsibilities and Rewards. The foregoing narative has outlined a great number of the issues involved, and no doubt gives some impression of the complexity of the exercise of creating BOT type

---

BOX2,
The Contract is made up of three components.

(a) The contractual provisions

(b) Schedules containing various technical requirements e.g.
- Management Control Plant for the design, construction and commissioning phase
- Quality Assurance requirement
- Commissioning criteria
- Raw water criteria
- Treated water criteria
- Water quality tests
- Records and reports
- Tariff
- Research and development

(c) Various exhibits provided by the water treatment company e.g.

- Quality Assurance Plan
- Description of work
- Preliminary Commissioning Plan
- Operation & Maintenance Manual outline
- Preliminary Emergency Response Programme

projects. The real nub of the problem however resides in the structuring of the project. This requires :
- the identification of all the risks in the project.
- the creation of a team that can face these risks
- their allocation to the party best able to carry each one
- and the agreement of a reasonable level of reward that each such party should have in compensation for the risk it takes.

The problem has to be solved in the context of the interplay of Economic, Technical, and Legal solutions as well as the constant search for the most competitive solution.

One of the interesting things about the "Drinking Water Programme", is the way it illustrates that each BOT has its own specific risk profile. Whilst setting out to achieve the same objectives, each of Prospect, MacArthur, Avon and Waroora have quite different risk profiles. It also illustrates how the way a project is structured can have a significant effect on the feasibility outcome and price. Each of the three succesful consortia developed slightly different institutional structures.

It is important to recognise that the interplay of these elements have to be examined on the level of the Client (Concedant or organising authority) to Contractor (Concessionaire or operator) relationship, on that of the level of the environment of the concedant (Corporation, State and Federal government etc.) and on that of each of the component organisations of the concessionaire consortium. They also have to be examined in terms of the time span of the contract and the phases it will pass through.

These considerations were central to all of the discussions between the Board and the various consortia at each of the stages of the process. This meant that as the projects each became more and more refined the balance between risk, responsibility and reward became better defined. In spite of this, the real form of the arrangements could only start to be finalised during the negotiation phase. Only at this stage could the final shape of the concessionaire team be fixed. As the negotiations progressed, the commitments of all the parties became more and more solid and the focus on the outcome more and more sharp.

One particular hurdle to be overcome was the fact that the project required the approval of the Federal Treasury under the rules referred to as "Global Limits". This meant that the treasurer had to be satisfied that the private sector assumes a significant level of risk. It also meant that no Federal or State guarantees were available on the project.

Conclusion

There are many traps and pitfalls that can upset a BOT project before it comes to fruition. Sydney was no exception as far as this potential was concerned. Among the keys to the success of Prospect were:

- The structured approach with three stages, pre qualification, tender and most importantly negotiation.

- A very high level of professionalism exhibited by the Board, the Consortium and their respective teams of advisors and the Banking Consortium.

- The positive effort made by both sides to foster co-operation and partnership.

- The time, care and professionalism dedicated by all involved in the negotiation process

- The very careful analysis of the risks, responsibilities and rewards of all the parties at every stage of the project.

These features combined created a unity of purpose between the public sector and the private sector teams, that enabled them to overcome all the difficulties in a timely manner. They enabled the Board to take the full advantage of the technical, financial and managerial strengths of a world class team from the private sector, and contributed to the establishment of relationships which should enable the project to serve the public of Sydney for the next 25 years.

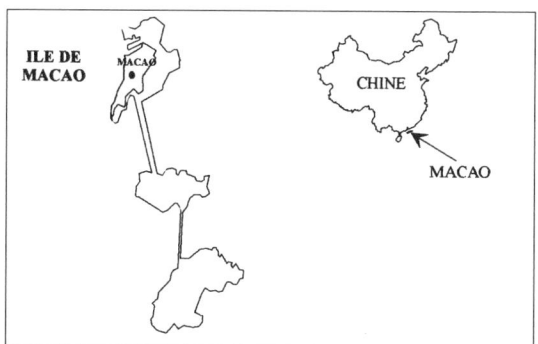

CHAPTER 12

Didier Rétali

From Macao to China

In 1985, the company Lyonnaise des Eaux, in partnership with the Hong Kong New World Development Group, took control of the Macao Water Supply Company (SAAM) which had been providing water services to a population of about 500,000 residents. A massive program of reorganization and capital investment has since been carried out in order to make this company a reference in Asia in the area of water distribution.

Located at the mouth of the Pearl River, some seventy kilometers to the west of Hong Kong, Macao lies within Chinese territorial jurisdiction, yet remains under Portuguese administrative authority until December 19, 1999. Thereafter, the Territory will be administered by China, in the form of a Special Administrative Region.

The Territory is composed of the Macao Peninsula (6.5 km² in land area) as well as the two islands of Taipa and Coloane (a total of 11 km²), connected to the mainland by permanent structures, both bridges and dikes.

Since the mid-1930's, water services management had been provided by a private company, SAAM, responsible for the entire span of operations. By the end of the 1970's, the situation had deteriorated to such an extent that in 1984, the Macao Water Supply Company was experiencing acute difficulties in adequately assuring water distribution, from the standpoint of both the regularity of supply and the quality of water being distributed:

- The water treatment plant was old and its capacity insufficient; as such, the Territory was often subjected to water service interruptions, and the quality of water delivered was rather poor.

- The distribution network was also quite old and in dire need of overhaul. In addition, its capacity, inadequate to maintain a satisfactory level of water pressure, had to be upgraded; at the time, water losses were in the order of 25%.

- The under-capitalization of the company along with its lack of technical expertise represented major obstacles to remedying the company's situation.

Against this backdrop, Lyonnaise des Eaux was invited by the Macao government, towards the end of 1984, to study the Territory's overall water problem and to formulate proposals for action; this step was carried out very quickly.

With the study having validated the plan for restructuring SAAM, Lyonnaise des Eaux went on to form with the Hong Kong New World Development Group, in June 1985, a joint venture company called Sino-French Water Development, in which each partner held 50% of the capital.

This newly-formed company then proceeded to take control of 85% of SAAM's capital through underwriting an increase in capital from a level of 3 million Patacas up to 51 million. The very next month, a new 25-year concessionary contract was signed between SAAM and the Macao Government.

Implementing a modernization policy

Measures were implemented as early as summer 1985 in order to bolster SAAM's management and to conduct a technical and administrative reorganization of the company. At the same time, a five-year capital investment program of 115 million Patacas (equivalent to 14.5 million US dollars) was being prepared. The execution of this program got underway at the beginning of 1986 and was completed in less than four years. A second program followed, covering the period

1990-1994. The third investment program, for the years 1995 to 1999, is in the process of being executed.

Since 1985, the Macao Water Supply Company has thereby invested over 350 million Hong Kong dollars, equivalent to 45 million US dollars, a sum which has enabled for the renovating of all the service's infrastructure facilities. In addition, actions have been undertaken in other non-technical areas that contribute directly to improving the quality of service being provided to residents as well as to enhancing the life of the company.

Bulk water supply

The Territory of Macao encompasses absolutely no water resources, given both the absence of aquifers and the excessive saline content of the Pearl River Delta. Under such conditions, the entire quantity of bulk water originates in China.

Since the raw water brought into the system was not of an acceptable quality, SAAM negotiated with Chinese authorities (the City of Zhuhai and the Pearl River Commission) for the construction of a new water supply system, which eventually began operating in 1988, measuring 16.4 km long and containing a series of canals, aqueducts, tunnels and pipes.

The supply of raw water was then secured with the construction in 1992 of an independent 140,000 m^3/day-capacity connection system in conjunction with the City of Zhuhai.

Ultimately, SAAM could make use of two reservoirs of bulk water as safety storage: one is located on the Macao Peninsula with a capacity of 1.2 million m^3, while the other at Coloane is offering 0.3 million m^3 in capacity.

Drinking water treatment facilities

Treatment capacity had more than doubled, progressing from 85,000 m^3/day in 1985 to 195,000 m^3/day, split between facilities at Ilha Verde (180,000 m^3/day) and Coloane (15,000 m^3/day). The treatment methods employed were reinforced in order to produce a water whose quality would meet European standards.

To reach this objective, techniques introduced by the Degrémont company were widely used, in addition to the construction of a 45,000 m^3/day-capacity Pulsator and Aquazur V filters, providing a total capacity of 180,000 m³/day. In the same fashion, the filters being utilized at the Coloane plant (15,000 m³/day) were also modified to incorporate the Aquazur V type.

The treatment facilities are completely automated, and the Coloane plant is controlled remotely from the Ilha Verde controlroom. In order to satisfy an increasing level of demand, a new treatment plant, with a capacity of 60,000 m³/day, is currently being built. Its design is based on the technology of a direct filtration.

The water distribution network

The total length of the distribution network is 239 kilometers, with pipe diameters ranging from 100 mm to 1,200 mm, thereby equivalent to twice the 1984 total network length. A special effort was undertaken to increase distribution capacity, with the installation of 33 kilometers of pipes whose diameters exceed 400 mm, thus enabling the delivery of water to users at a sufficient level of pressure throughout the Territory.

A strong-willed policy of network renewal was implemented so as to eliminate the majority of asbestos-cement and cast iron, which had been the causes of many leaks; 60% of all the pipes existing in 1982 have, under this impetus, been replaced. In addition, a program of systematic leak detection was launched. The combination of these measures enabled reducing the rate of leakage from 25% in 1984 to roughly 12% since 1990.

Finally, the total capacity of the reservoirs of treated water has almost tripled: from 17,000 m3 in 1985 to 45,000 m3 at the present time. These reservoirs are equipped with automatic rechlorination devices, which allow maintaining an adequate level of chlorine throughout the entire network. For managing its distribution network, SAAM uses the APIC software developed by Lyonnaise des Eaux; the sizing of network extensions and reinforcements is performed with the help of the Piccolo software.

Customer relations

SAAM has taken various measures in order to improve its relations with users:
- A vast program to replace water meters has been conducted, and SAAM is now equipped with a testing apparatus to check the meters acuracy.
- Meter-reading is performed by means of hand held computers.

- Users are informed in advance of any water service interruptions necessitated by network operations.
- Controlling meters on site can now be carried out thanks to ultrasonic meters. Meters can also be tested with a specialized testing apparatus upon request of the customers.
- A special service, set up with easily-accessible offices open to the public, has been created to handle information requests and complaints from the service's customers.

The Laboratory and Research Center

A new laboratory was placed into service towards the end of 1987; it contains the most modern set of equipment for controlling the entire range of parameters for maintaining European standards, which consist of over sixty measurable values. Worth highlighting among this array of equipment are a gas chromatograph, a liquid chromatograph, an atomic-absorption spectrometer and a GC/MS unit.

Moreover, SAAM has been conducting since 1988 a research program, in coordination with the Lyonnaise des Eaux's Central Laboratory. The company has thereby been able to test, from the end of 1989 on, the ultrafiltration membrane developed by Lyonnaise des Eaux, and has been operating since the end of 1991 a 3,000 m^3/day-capacity demonstration unit.

SAAM is also carrying out studies on the evolution of water quality throughout its networks, on the reduction of prechlorination treatment and on the analyses of water's tastes and odors.

Lastly, SAAM has organized, in conjunction with Lyonnaise des Eaux, two international conferences: the first being held in 1989 on the topic of treatment techniques, and the second in 1992 on automated systems and computerization applicable to the water services.

Personnel training

The total number of employees has remained relatively stable since 1984, at a level of approximately 250. This feature signifies that substantial productivity gains have been realized through the company's reorganization as well as through its automation and computerization. As of 1984, an annual productivity increase of 9% has thus been attained.

In order to accomplish this feat, the personnel's qualification levels have been measurably upgraded, with the number of university graduates rising from twenty-nine to over sixty in 1993. A major training program for employees, consisting in certain cases of sessions held in France, has been instituted in order to assure a satisfactory effort for technology transfer. As a result, SAAM counts only one full-time French expatriate among its staff members.

Employee training also extends to customer and public relations, both key components for a service-oriented company.

Rate structures

The company bills its customers directly. No automatic rate revision clause has been written into the contract, and rate increases must be submitted for approval each year to the Macao Government. In applying the concessionary contract, SAAM is subjected to governmental controls. In particular, a government representative attends all Board of Directors meetings, and all important decisions must go through the approvals process. In addition, SAAM is subjected to the same kinds of accounting controls that would pertain to any company's operations.

Each service user, including those residing in multi-family dwellings, is equipped with an individual water meter. Billing takes place on a monthly basis, whereas meter reading is only performed once every two months, with the intermediate bill amount being based on estimated water consumption levels.

The rate structure consists of a monthly tax for meter rental and maintenance, along with a use fee based on the volume of water consumed, evaluated at a price of 4 Patacas/m^3 (equivalent to US$ 0.50/m^3).

A minimum consumption threshold is applied, varying from 5 m^3/month for a 15-mm diameter water meter up to 500 m^3/month for a 150-mm meter.

In 1985, the rate was 2.5 Patacas/m^3, corresponding to an increase of 60% between 1985 and 1995. Nonetheless, in constant currency terms (base 1985), the rate actually dropped from 2.5 Patacas in 1985 to 2.09 Patacas in 1995 (see Figure 1). This evolution demonstrates that the water rate in Macao has risen on average 2% less than the rate of inflation since 1985.

This overall result can be broken down into stages: between 1985 and 1986, the rate in constant currency terms increased from 2.5

Patacas to 2.67 Patacas, due to the sizable capital investment effort being undertaken at the time the company was absorbed. Thereafter, taking the rate level reached in October 1986 as a reference, the drop recorded in constant currency since that time has been 22%, which would correspond to an average rate increase of 3% less than Macao's rate of inflation.

Thanks to measures aimed both at the economy and at the company's restructuring, this result has been obtained while insuring an adequate level of profitability for shareholders.

FIGURE 1:

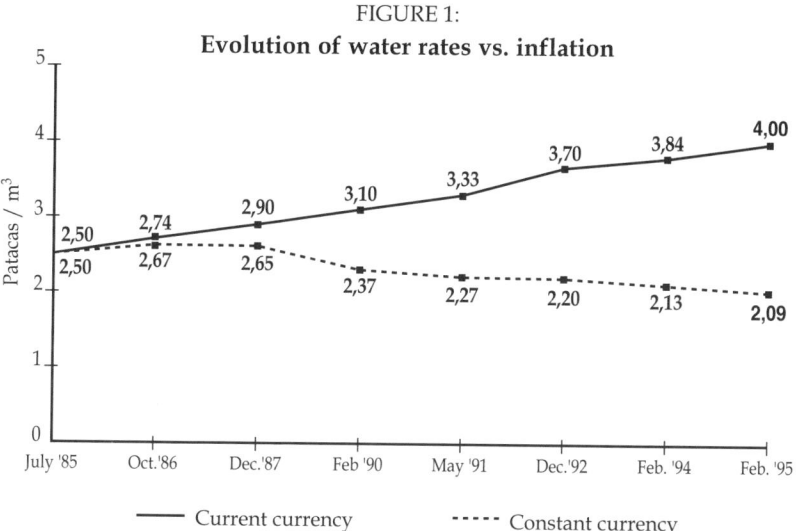

Evolution of water rates vs. inflation

The keys to success

Several factors have enabled conducting this services modernization policy successfully.

Macao's economic environment constituted a favorable backdrop: a liberal economic policy outlook, low rates of income taxation, full currency convertibility, growth in both population and income levels. In addition, the Territory of Macao possessed the necessary institutional and legal framework to undertake concessionary projects of this nature.

Under these conditions, the project could be completed by Lyonnaise des Eaux under "project finance", meaning that no financial guarantees have been provided by the shareholders for the bank loans.

It should be added that the concession's contractual regime did offer a flexible framework within which the operator shouldered the obligation for results, such as supplying in sufficient quantity and quality the entire Territory, yet at the same time retained the choice of means to be utilized. SAAM could thereby perform an overall optimization of Macao's water supply system in proceeding with the appropriate adjustments on a year-by-year basis.

Lastly, operational savings realized following the company's re-structuring, carried out by Lyonnaise des Eaux have generated financial resources and, as a result, enabled implementing a thorough modern-ization program while according users inflation-adjusted rate reductions.

Heading towards China

This experience has, over the past several years, proved to be a reference for the Lyonnaise des Eaux Group's activities in Asia. It has, in particular, helped the Degrémont company to set up operations in China. Degrémont has signed more than 40 contracts for water treatment plants, including the Daya Bay facility, the drinking water production plants at Xian (600,000 m^3/day), Shenyang (400,000 m^3/day), Chongqing (200,000 m^3/day) and Zhaoqing (200,000 m^3/day), along with the wastewater treatment plants located in Tianjin (400,000 m^3/day) and in Shenyang (400,000 m^3/day).

More recently, Lyonnaise des Eaux, once again in partnership with New World, began investing in water distribution in China. An initial contract was signed in October 1992 with the Municipality of Tanzhou (Zhongshan - Guangdong Province) for its water production and distribution concession. In order to promote this aim, Lyonnaise des Eaux and New World created, in conjunction with the Municipality of Tanzhou, a 50/50 joint venture which assumes the role of concessionaire over a thirty-year period.

This joint venture took over the water production and distribution service as of May 1st, 1994, and a new 60,000 m^3/day drinking water production plant began operations towards the end of 1994. The plant, built with the assistance of Degrémont, produces water in conformance with European standards.

Other contracts have been signed with the City of Shenyang (Liaoning Province) for the buyout and operation of the 400,000 m^3/day-capacity plant built by Degrémont, as well as with the City of Nanchang (Jiangxi Province) for the construction and operation of a 200,000 m^3/day facility.

It should nonetheless be highlighted that projects set up as concessions or as B.O.T.s (Build, Operate and Transfer contracts), approaches that are still quite new to China, do present some difficulties:

- China's institutional and legal framework, especially with respect to property rights, has not yet attained an appropriate level.

- The absence of a real capital market in China is currently necessitating heavy recourse on foreign financing, which has rendered projects very vulnerable to fluctuations in Chinese currency in relation to foreign currencies.

- Owing to the lack of convertibility of the Chinese currency and given an insufficient experience with concessions or B.O.T.s, foreign banks are now stipulating that all loans granted be guaranteed by shareholders.

Against this backdrop, concessionary or B.O.T. projects in China are requiring, at the present time, extremely high levels of financial commitment on the part of shareholders, thus serving to hinder the further development of these approaches.

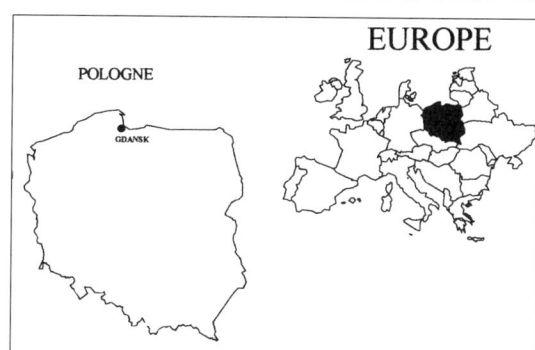

CHAPTER 13

EUROPE

POLOGNE

GDANSK

Zbigniew Maksymiuk

The transformation of a municipal enterprise into a joint venture company

The first joint venture-type company ever set up in Central Europe, Saur Neptun Gdansk S.A. (SNG), responsible for operating and managing a municipality's water supply and wastewater facilities, was created in Gdansk on July 1, 1992.

Gdansk is a city that symbolizes Central Europe. Throughout history, it has always been subjected to a dual Slavic and Germanic influence - a city under Teutonic rule, followed by periods of Hanseatic and Prussian control, before becoming a "free" town. Gdansk's function as a major port city has thrust it into a role of exchange center between the agricultural hinterland and export markets. Finally, Gdansk is the city where the Communist bloc's democratization movement first got its start. The "Gdansk accords" changed the face of Poland and marked a turning point in the Central European political context.

The technical system of water and wastewater services

The water supply and wastewater facilities that provide service to the cities of Gdansk and Sopot (460,000 and 50,000 population, respectively) are one hundred and twenty years old. The drinking water purification plant and the wastewater treatment facility were both built in 1869, and thereafter, other facilities contributing heavily to the system's expansion have been added every thirty years or so. Some of the system's oldest elements are still being operated. For example, it could be noted that roughly 20% of all network pipes in place are more than 100 years old (see Figure 1).

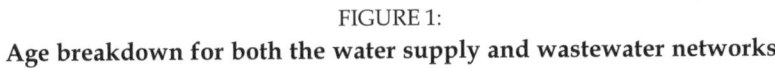

FIGURE 1:

Age breakdown for both the water supply and wastewater networks

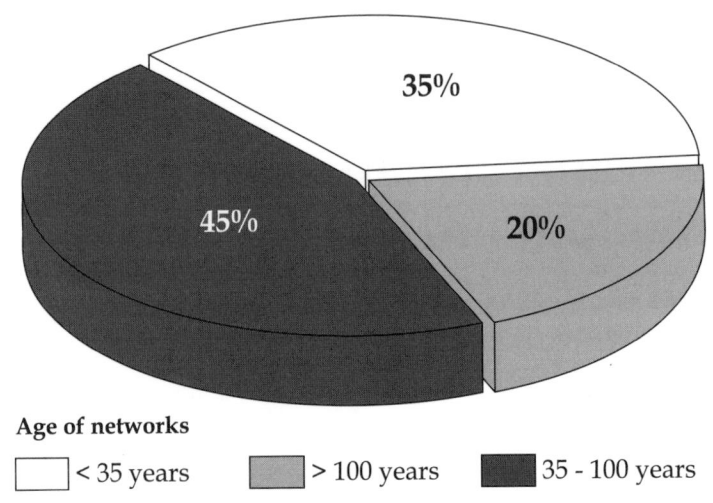

Age of networks

☐ < 35 years   ▨ > 100 years   ■ 35 - 100 years

The typical characteristic of Gdansk's water production and purification system[1] is: an abundant resource along with varying degrees of treatment for all effluent. At the end of 1993, the water supply system included a total network length of 678 km (without counting the connection pipes, whose total length amounted to 157 km) and a pipe diameter ranging from 50 to 1,200 mm. In general, a significant portion of the city is not equipped with large-diameter pipes, and no interconnections among major water mains is in place. The network is supplied by twelve plants producing on average 170,000 m^3/day. These production facilities are composed of a dam accounting for 30% of all drinking water production, nine wells for another 60%, and two drainage sites comprising the remainder.

1. The data concerning the volumes of both water supply production and wastewater generation also include the City of Sopot as well as three municipalities located adjacent to Gdansk, which are all kooked up to the City's facilities (in general, for wastewater services.

The geological configuration of the land area is quite varied and complex. Five pressure zones, six water supply recovery stations and eleven primary pressurization tanks connected to the network were all created to help provide service. In addition, the system contains five reservoirs providing a total capacity of 49,500 m³/day, which yields a reserve of around 30% of the average daily water production.

Breakdown of the service's customer base:

Households	80.0%
Industries	8.5%
Other	11.5%

The wastewater network is separate, and the operations of the rainwater collection network are run by another company. As of the end of 1993, the total length of sewers was 536 km, and the length of all user connection pipes was another 208 km. The sewer pipe diameters vary between 0.15 m and 2.7 x 2.3 m. Two wastewater treatment plants are part of the overall system: one with a capacity of 35,000 m³/day, the other serving a portion of the city along with the adjacent municipalities at 130,000 m³/day. Despite the relatively weak elevation differential of the gravity collector system, twelve pumping stations are nonetheless in operation throughout the wastewater network. This situation is caused by fundamentally different conditions affecting the construction of the gravity network on the lower terrace - flat topography - as opposed to the upper terrace - hillier topography. About 20% of all wastewater is treated by a mechanical and biological process, while the remaining 80% is subjected to a mechanical and chemical treatment.

The transformation of water service institutions since the Second World War

Following the war, the company undertook transformations to both its structure and the geographical scope of its activities (see map below).

1946 saw the creation of the company: City of Gdansk Water Supply and Wastewater Services, along with its eventual transformation into a municipal enterprise. Gdansk needed to be rebuilt at that time in its history. Its town center had practically been destroyed. The transplanted communities from former Eastern regions, annexed by the Soviet Union, had to be rehoused. The economy was being revamped for mass production capabilities, yet devoid of technical quality; suppliers were imposed; competition was inexistent. The water and

FIGURE 2:

Geographical coverage of the services provided by the O.P.W.i.K. in Gdansk

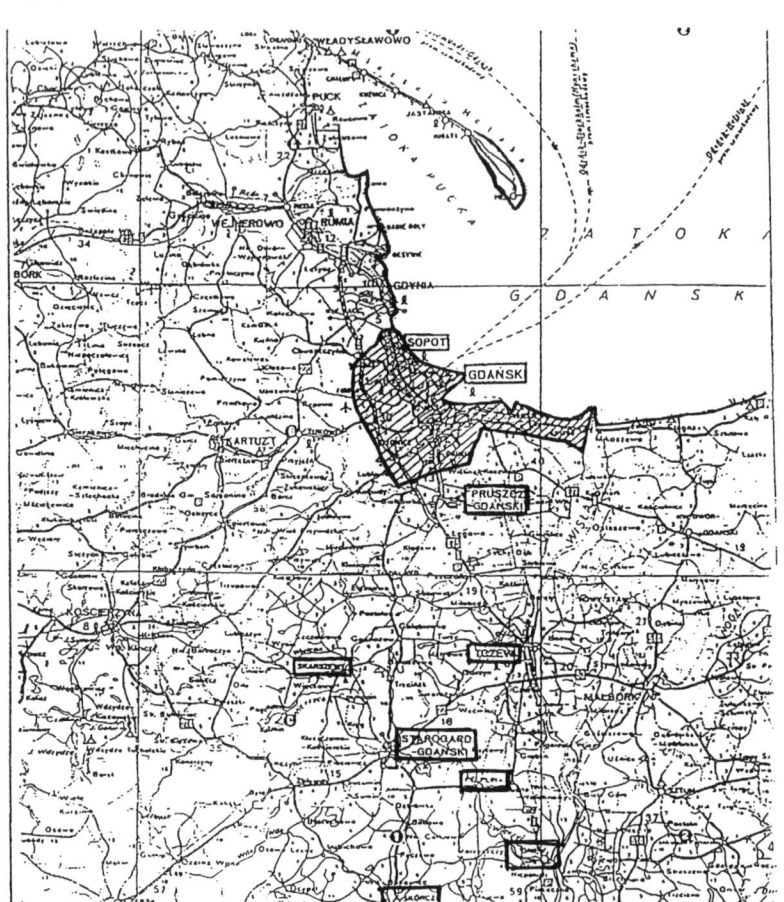

wastewater networks that date back to this period and still in use at the present time are, in fact, the most vulnerable, and their taps the most defective. Operating equipment were in serious short supply: the wheelbarrow was considered a high-technology tool. Service staff was being recruited from amongst the ranks of prisoners, since the work was so tough and so thankless. Needless to say, the company's image was rather tarnished.

In 1974, through application of the government's new liberalization and development policy, the Voivodie Water Supply and Wastewater Services Company, whose coverage spanned Gdansk's Voivodie (territorial jurisdiction), was created. Its activities were being performed under the control of the "Voivode" (Prefect). This was a very timely period within recent Polish history, where money, loaned from abroad, was plentiful. Water distribution facilities at the time expanded out to smaller cities and rural areas.

1980 was the year when the Regional Water Supply and Wastewater Services Company - O.P.W.i.K. - was created in Gdansk. Its geographical coverage included the cities of Gdansk, Sopot and nine others (see map); 75% of its activities were concentrated in Gdansk proper. Once again, activities carried out fell under Voivodie control. This represented the beginning of the process to dismantle State-held companies. The scope of their involvement had been restrained, and empowering the cities with oversight authority had just begun. The western part of the department didn't fall under the jurisdiction of the company. Following the shipyard strikes, Solidarnoz's victory was followed by the "state of siege" and the show of force that characterized the events of December 1981.

In 1982, control of O.P.W.i.K. was taken over by the President of the City of Gdansk; this transformation symbolized the return of municipal responsibility to the sector of water services. Capital investments were budgeted at the municipal level; setting the price of water required Municipal Council approval; nonetheless, the company remained the property of the State.

A revised organization

The grip held by the regime in power was weakening. The country was bankrupt, overwhelmed by the weight of its tremendous debt, by obsolete means of production and by a completely unmotivated workforce. The "state of siege" had come to an end. The regime was required to call upon the opposition for assistance. Semi-free elections were organized in 1989; the outcome saw the Solidarnoz party assume power at both the national and municipal levels.

With respect to local affairs, a revised legal system was gradually being implemented, intended to "liberalize" the economy. Two laws resulted from the initiative:
i) a municipalization law that placed all infrastructure facilities in the hands of the municipalities. This law actually served to separate the networks and facilities transferred over to their founding municipalities along with the land ownership for those parcels on which they were located; and
ii) a law transforming the State-held companies that, concerning water supply and wastewater services, gave rise to several potential solutions: integration within the city's services departments, "privatization" through a single-shareholder limited company, where

the sole shareholder would happen to be the municipality, thus a veritable privatization scheme.

Following the enactment of these laws, between 1990 and 1992, the various municipalities comprising the pertinent geographical jurisdiction left the O.P.W.i.K., which only retained the cities of Gdansk and Sopot. The "steering" directives instituted the transfer of a certain number of activities from the State level to the cities, yet without guaranteeing their adequate resources. Municipal budgets were unable to easily cope with these new service charges: roads, hospitals, schools; it had become impossible to finance the renewal or the further development of both the water and wastewater facilities. It's against this backdrop that the creation of SNG took place, a process consisting of the legal liquidation of O.P.W.i.K. as well as the transfer of property to the new company.

Direct contract negotiations lasted over a year and were ultimately finalized in November 1992. They were led by a special commission appointed by the City of Gdansk's Board of Supervisors. Experts were called on in the fields of law, finance and foreign trade. The text of the contract was submitted for review by the five consulting firms designated jointly by the City's Municipal Council and its Board of Supervisors. The City of Sopot was not involved in the negotiating process, and simply retained the right of access to service provided by its infrastructure facilities under SNG control, in conformance with the pertinent principles in application up until that time, as stipulated in the operations agreement.

The negotiations relative to the definition of terms of the company's statutes took eight months, from the end of 1991 to the beginning of 1992. The City of Gdansk was represented by the Judicial Chancellery that was executing the orders given by the City's Board of Supervisors. Throughout the entire negotiating period, the Polish delegation was being directed by three successive Boards of Supervisors, while two successive management teams were participating on behalf of the company.

On the 1st of July, 1992, Saur Neptun Gdansk S.A. was officially created, with a capital of 77 551 000 zlotys ($30.5 million), split 51%/49% between SAUR and the City of Gdansk. SAUR's contribution to the joint venture company took the form of a financial contribution for the development of a service quality improvement plan. The City's contribution was material in nature, consisting of land, buildings and equipment (vehicles) from the former O.P.W.i.K. head office. This transaction would signify that SNG had become owner of the offices, the workshops and the means of transportation held by the former

BOX1
Chronology of Negotiations

February 1990: representatives from the SAUR Group visit the city upon the invitation of members of Parliament from the Gdansk region as well as of Solidarnoz union leaders.

August 1990: signature of the letter of intention between the City of Gdansk's Board of Supervisors and SAUR.

March 1991: decree promulgated by the City of Gdansk's Board of Supervisors concerning the initiation of O.P.W.i.K.'s liquidation.

July 1991: approval on the part of both the Independent Workers Organization and the O.P.W.i.K. Workers Council for the privatization of the company into a joint venture with the French firm SAUR.

July 1991: signing of the preliminary contract between the City of Gdansk's Board of Supervisors and SAUR.

December 1991: decree issued by the City of Gdansk's Board of Supervisors on the choice of the legal and organizational form retained for O.P.W.i.K.'s activities through the creation of a joint venture company in conjunction with SAUR.

December 1991: decree issued by the City's Board of Supervisors regarding the initiation of O.P.W.i.K.'s liquidation.

March 1992: favorable judgement rendered by the Anti-Trust Office on the layout and creation of the joint venture company, based on the liquidated O.P.W.i.K.'s operation.

April 1992: notarized deposition of the SNG S.A. corporate statutes.

June 1992: approval by the Ministry of the Interior for the City's contribution to the company in the form of land and buildings.

June 1992: notarized act for the founding of SNG S.A.

June 30, 1992: decision rendered by the Gdansk Circuit Court to approve SNG's listing in the Business Registry.

July 1, 1992: initialing the contract between Gdansk's Board of Supervisors and SNG.

December 1992: confirmation of the contract by decree of the Gdansk Municipal Council and the contract's signature by the City's Board of Supervisors and by SNG.

June 1993: confirmation of SNG's listing in the Business Registry, upon approval by the Minister of Industry and Commerce.

operating company. Its scope of activity covers the whole city of Gdansk (in accordance with the terms of the contract) and the city of Sopot (in accordance with the applicable operations agreement). Oversight of company operations is exercised by its shareholders: the City of Gdansk and SAUR. Control over the company's service provision activities is performed by the cities themselves receiving the service.

Why did the City decide to create a joint venture company? Put otherwise, why privatize a typical municipally-run enterprise like O.P.W.i.K. that was operating well (in respecting local-based criteria)?

From the standpoint of the City, three factors served to support the ultimate decision:
- the quantity of water. In 1986, a surface water pumping facility was placed into operation in order to supply 30% of the service's customer base. This effort represented a vital capital investment given the limited production capacity of the aquifer. Yet, at the same time, residents began receiving chlorinated water which was of rather poor quality, a fact they obviously couldn't accept;
- the absence of guarantees with respect to maintaining continuity in service provision (the poor state of the previous facilities causing a good deal of damage) and to the system's water losses; and
- the lack of sufficient financial resources to enable upgrading the current state of affairs both quickly and efficiently.
Generally speaking, the City was keen to improve the quality of its services, to realize cost savings in its management and in its investments, as well as to satisfy needs. In addition, the price of water had to remain within reasonable limits after the increased level of quality.

From the standpoint of the Municipal Enterprise, we can list a set of other motivations:
- lack of resources necessary for its operations and subsequent development;
- need to distinguish responsibilities between the company and the City; and
- motivation to access to the most up-to-date technologies and to methods for managing the financial and technical parameters from an overall perspective.

In this context, the company sought to establish more optimal relationships with both the City and the service's users, even though these relationships meant additional commitments and additional responsibilities. At the same time, the company was also seeking the guarantee of its continual development, accompanied by the guarantee of economic growth.

The new relationship between the City and SNG

The contract. The contract constitutes a specific document describing, through over 100 articles, the conditions under which the City has leased to SNG the infrastructure facilities comprising the water supply and wastewater systems. Moreover, it lays out the responsibilities and commitments of SNG (the service operator) along with the methods for their proper control, which are to be administered by the City (in its role as the facilities' owner). This split in domains of authority can be summarized as follows:
   a) the City
   - remains owner of all infrastructure,
   - carries out capital investment planning (for infrastructure),
   - procures financing (for infrastructure), and
   - sets the rates charged for services (price of water).
   b) SNG S.A.
   - is responsible for the equipment it has been entrusted,
   - assures the high quality of water,
   - guarantees upholding service continuity and service quality, and
   - is responsible for customer relations.

The contract applies for a thirty-year period, since, according to the advice of the parties to the contract, only a long-term engagement can guarantee complete respect of the entire set of commitments. Such is particularly true in the case of a foreign firm, which has to carry out the transfer of the most up-to-date technical and organizational solutions, along with the upkeep of the facilities entrusted.

SNG's commitments. By signing the leasing contract with the City's Board of Supervisors (the new relationships are presented in Figure 3), the company assumed a series of precise commitments:

 * technical:
   - raise the quality of Gdansk's water supply to standards applicable in European Community member countries, within a period of three years for aquifer-drawn water and a year and a half for water drawn from surface sources,
   - reduce the rate of water supply losses,
   - inventory the entire extent of both the water supply and wastewater networks,
   - develop a water resources program for the city of Gdansk, and
   - implement a "pollution watch" control post on the Radunia River.

 * economic:
   - decrease by 7.5% the operating costs within a three-year period,

FIGURE 3:

Diagram of the new relationship in effect in Gdansk

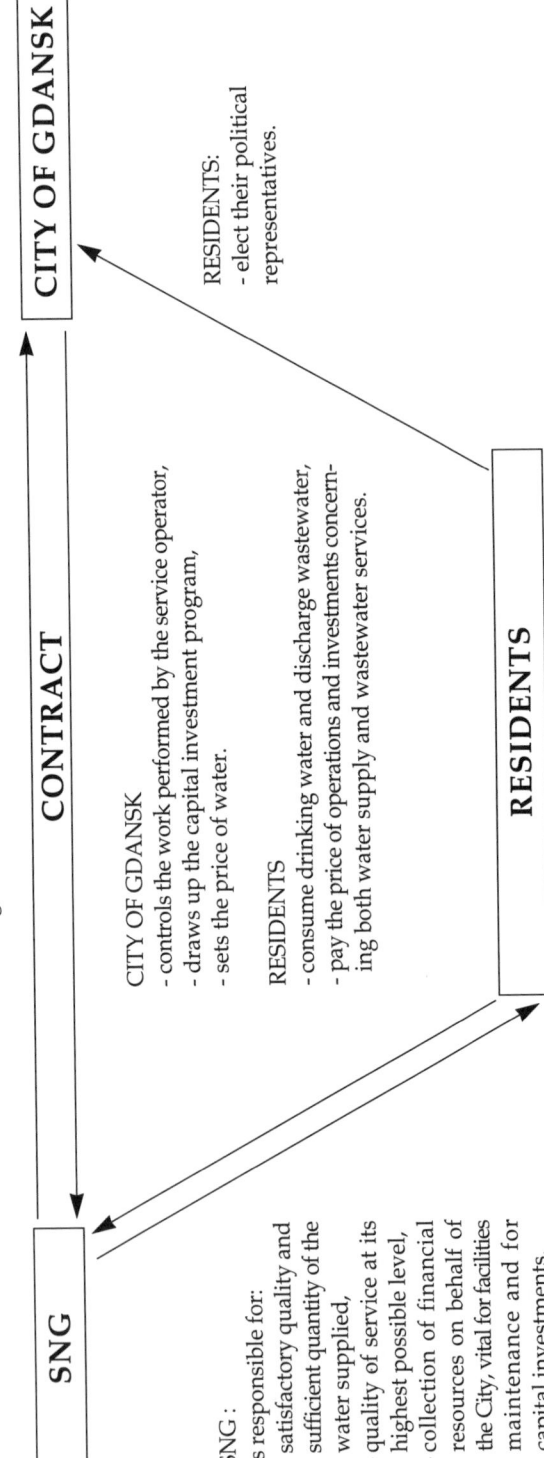

CITY OF GDANSK

RESIDENTS:
- elect their political representatives.

SNG
- operates the facilities remaining under City ownership,
- acts as adviser to the city for planning the development of the infrastructure network and for selecting the technological solutions.

CONTRACT

CITY OF GDANSK
- controls the work performed by the service operator,
- draws up the capital investment program,
- sets the price of water.

RESIDENTS
- consume drinking water and discharge wastewater,
- pay the price of operations and investments concerning both water supply and wastewater services.

RESIDENTS

SNG

SNG :
is responsible for:
- satisfactory quality and sufficient quantity of the water supplied,
- quality of service at its highest possible level,
- collection of financial resources on behalf of the City, vital for facilities maintenance and for capital investments.

as measured in constant prices, and
- set up a more modern service fee structure for both water supply and wastewater by separating out an operations component and a volume-based service charge, a split which would enable the authorities to undertake a beneficial capital investment policy.

* organizational:
- provide ongoing training for the company's workforce and for the regional authorities' professional associates to be conducted at the Training Center created for this particular purpose,
- undertake the computerization of the management system along with the customer service operations within a period of one year; furthermore, significant progress having been made in the area of computerization and automation of technological processes within three years' time, and
- devise a detailed breakdown of authority and responsibilities between the City - owner of the infrastructure facilities - and the company - user of the facilities.

These commitments are intended to improve the quality of service through: i) reliability of the equipment and networks, ii) identification and expeditious elimination of service malfunctions and network failures, iii) an up-to-date system for providing service and for billing customers, and iv) a widespread information campaign designed to instruct the residents of Gdansk on the value of the potable water supply and of its economic use.

The rule of service. As an appendix to the contract document, it signifies that the contract has been submitted for approval by the City of Gdansk's Municipal Council. This code of conduct stipulates the reciprocal sets of responsibilities as well as the breakdown of authority between SNG and its customer base (see Figure 5).

The price of water. The modification in the approach employed to set the price of water constitutes a fundamental element in the system's transformation. The price structure is built upon two primary components: the water use fee and the leasing amount (see Figure 4).

The former has since been applied by SNG. It has been designed to cover operating costs, along with all maintenance work. In addition, it provides a source of profit for the company. The latter component of the price is collected by the City - the amount thus generated is then allocated to the municipal budget, thereby creating the means for financing major repair work and capital investments in

FIGURE 4:

Pricing structure for water in Gdansk

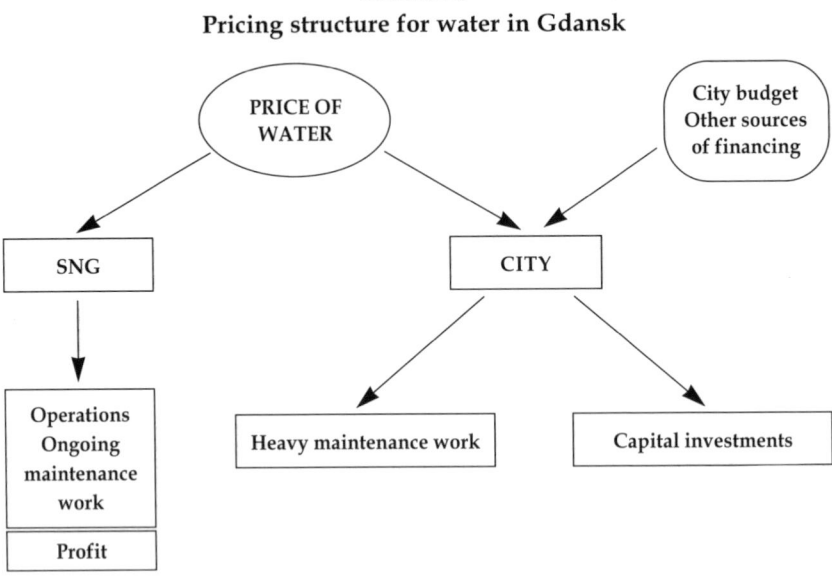

the areas of water supply and wastewater, both vital to the system's functioning. The City most certainly can earmark additional resources for the financing of other capital investments, originating for example from borrowing, budget subsidies, etc.

The price of water is confirmed by decision of the City of Gdansk's Municipal Council. In contrast, the budget of the company SNG is approved by shareholder vote, provided that this approval is unanimous. The leasing amount - the portion of the price structure that is attributed to the City - is set according to the list of needs laid out in the investment and reparation schedule established by SNG. This schedule is submitted to the City for approval.

The leasing amount remains the property of the City; the lease payment is directly deposited into the City's budget. These financial resources must be slated to financing major repair work and capital investments in the areas of water supply and wastewater. These works are carried out by delegated investors chosen by the City; the company SNG is an eligible candidate in this selection process.

All works are commissioned by the tender committee. This committee is composed of representatives from the Gdansk City Hall, the City's Municipal Council and SNG. The detailed set of rules governing the tender procedure was stipulated by the City, which holds a majority of the seats on the tender committee.

Current results achieved from SNG operations

Meeting commitments. SNG's operations, which have been ongoing for over two years, enable drawing up an initial assessment of operations, to be compared with the set of commitments outlined in the contract.

- With respect to the commitment concerning the reduction in operating costs of 7.5% within a period of three years, the target was reached well ahead of schedule. In fact, a decrease of 15.5% was actually recorded only after eighteen months of operations;

- The improvement in water quality of surface sources, contractually required within eighteen months, up to standards imposed by the European Community was attained ahead of time. In June 1993, the activated carbon treatment process was installed, and the definitive system (ozone) was in place in June 1994. Work performed on the technological design for treating water from underground sources has been finalized, with the initial system elements being slated for completion in 1995;

- SNG has devised a biological treatment technology for underground water; the chemical purification process for wastewater has been implemented; the treatment of surface water supply through two-level ozonization technology and activated-carbon filtration has been developed;

- The commitments concerning the application of up-to-date technologies and the computerization of the company are also in the process of being met; both the technology and the working tools utilized by SNG are among the most modern seen in all of Poland;

- Thirty-seven computers are dedicated to the management control function, and twenty-six to operations; the company is equipped with a complete array of measurement and operations apparatus, such as: quantifiers, correlators, television cameras and so forth, as well as a computerized hydraulic model of the water supply network;

- In conformance with the executive training program, we have completed training for 920 staff members; our in-house Training Center satisfies the company's needs entirely;

- The principle behind the rule for setting the maximum repair response time for mechanical failures at 24 hours has never been compromised; the number of occurrences of equipment failure has been decreased by 40%, which has served to significantly improve the reliability of the water supply system and has enabled initiating the prevention treatment of the network; and

- The commitments of SNG with respect to conducting expert appraisals on the facilities and networks have already been fulfilled; these appraisals constitute the basis for planning system reparations and modernization programs over the next ten years.

These spectacular results have been realized thanks in part to the implementation of:
- a detailed system for control and evaluation, whose basis consists of an analytical accounting approach along with a system of technical and economic parametric comparisons,

- an up-to-date and straightforward organizational structure: following both a general and detailed assessment, the company's organizational chart was modified; the operating principles for the majority of its departments were revised as well, and

- a relatively stabilized social and financial context for the personnel. After five months of negotiations with both labor unions, a collective bargaining agreement was signed along with a new working code of conduct. The component of the base salary was raised from 50% to 80%.

The new spirit behind SNG. The development of the company through acceptance of a revised working philosophy has necessitated changes in the ways of thinking at all levels. The new mentality has been stimulated by the Board of Directors, by instituting a process of delegating responsibilities, defining responsibilities, setting objectives, focusing on economic parameters and improving skill levels. In fact, a whole new set of general guidelines had been put into effect, along with specific solutions in the areas of technical, administrative and operating activities. These guidelines have been accepted by the personnel, and, most importantly, staff proposals have indeed given rise to a good number of modifications.

Typical examples of the changes introduced by the updated organizational chart were the delegation of responsibilities to younger engineers as well as the creation of horizontal structural relationships between groups with specific sets of aims. Responsibility placed in the hands of one individual favors a concentration around that individual's particular domain of specialization. A detailed planning schedule and a set of prescribed relationships have been accompanied by methods for optimizing employment resources, use of facilities, and the management of equipment and budgets at the local level. At the same time, the company began preparing for the following series of projects utilizing its own resources.

The response of the personnel lies in its determination to participate in the training sessions proposed as well as in a keen level of awareness for new methods and technologies. The notion of well-roundedness has been adopted; extending working hours actually emanates from the staff itself. Concurrently, a strong identification of the personnel with the company and its missions has been ever more present. The responsibility for decision-making and for their eventual consequences have become ever more prominent. The need to construct horizontal working relationships and the spirit of teamwork has been gaining considerable strength.

Public relations policies. Ever since the beginning of its activities, the company has been striving to develop both internal and external relationships. Regarding internal relationships, we have focused upon the organization of topic-specific and interdisciplinary meetings. An in-house publication (quarterly) is distributed in order to provide information on all major events related to the company as well as to its workforce.

The purpose of pursuing external relationships aims at guaranteeing the widespread dissemination of the approaches adopted - each month, the results of the water quality analyses conducted at the system's treatment plants and across the city's various districts are communicated to the media. The color of the company's fleet and the work uniforms worn by personnel have been standardized and coded - every resident is thus able to evaluate the work being performed by the operations services. Seminars and presentation sessions have been organized for representatives of City Hall, the Municipal Council, local residents and the press.

Contacts with both local and national organizations and institutions have been established. SNG is the member-founder of the "Polish Water Supply" Economic Chamber and the Polish Ozone Technical Organization. A cooperation agreement was entered into with the Hydrotechnical Department of Gdansk Polytechnic as well as with the Mechanical and Electrical Vocational High School and the Environmental Engineering Vocational High School in Gdansk. Efforts to organize the Water Resources Center have been carried out in conjunction with the Gdansk Voivodie.

In general, a great deal of attention is paid to building a cooperative spirit with the local youth population. In 1993, a hundred high school and university students fulfilled their professional training programs inside the company. SNG organizes ecological-oriented outings, company visits preceded by classroom instruction - for over four hundred primary and secondary school students.

Conclusion

All Polish cities are faced with similar types of problems: water quality not in compliance with required standards, poor technical state of both the network and the system's equipment - an incomplete and defective wastewater network. In practical terms, three methods are available to resolve such problems:

First method: accepting the current methods in operations and management. This solution could be considered as a strategy that doesn't foster any significant changes or, apparently, any risks. Yet, these risks do exist, in particular the lack of a guarantee for the renovation and development of infrastructure facilities (incurring the risk of devoting budget resources, or even depreciation towards other objectives). A more local-based approach to problems may give rise to simply accentuating the openings already created, which would signify expending energy and resources on identifying solutions already tested elsewhere.

Second method: renovating existing facilities (both technical equipment and networks). Suppliers of new technologies, along with the lending institutions, are obviously striving to promote this solution. This method can also be appreciated in that the purchase of new materials tends to upgrade the system's value, but here once again, certain dangers are present. The strategy retained necessitates heavy investment. The financial resources are in fact held by the banks, yet afterwards, the loans must be reimbursed (either through the City's budget or through the price of water; in any event, it's the residents who foot the entire bill). New technologies could wind up as mere gimmicks, lacking the necessary complementary training or the accompanying changes in organization and in mentalities.

Third method: optimizing the existing infrastructure and organization. Included herein would be conducting detailed systems analyses (facilities for producing drinking water, for purifying wastewater and the networks themselves), along with judging between the modernization of existing system components and the use of new technologies. The level of technical and economic expertise forms the basis of the decision-making process that takes into account the potential and the expectations of both the City and its inhabitants.

The City of Gdansk, conscious of its limited financial resources in comparison with the level of current needs and without spurning modern organizational solutions, has opted for the path of cooperation with a professional foreign partner. This approach has provided the City with the guarantee of obtaining the best results within the shortest time frame at the lowest costs. An assessment of the accomplishments posted by this limited company, Saur Neptun Gdansk, has served to confirm the effectiveness of the adopted solution.

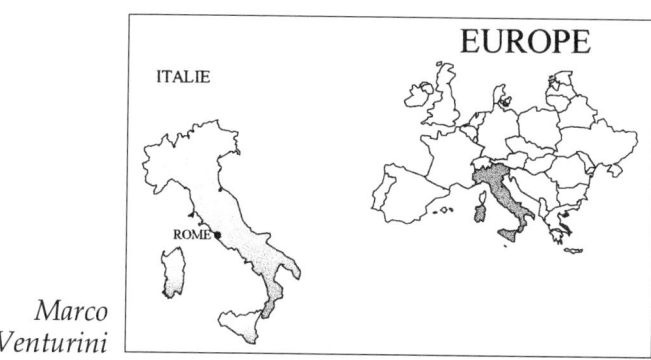

CHAPTER 14

Marco Venturini

Italy : the paths to reform

When comparing the quality of electricity, telephone and natural gas services provided the residents of various Western nations, it becomes readily apparent that Italy exhibits levels of quality and technological achievement undeniably on a par with its neighbors. The state of the Italian railway network is indeed comparable to Great Britain's, even if it does remain behind France's and Germany's in the development of high-speed rail ; the rate of cellular telephone use in Italy and the level of coverage of the country's land area do rank with that of Germany, and are considerably higher than those experienced in France. Furthermore, in the area of natural gas provision, Italian companies display an expertise at least equal to that of the major French and English public service monopolies.

In contrast, within the sectors of water and wastewater services, Italy could be considered, from several vantage points, as a somewhat "backwards" country. Entire cities, especially in the southern part of the country and the islands, periodically face shortages in drinking water supply despite capital investment programs carried out over the past few decades that at times have reached tremendous proportions. These programs have been implemented by the Mezzogiorno Development Fund, a public-sector financial institution which had been responsible, up until its recent dissolution, for managing the State's economic development subsidies targeted for southern Italy.

Within some of the more heavily-industrialized regions in the northern part of the country, pollution of aquifers from both agricultural activity (pesticides, atrazines, nitrates, etc.) and industrial activity (chemical pollutants, heavy metals, etc.) has been observed on a recurrent basis.

From the standpoint of wastewater services, it has been estimated that just 60% of the effluent generated undergoes any kind of treatment prior to being discharged into the environment. Entire metropolitan areas, such as Milan and Florence, are simply devoid of any water treatment plant.

Background

In seeking a broader understanding of the rationale behind the current situation, it would be appropriate to review the fundamental stages in the evolution of public services during the previous decades, beginning with the wave of nationalizations in the 1950's, spanning the grand-scale projects of the 1970's and 1980's all the way up through the recently-enacted water services reform law of January 1994.

In the 1950's, the pressing need for reconstruction and accelerated growth necessitated all European nations to devise systems for regulating public services that had the capacity to respond to rapid urban expansion as well as the changing demands of industry. While France was, at this time, pursuing the strategy of a mixed system, which allowed localities the latitude to choose between purely public-run services ("in-house" management by municipal staff) and contractual delegation to specialized service operators (leasing and concessionary contracts), Italy's government was organizing its water services exclusively around public-sector management schemes. This trend resulted from the absence of viable private water service operators along with the prevailing political support for the nationalization of certain sectors of the economy. The primary forces acting upon this process were: the municipalities, the rate structure imposed by the State, a populist pricing policy based on the notion of water as a social right being both vital and guaranteed (and thereby relatively free of charge), the investments carried out essentially through public subsidies, and a management approach (in terms of maintenance, periodic replacement, investment scheduling and operating cost optimization techniques) that was heretofore practically unknown. If the fact that Italians are traditionally outstanding builders yet poor managers were added to this backdrop, it can clearly be understood why the massive capital outlays carried out in this sector have not yielded the kinds of results expected.

During the past few decades, Italy has invested in major water storage and delivery systems, as well as in wastewater collection and treatment facilities, on a par with its European neighbors. The large-scale water-related infrastructure projects have enabled Italian construction firms and design practices to attain a level of competence recognized the world over. However, once built, these facilities were then placed in the hands of local government, which simply did not possess the staff size (or skills) necessary to manage them; as a result, other public monies had to be allocated to finance major repair work or service extensions. It was only logical that such an approach would lack both scheduling efficiency and a real consistency in implementing action. This functional weakness on the part of Italy's local authorities, in comparison with France's, highlights a significant difference between the two countries and one that must be taken into account in order to fully assess current trends and recent Parliamentary decisions.

With respect to environmental protection regulations, Italy has, in theory, been far ahead of other countries. Back in 1976, a wastewater pollution clean-up law set out rules that were in some cases as strict as those specified in the newly-published European Directive No. 91/271. Following enactment of this law, ambitious collection network and treatment plant construction projects got under way throughout Italy's larger cities. But, here again, poor management and disorganization among the institutions assigned operational oversight resulted in a highly-dysfunctional environment and ultimately in additional expenses for the municipality. It's for this reason that the treatment plants in Naples and Bari do not run smoothly; furthermore, certain major treatment plant construction projects to serve cities like Milan and Florence have simply never come to fruition.

Warning signals and calls to reform the system have been heard ever since the end of the 1980's, also perhaps owing to the severe drought that hit the entire Mediterranean Basin between 1988 and 1990. Whatever their origin, these reformist trends (very popular in Italy during the *"Mani pulite"* campaign and the "Second Republic") have attracted the attention of the public, the media and industry both in Italy (ENI, Italcementi, FIAT, to cite just the big names) and abroad (besides French, also German, English and American firms). All those concerned have acknowledged that the time has definitely come to modernize Italy's water system.

The Parliament thus decided to drastically alter the applicable legal framework. A proposed legal reform, called the "Galli Law" after its sponsor, was introduced in 1990 and eventually approved, following a good deal of modification and adjustment, in January 1994, just a few days prior to the government's dissolution.

However, before proceeding with an analysis of the new law and its likelihood of success in advancing the system, it would first be necessary to describe the set of ground rules as well as the main problems being encountered, and rather systematically at that, within the water services sector in Italy.

The legal framework

Initially, it is important to specify the actual legal framework in place. Much like in France, the water services sector is considered a "public service", denoted as a provider of "industrial or commercial services" under the responsability of the public authority. Since the enactment of Law No. 2578 of 1925, the organising authority entrusted with overseeing this service has been the municipality itself, which is able to choose from among several types of management formulae, public or private. When it's the municipality that directly manages the service through one of the forms referred to as "public-sector management", it can select between an "in-house water services department" (analogous to the version known in France) and the "*Azienda Municipalizzata*" (a kind of municipal services establishment with its own accounting status, corporate identity and operational independence, yet lacking both financial autonomy and the status of a real private company). When the municipality elects one of the so-called "private" forms, it can either delegate management of the service to a specialized company through a concessionary contract or constitute a mixed public/private company. In either case, it is obvious that the choice of concessionaire or private partner is conducted in strict accordance with the European rules governing tender procedures within those excluded sectors.

Municipalities are entirely free to select any of the management formulae proposed, since the central government is in no position whatsoever to constrain them into opting for one particular approach. This breadth of latitude accorded local authorities is counterbalanced by a system of centralized and peripheral controls pertaining especially to sales prices (set by a Price Commission which is under the supervision of the Ministry of Industry), to water quality (controlled by State laboratories under the Ministry of Health), to water resources management (pumping and discharging in natural settings, whose oversight is shared between the Water Basin Agencies ("*Agenzie*"), provincial government and the Ministry of Environment), and to capital investment programming (determined by the Ministry of Public Works). The maneuvering room enjoyed by municipalities was noticeably restricted due to the low service rates and, consequently, due to the incapacity of financing services through exclusively municipal means, with respect to both capital investments and operations. This incapacity has only served to strengthen local-level dependence on central government. The Italian government's recent financial crisis has engendered a significant reduction in the size of public subsidies awarded to local authorities along with the push towards privatizing those sectors of the economy responsible for generating deficit.

In terms of the level of service provided to users (water pressure, flow rates, on-call services, customer services, response time, public information, etc.), the set of rules that normally apply in Italy are quite similar to those encountered in France; however, their effective compliance varies markedly from one municipality to the next. Calls for improved service lodged by citizens' groups and consumer associations are just starting to be heard. Their demands are being felt even more strongly now that mayoral races, after forty years of a proportional-based electoral system that favored the national partys' political machines, are now being decided by popular vote.

As mentioned previously, rate structures had tended towards moderation up until 1988, the year in which finance legislation required all municipalities "to set the price of water to cover at least 100% of the operating costs" (also noteworthy herein was the "obligation" for the municipalities to insure that the service was paid for). This measure, while far from being sufficient, was also somewhat ambiguously introduced since successive rate increases could not exceed the national government's projected rate of inflation. Besides, rate setting relied closely on a complex and bureaucratic system of rules that was too heavily subjected to changes in the political winds. Finally, absolutely nothing was stated concerning the ultimate investments and financial charges. (It is quite simple to imagine that, against such a backdrop wherein projecting future sales prices was impossible, private-sector investment did not appear particularly appealing.)

In exchange for keeping water and waste water bills so low (the equivalent of four to six French francs/m^3, being half the average price in France, a level which doesn't enable financing investments for building water supply facilities), municipalities and their Water Services Syndicates are eligible for long-term loans at preferential interest rates from the "Caisse des Dépôts et Consignations" (public-sector development fund). This eligibility is reserved for local authorities, since private concessionaires are not granted direct access to these funds. Such a situation has obviously favored growth among construction firms as well as specialized suppliers of plant and equipment for water treatment, whereas the service operations professionals, not easily accommodated into this framework, have been to a great extent bypassed.

The guiding legal framework is further complicated by the sheer number of applicable laws (we are aware of 62 concerning drinking water alone!) and by the fragmentation of decision-making responsibilities pertaining to water services.

The fragmentation of service operators

Fragmentation is undoubtedly another fundamental characteristic associated with this sector, not only from the standpoint of resource management, but also from that of public service operations at the municipal level. Water resource management (concerned with the entire set of problems related to extraction and discharge within the natural environment) has been placed under the formal control of the Water Basin Agencies (like in France). Yet, the lack of financial autonomy and vetoing power of these institutions has rendered them unable to achieve their designated mission, which has in turn been jointly assumed by the State, the Regions, the Provinces and local health and sanitation authorities. As far as the operations of municipal public services are concerned for Italy's 8,000-plus municipalities, a total of about 12,000 operators (public, private and mixed), responsible for managing both water and wastewater services, has been estimated. In France, England and Germany, in contrast, development of the water services industry has led to significantly higher concentrations in the number of operators.

The number and diversity of operators would not be a detriment in itself except for the fact that each case is treated practically independently from the rest. Individual operations are thus subjected to countless controls on the part of the widest array of authorities, within a chaotic legal and regulatory framework.

Among these 12,000 operators are the approximately 6,000 in-house municipal water departments (or 50% of the total) of those municipalities that manage their services through personnel reporting directly to City Hall. This type of service organization affects 32 million residents (or 57% of Italy's 56 million population). It's primarily the small and medium-sized municipalities, those most in need of technological and financial assistance and, paradoxically, those most often "overlooked" by the State, that are specifically concerned. The majority of cases of poor management, technical dysfunction and real threats to public health, which occasionally attract widespread media coverage, have arisen in these smaller municipalities. This is the jurisdictional level where appropriate water resource management is still dependent upon the personal drive of a few elected officials and technical staff, whose efforts are often disproportionately low in comparison with the magnitude and complexity of the problems faced.

A second group of operators is represented by the municipal service enterprises (called *"Municipalizzate"*), the municipal syndicates (*"Consorzi"*) and the public-sector development corporations (*"Enti Acquedottistici"*), within the regions of Sicily, Sardinia and Pouilles). This group provides water services to another 20 million residents, or 36% of the country's population.

These types of companies are wholly-owned by either the municipalities or the State, and their operating procedures have been designed along the lines of an administrative organization (hence a bureaucracy) rather than a business venture. This orientation has not, however, prevented some of these companies from enjoying a stature of considerable economic influence and outstanding service quality. This position tends to be more often encountered when they jointly run all of the so-called "technological" utility services (water, gas, public transportation, district heating, waste disposal, etc.) for large northern cities at relatively high prices and benefit from financial assistance (if not outright subsidies) from the public authorities. Such is the case for the municipal water departments in Rome, Bergamo, Bologna, Genoa and Padua, whose strong economic performances have even enabled investing significant amounts in providing services to neighboring municipalities. Rome's Municipalizzata (whose annual turnover surpasses the one-billion franc) has announced its intention to be listed on the Milan Stock Exchange.

The third group of operators consists of private firms. Within the area of drinking water supply, these companies control distribution for some 4 million residents (5% of the nation's population), under public service delegation-type contracts, that resemble the French-style concession, as well as in the form of mixed public/private companies or short-term management services contracts. In addition, cases where companies simply retain direct ownership of infrastructure networks, and thereby of a "perpetual concession", are also to be found.

Worthy of special mention within this private sector grouping would be the State-held ENI, acting through its subsidiary Italgas, which manages roughly three-fourths of all municipal services delegated to the private sector. This feature further reduces the share of the market being conferred to purely non-public firms.

In the area of wastewater services, a rather distinct difference can be noted between the management of sewer collection networks, which is carried out in practically all localities by municipal staff, and the management of water treatment plants, which is usually commissioned to specialized private firms. Treatment plants are generally subjected to short-term management contracts, often associated with maintenance and repair work or facility expansion projects wherein legal, financial and technical oversight remains with the municipality. Several hundreds of private companies operate wastewater treatment plants; outside of twenty or so medium-sized operators, this group is normally composed of smaller organizations (and in some cases family-run businesses) whose range of competence is limited and whose approach is more entrepreneurial than that of a conventional public services operator. Moreover, it should be remarked that up until the end of 1994, the service rate for collecting and treating wastewater had been established by the State at 570 liras per cubic meter (equivalent to less than two francs), an amount which didn't even allow, in the majority of instances, depreciating capital investment expenditures on the service's sales price. Public-sector financial assistance has thus become the rule in this service area, and, along the same lines, the use of concessions is next to unknown.

Guiding principles behind the sector's reform

The portrait of the current situation could appear a bit bleak. The fact that most Italians have learned to adapt to crisis situations concerning their water's quality or quantity means the problem has not yet developed to a state of real emergency. A sort of tentative equilibrium has been reached: for example, the population's reflex to never drink tap water limits the impact of occasional accidental contamination. In return, the market for bottled water has exploded over the past several years, generating jobs and a whole new set of small-sized companies. Another example: within municipalities where the quantity of water is not sufficient to provide a 24-hour-a-day level of service, households have procured small tanks, with enough capacity to meet daily consumption needs, which automatically fill up whenever water is flowing in the distribution mains. It is true however that water services in these municipalities are typically provided free of charge.

Such a fragile equilibrium could evolve towards a more modernized system by means of massive capital investment to put this sector's "house in order", something the current state of public finances can no longer permit. Faced with a shortfall in public monies, local authorities are being forced to seek alternative solutions for financing and running these services. They have increasingly been relying upon private concessionary companies or upon public-sector development corporations prepared to invest in this sector. The pursuit of a new balance between actors, financial considerations and remaining technical problems have all been catalysts behind the recently-adopted legislation governing water.

The new legislation on water services

First and foremost, it should be mentioned that this law (Law No. 36 of 4 January 1994, entitled "Measures concerning water resources") has been shaped along the lines of both England's privatization reform of its Water Authorities and the French model for delegating public services to specialized firms.

Among its distinct features, the law calls for dividing Italy's land area into "optimal hydrological basins" (*Ambiti Territoriali Ottimali*, or ATOs), which correspond to homogeneous zones from a hydrogeological perspective (for example, by equivalent water resources, by homogeneous wastewater disposal environments, by the presence of extensive water distribution piping networks, etc.) as well as from an economic one (sufficient number of users to justify sizable capital investments, similarity of operating conditions, etc.). These territorial divisions (whose governing principles were established by law and applied by the Regional authorities) have created a kind of "concentration" whereby all problems related to service fragmentation could be resolved simultaneously. Such a concentration is witnessed from a geographical standpoint, by the grouping of water and wastewater services throughout all localities situated within the same ATO, in addition to a technical one. It has been planned that all activities in the areas of water production, conveyance and distribution, along with those in the collection and treatment of wastewater, be managed by one single operator covering the entire ATO. As an example, plans project that future ATOs will encompass at least 100 municipalities, comprising a minimum of 200,000 population (and up to 4 million in the case of the Rome Metropolitan Area). On this basis, the number of ATOs for all of Italy has been estimated at between 100 and 200. Municipalities remain responsible for service provision, even though they're being collectively represented by Municipal Syndicates, called *"Autorita di ATO"*. The relationships between local authorities -ATO-

and the operator are to be regulated by a Collective Management Agreement, which will be drawn up by the regional government.

Each operator ("*Soggetto Gestore*") within each ATO must achieve a set of ambitious objectives consisting of managing, financing, scheduling, building, maintaining and fully developing all facilities and services for every locality constituting the ATO. The operator alone will oversee all relationships with the service's users, control agencies, financial institutions and elected officials. It will be held to offer a service of exceptionally high quality in strict accordance with the rules adopted by the European Community. Its sole source of remuneration will consist of the "S.I.I." sales price (Integrated Hydrological Services), which will be specific to each ATO.

Application of the reform

While the reform's more theoretical framework would appear rather straightforward, its application has been slowed (or even thoroughly reconsidered) because of a number of obstacles. In the first place, the law sets out the general rules but, with respect to their application, refers back to decrees issued by the Ministry of Public Works and the Ministry of Environment as well as to the body of laws governing Italy's nineteen administrative regions and two autonomous provinces. For the time being, one single ministerial decree has been promulgated. The regional authorities have been very slow in defining geographical boundaries for the ATOs and in drafting the "Operating Agreement". The local authorities have not yet even been consulted. The updated rate structure is still being negotiated... The first obstacle to tackle therefore is the bureaucratic slowness of the State and the Regions in applying the law.

In reality, this slow response is justified to a large extent when the specific problems that the application decrees were designed to solve are examined closely. The price of water is too low and doesn't cover the operating and investment charges. Its increase is considered by all concerned parties as a vital precondition for this sector's reorganization. However, price increases translate into highly unpopular measures, and no elected policy-maker wishes to assume the responsibility of announcing such a decision in front of his electorate. The leaders of the parliamentary majority (Forza Italia, Alleanza Nazionale and Lega Nord) campaigned under the banner of no new taxes, and thus cannot make any exception for water services (which are considered, as mentioned earlier, to be social, guaranteed services whose price is often absorbed into a local tax). In addition, mayors do not relish announcing severe measures, inasmuch as they know that reforming this sector will deprive them of control over their own municipal services. Regional governments, assigned to carry out the reforms, are in fact furthest from the reality of the situation: the resources (in terms of personnel and financial support) at their disposal are extremely diminished; their expertise in handling technical operations problems for local water distribution is often limited. This absence of power and responsibility during the service's transitional period is another quintessential characteristic; yet, it's one that mustn't frighten, since it's only normal that reforming such an important sector for a country be conducted with serenity and respect for the necessary scheduling constraints.

Another obstacle however remains to be overcome, one that concerns the choice of firms intended to become "*Soggetto Gestore*" for one or several ATOs. It's thereby necessary to establish effective ground rules by applying the appropriate European Directives for awarding public-sector contracts. These rules are intended to stimulate competition between, on the one hand, municipal service enterprises and public development corporations, which seek to maintain (or even expand) their service territories, and, on the other, private firms attempting to increase their share of the market. And this competitive battle promises to be especially hard-fought.

The municipal service enterprises can at times be solid and well-structured enough to take on new capital investments in other municipalities. These operators are thus considered, and deservedly so, as preferential candidates for absorbing small municipal water service departments. In this sense, they are expanding their service territory within the defined ATO boundaries by incorporating additional municipal operations into the originally-created water service enterprise (which is often located in the ATO's largest city). The ultimate goal would be to develop organizations sized in what may be considered an "optimal" fashion. According to some observers, this process of concentration could be performed as a gradual, "soft-pedaled" approach without resorting to a tender procedure. The fundamental problem is specifically ideological in nature. Against the backdrop of a historic period, during which all nations including Italy are favoring economic privatization, this growth in municipal service enterprises represents a countertrend moving towards nationalizing a promising sector of activity.

Private firms, in contrast, will be systematically subjected to competitive bidding procedures for contracts involving construction and services management. They would prefer competing directly with public operators for the ATO operations assignments, and look on with interest at the concentration of municipal departments within certain organizations that hold substantial economic clout.

Future trends - Conclusions

For the time being, however, no ATO has been created; the decrees enforcing application are still pending; and the new rate structure is still being defined. The situation would appear once again to have reached a standstill.

And yet, private firms possessing high levels of technical competence are starting to be commissioned by municipalities. Growing tired of waiting and wary of neighboring cities' municipal enterprises, they have conferred their water services to private operators through a tender process. As a result, water rates have started to rise in proportion with actual operating charges and with improvements in the quality of service.

In this context, even though it remains difficult to project evolutions and trends, one thing is certain: the current system is in the process of transforming towards more modern and efficient means of management, with more realistic price levels. The presence of a distinct split between the operations activity, contracted out to either public or private specialized firms, and the activities of programming and control, reserved for public-sector institutions, is now readily apparent. The market share that will open up for private firms depends primarily on the capacity of each party to be present, convincing and effective. Refining the legal and regulatory framework will be carried out at a determined pace, and a host of different solutions will most likely be developed. Italy is distinguishing itself, in this sector like in many others, as a country that's difficult to describe, to comprehend and to assess.

Dominique
Lorrain

Lessons from the experience

Several notions serve as a backdrop for this book's chapters. Urban growth and environmental concerns give rise to new problems in urban history and have resulted in the involvement of major firms. The entry of the large firm within the "local" universe of city government is creating a totally novel situation. An asymmetry that we deem structural exists between these firms and local public authorities. How should one thereby go about organizing these markets under satisfactory conditions for public authority, user and firm alike.

One response comes to us from the latest developments in economics derived primarily from the regulation of the telecommunications and electricity industries - theories of imperfect equilibria, contract economics (see references at the end of the introduction). The use of incentive-based contracts, the separation between monopoly-run infrastructure and services open to competition, the theory of the principal agent, the transition from "cost plus"-type remuneration formulae to those featuring a "price cap" are but some of the improvements that have enhanced techniques for organizing urban infrastructure markets. Do these solutions comprise an appropriate response to the problem of urban utility networks? only in part.

Let's begin with the contributions presented in this book. Without admitting so, they do draw the contours of one approach to formulating the question. All speak about the role of geography and of economic conditions; they've all felt the need to lay the historical context. Some have described the utility network - length, age, state of repair. The message is clear: the socio-economics of urban utility networks cannot be dissociated from their long-run historical experience, from technical and geographical constraints, from lifestyle considerations or from politics. In other words, the analysis of urban utility services cannot be boiled down to a few financial indicators. The solution won't be derived from a unique "mathematical formula" that would adjust the relationship between public authority and operator. This manner of presenting the problem leads us to position urban utilities at the crossroads of three major bodies of social theory: constitutional economics along with Law Economics, since the intention herein is to examine "the choice of constraints" before tackling the "choices within the constraints"; Industrial Economics, to help devise solutions that are optimal from a technical/financial standpoint; Political Science and Law, which draw us to assess the foundations of public service categories (in France, Duguit, Aurioux) and to reread Rawls and his "theory of social justice".

From this base, several lessons stand out from a reading of the various chapters. First and foremost, the *time factor* appears critical, as exposed by the experiences of French cities. The problem of long-run management - inherent in this type of service network - constitutes a limitation to contract economics. The examples, which we've addressed in this book, highlight that the predictive power of contractual parties, over periods of several decades, diminishes and contracts tend to function much like learning processes for both the public authority and the firms.

Next stands out *the political dimension*. It can virtually be deleted in the case of electricity and telecommunications; this deletion becomes all the more difficult for urban utility networks, which are too closely-tied to the physical structure of cities, to their way of government and to issues concerning justice and fairness. The action framework must also encompass, right from the outset, the politician himself, who introduces the notion of limited rationality, a classic result from organizational sociology and one that's built as a reaction to the all-powerful rational actor "homo economicus". The examples from various foreign countries serve to reinforce this dimension that the French cities have also exhibited.

These two dimensions - long-run time frame and limited rationality - thereby combine with one another to shape the contract not as an ultimate moment in itself but instead a step that stabilizes a relationship at a given point in time and that must be allowed to evolve.

Another key result has to do with the "how" side of the question. How is it possible to obtain a stable and fair relationship between public authority and private firm? Consideration accorded these various case studies, within the scope of their overall diversity, leads to focusing on two critical notions - *conditions preliminary to action* and the *means of system calibration*: prior to the contract? vs. during its execution? These two notions together thus enable tracing the complete spectrum of situations, from the most satisfactory to the most difficult. At one extreme, we encounter the case of Sydney which combines good preliminary conditions with quality preparation before the contract. At the other extreme is the Caracas example, or that of French cities at the beginning of the history of urban utility services, towards the end of the XIXth century, at a time when preliminary conditions remained insufficient.

How should these borderline cases be handled? If the preliminary conditions are essential to stimulate collective action, how can action be undertaken as long as what's preliminary remains deficient? In short, to break through this impasse and since waiting does prove impossible, actors commence their work under imperfect conditions. The examples treated herein provide support for this vision of collective action. The shaping of an action framework entails preliminary phases, tenuous stability, with experiences turning out for better or worse, partial agreements, followed by tentatives that can sometimes be premature. Action can be carried out in a precipitated manner, without any kind of rational approach; it can also be criticized, yet it remains the necessary detour for actors to begin their learning process. This way of describing situations incites variable action strategies, depending on the scenario in question.

Management over the long run

In reading over the chapters covering the case studies in France, the feature that emerges with the most salience is the length of the relationship developed between large service provision firms and city government: nearly one hundred and fifty years in Lyons, and ninety-two in Bordeaux. What is behind this exceptional durability? The obvious response would be the particular strategies employed by companies, which consist of setting up operations in a municipality, striving to win the trust of local elected officials and municipal employees alike, as well as pleasing its customers. Once this territorial base has been secured, firms expand their "turf". In the city of Lyons, the Compagnie Générale des Eaux started with the metropolitan area's central city, though at the time relations were not smooth. The company then set up a base in the surrounding areas, thus enabling it to remain within the metropolitan area when its role as service provider for the central city was lost in 1900. It would eventually come back eighty-six years later as the entire metropolitan area's sole operator. Quite the opposite scenario in Bordeaux where the Lyonnaise des Eaux began operating rather modestly in 1903 in the suburbs, only to focus its activities on the central city at a later date. Essentially, these relationships owe their durability to the establishment of a legal framework that's both detailed enough to focus activities yet flexible enough to allow managing over the long run.

Time as a critical factor. Implementing the kind of solutions that can cover an entire urban area did not happen all at once. A long period of time, from 1928 to 1949 to be precise, was necessary to merge each of the contracts signed with individual suburban municipalities around Lyons into one single contract governing all the member municipalities of a joint syndicate together. Time was also required to assuage political tempers stirred by the debate pitting public management and private management against one another as was the case in Lyons. Time was once again needed in order to reduce tension between central city and suburban communities. In Bordeaux, Lyonnaise des Eaux began in 1903 with a concession to serve two suburban municipalities; its service area expanded between 1925 and 1933 with other operations contracts, still exclusively in the suburbs. In 1949, it became responsible for service throughout the metropolitan area, yet in this instance under an incentive management formula, before finally being granted, in 1992, a water and wastewater services concession covering a large portion of the whole area.

Worth retaining from the example of these two cities is the gradient of institutional approaches available that enable adapting to the wishes of elected officials, over time.

Flexibility or imprecision in system design? It is clear that for a long time, elected officials were entering into contracts which were not sufficiently prepared - at least in comparison with current standards: ninety-nine-year contract, irrevocable before thirty years, signed by the City of Lyons in 1853; separate contracts signed by the suburban municipalities without any coordination whatsoever among them and whose standardization would require waiting twenty years. Retrospectively, it could be stated that the local authorities took risks. Nonetheless, over time, satisfactory solutions were indeed found.

In Bordeaux, it could also be observed that relations have not always been optimal. The incentive management contract, along with its "cost plus incentive" remuneration scheme, provided a comfortable position for the firm from a financial standpoint, even if its position, from the standpoint of industrial strategy, proved rather uncomfortable. In 1990, a new concessionary contract was drawn up very quickly; some would even say too quickly. And yet, it works; the system is balanced. The various actors are redefining the action framework and addressing all outstanding points.

The contract as a learning process. It's necessary to recognize in these results one very important property. These long-term contracts, dedicated to the resolution of practical problems, also perform the function of learning tools both for local authorities and for urban services companies. The two contractual parties set out with a "soft framework", a limited set of objectives, and act within the dual constraint of performance and profitability. With this as a backdrop, they work to build a collective action framework, which is distinguished by the partial revision of contracts and the adoption of amendments. "The agreement of 1970, signed in Lyons, has experienced an average of one amendment every two and a half years." It's a building process that can take a good chunk of time.

The system is also an interactive one. While the firm does make proposals to the local authorities, it nonetheless evolves in relation to the authorities' requests. The quality of the institutional framework helps explain the behavior adopted by the firm. In Lyons, for example, C.G.E. would only evolve once the suburban communities had formed one unique syndicate in 1928 to express their requests with more clarity. The company would adjust its behavior to the expectations of its partner. Even to this day, the quality of the requests formulated by the local public partner - elected officials and municipal staff - plays a key role in guiding the firm's actions.

From this discussion, one should retain: i) within an interactive setting, clearly laying out the ground rules on the part of the public authority tends to raise the level of performance; ii) yet, since forecasting all eventualities is impossible, some amount of flexibility should be built in so as to allow the actors to modify the rules with respect to observed results.

Cooperation through technical means. Water represents the public service area in which the very first intermunicipal organizations were implemented. It was at this point in time that local elected officials learned to work together with a scope much broader than the immediate concerns of their respective municipalities. As demonstrated in the example of intermunicipality in Bordeaux, the application of a single service fee served as a mechanism to equalize rates between wealthier and poorer municipalities, as well as between central city and outlying areas. The rate structure utilized in the central city enabled equipping the suburbs, thereby providing for the expansion of the urban development zone. In accepting such a mechanism, municipal officials acknowledged the loftier principle of serving metropolitan-wide interests.

Urban utility networks have been, for French politicians, a sort of management training ground. They got exposure to other approaches; they learned to combine technical efficiency with the principles of social justice by means of a service rate, to incorporate a wider concept of metropolitan territory into their decision framework, and to reconcile day-to-day management with major, long-run capital investment programs. This evolution in methodology has been very important not only for city government but also for the policies adopted by the urban services firms. Smoothing political tempers and acknowledging economic arguments on the part of elected officials represent the kind of factors that foster the development of firms; an inverse approach would limit them into sub-optimal solutions.

Also to be retained from the discussions presented herein is that the introduction of private-sector operators within public service areas, dominated for the most part by public actors enjoying territorial monopoly statuses, has given rise to a certain level of competition. The existence of a highly-efficient private component has spurred reforms in the domain of city management.

Another notion worth retaining from these lessons is that of a dual vector for modernizing city management: i) the transfer of know-how from the service provision firm to the body of elected officials, and ii) the introduction of a competitive environment including public actors.

Two ways to structure the transfer of knowledge. The history of delegated management for water services displays several distinct approaches to structuring public authority control over the contracted firm. In Nimes, France, between 1969 and 1983, local officials were heavily involved with managing the city's water service, most certainly to a greater extent than explicitly specified in the leasing agreement. Representatives from both the contracted firm and the municipality met on a regular basis. From 1983 on, the new municipal team began applying more private-sector-oriented management practices -objective-based management. The primary advantage registered from this revised approach: a clarification between decision-maker - the public authority - and operator. Another advantage consisted in time savings for each party, by cutting down on the number of meetings. Yet, with the experience gained over time, reliance on these applied management methods in performing city management can raise some serious questions.

How exactly do control procedures facilitate the transfer of expertise from firms to municipal officials? This issue of stimulating the learning process, raised forcefully in developing countries, is brought back to the fore. The Nimes example serves to highlight that the informal procedures drawing extensive participation from local political figures offer the advantage of being quite rich in terms of information actually exchanged. In contrast, stricter management control procedures, emanating from corporate control methods, fosters the separation of the two worlds, requires just a very limited amount of information, and only works well when both partners are placed in positions of equal strength.

Limited rationality and the political dimension

A major part of the economic theory of monopoly market regulation for utility services was originally developed from the sectors of electricity and telecommunications. These sectors were predominantly set up, in France as well as elsewhere, without the involvement of local public authorities, thereby centering the issue on the behavior of firms, the rationality of the engineering methods employed and the behavior of consumers. Against the backdrop of urban utilities, and water services in particular, enters the figure of the elected representative. Such a scenario is especially accurate in France where the local elected official is definitely the organising authority. In other countries, even if the guiding legal framework is different, political impacts can't be altogether excluded as long as certain decisions depend either on input from politicians -setting rates, collecting outstanding payment - or directly on city management functions-implementing a works program. This figure of the elected official introduces into the public service provision models another dimension to the process's rationality.

The water cycle is a complex system supporting diversified use patterns at various territorial scales. Managing this resource in a rational manner, given this level of complexity, requires several actors and cooperation among several territorial jurisdictions - the localities at the site of operations, the river basin to control allocation of water and the State in a coordinating capacity. Accommodating these various interests cannot solely be carried out by technical institutions. The presence of the political perspective along with conflicts of interests can simply not be circumvented.

At the time Bordeaux's "Communauté Urbaine" was created in 1968, water and wastewater services were considered part of its obligatory domain of responsibility. Nonetheless, a few municipalities did prefer maintaining their independence, while some municipal syndicates outside the Communauté Urbaine joined in the overall provision of water and wastewater services metropolitan area-wide. Same sequence of events took place in Lyons in that when the first intermunicipal syndicate for water distribution was created in 1928, all of the suburban communities didn't necessarily participate outright. It took waiting until the creation of the Communauté Urbaine in order for the geographical boundaries of the intermunicipal syndicate to coincide more closely with the urban services zone. The net result was an obvious increase in the complexity of institutional organizations. Querying more deeply into the meaning behind these systems can sometimes lead to the conclusion that the entire process would be smoother with a broad-based and mandatory intermunicipal framework, or even with one sole institution. Quite possibly so.

The following long-run observation stands out: patterns of collective action simply reflect the morale of the day, the practices at a specific point in time. They represent a pragmatic social construction associated first of all with resolving problems and not with illustrating a particular dogma. Over time, flexible and adaptable approaches prove their worth over more rigid ones.

Political rationality of decision-making processes. Decision-making relies on more than just purely rational logic. The political equation also enters into play. In 1969, Nimes city officials opted for the solution proposed by the SAUR most certainly because it spared them a costly capital outlay - a new water conveyance pipeline - that the electorate/taxpayers didn't consider a priority. For twenty years, they put off the decision to replace this piping system which had been built back in 1904. Over more than thirty years, from 1930 to 1963, Lyons' municipal water department, which had taken over the service from C.G.E., would not carry out any major investments, as residents and politicians alike were content with the infrastructure completed in the 1920's. Additional expenditure didn't strike them as a priority.

Decisions are made under the dual condition of technical imperativeness and political acceptability.

Variable appreciation of time scales depending on type of actor. Program implementation is not performed in a strictly linear fashion. Two distinct time scales are observed:
- The long run of facility construction programs that often exceeds the planning horizon, quite simply because revenues are lower than

expected, new needs arise, and the development of major, highly-technical infrastructure remains a distinctly complex operation; and
- The short run of politicians, punctuated by elections and crises. Decision-making often takes place amidst a climate of urgency, as was the case in Lyons and Bordeaux, and is so nowadays in Gdansk, Caracas and Indonesia.

This observation lends a practical result. While the juxtaposition of short run with long run proceeds from decision-making mechanisms in democracies, it is undoubtedly quite utopic to imagine that rational preparedness could actually envision all potential events. The case studies presented herein reveal that defining the contract is just one of the milestones within a much longer process.

The role of crisis moments in decision-making and adopting new strategies. The operative mechanism that has served to shake decision-makers out of their routine appears as an invariant:
- cholera epidemic in Lyons in 1928 that incited suburban municipalities to form a single syndicate following several years spent in the planning stages, - water intake at the main pumping plant being shut due to freezing in Lyons in 1963; the City would discover the work schedule delays present within its department, and would thereby undertake a very ambitious capital investment program that would require thirty years to complete. - flooding in Bordeaux (1982) and Nimes (1988) serving to stimulate sizable rainwater collection investment programs. - collapse of the public model in Caracas and Buenos Aires, - system-wide crisis in Gdansk,
- a multiplicity of problems, delays and underinvestment in Macao.

These examples display a gap between the decision-making context characterized by a sense of urgency, high drama and even sometimes the fervor and recommendations of consultants who envision a purely rational process, where all parameters could be exposed, compared and evaluated. If the "crisis", the unforeseen occurrence, is an integral component in the process, then what transpires following the decision takes on fundamental importance. Put otherwise, a balance must be held between the quality of the preparatory procedures and the mechanisms of self-correction. The proper balance in reform measures must accord as much emphasis on preparation as on ongoing control.

Contributions of the large firm

Two years after the start-up of operations at Aguas de Argentinas, tangible results have been recorded: 530,000 additional residents receive household water service; 300,000 more are hooked up to the wastewater collection network; service has been improved for all users; 250 million US$ have been invested throughout the service network; the firm has realized profit thanks to better commercial management and productivity gains; and the user has witnessed a drop in service rates of 14% on average in comparison with the rate at the time the tender was announced. This highly-exemplary case, by virtue of its sheer magnitude, illustrates the contributions provided by a specialized large firm.

The same observations could be evoked in the cases of Macao, Gdansk and Sydney. By carrying out investments rapidly, by optimizing management of the technical system, by reestablishing commercial policies and to a wider extent customer relations, the presence of these firms on the scene has enabled, over relatively short time spans, substantially improving service to consumers.

As a consequence these results are merely verifying economic properties. In being transformed from the state of a natural resource to one of an industrial commodity, the area of water services is thereby subjected to the same economic rules as are other industrial sectors. The key strategic issue brought to the fore is to determine the conditions under which productivity gains can be realized. It's the debate on the means for structuring markets that reappears in this context: a dispersed competitive market of medium-sized firms vs. a monopoly market exclusively for large firms. This issue warrants in-depth examination from a strictly economic perspective based on observations of contrasting situations.

An actor for change. Several examples, water in rural Mali, Italy and Caracas, remind us of Schumpeter's truth: a market economy cannot exist without enterprise and without entrepreneur. The importance of the individuals and their direct involvement is one of the lessons to be retained from Mali's rural water services. This example clearly highlights the necessity of an "active actor" who mobilizes resources, insures service continuity, maintains equipment and charges a fair price since free water obviously gives rise to wastage. The stalemate encountered in Italy can be interpreted from the standpoint of this market entry. The heavyweights in the field demonstratively line up in support of the city, while the reformers have already been opting, for a good length of time now, for transferring responsibilities to the regional level. The corresponding legal framework exists, yet it has only been partially developed. Regions are supposed to organize service provision; however, responsibility for operations will remain with the cities.

The service approach, be receptive to deciders. One factor in the success of these firms relates to their capacity to respond to the expectations of elected officials. Several of the cases presented illustrate this point perfectly.

In 1969, Nimes' Communist city councillors, who were delegating the city's water services at the time, wanted the firm to carry out certain capital investments, to assume control over existing facilities and to take over their operations, hence responsibilities which normally place the contract somewhere between a concession and a lease. Yet, they also sought to be tightly associated with the management function. The firm adapted its strategy: it created an ad hoc subsidiary; it adopted a type of operating approach very close to that of a fixed-fee management contract.

In Bordeaux from 1949 to 1992, the operator provided service according to an incentive management contract formula; nonetheless, on several occasions, he additionally participated in specific investment programs, most certainly in order to compensate for public finance restrictions.

These instances indicate that firms are adaptable to the requests placed upon them by organizing authorities and that the contractual formula originally adopted never actually constrain the behavior of either party.

The service approach, training staff members and educating the consumer. This aspect represents a factor that helps distinguish a service-based approach from a public works based approach. For an urban service operations company, the quality of its personnel, its level of technical competence and its overall motivation are very critical factors. This feature is especially apparent for work performed outside of France. In Macao, Gdansk, Buenos Aires, the Ivory Coast and Guinea, operators have developed their own training programs; in essence, they've been transferring their know-how. Eventually, they'll provide service with local staff who will be able to participate in the group's other expansion policies. Herein lies the special attention these operators grant their workforce right from the time the network's service is first taken over.

On several occasions - Gdansk, Ivory Coast, Guinea - they've also focused on consumer behavior in order to avoid wastage and to fully explain the rate structure.

The importance of preliminary conditions

For a relationship to bond, it's initially essential that the set of preliminary conditions for action be satisfied all at once: an empowered public authority, a financial market, legal rules, standards and norms, a rate revision procedure, etc. These stipulations, if well-structured, tend to fade into the backdrop for the actors within the process, yet quickly return to center stage if they prove insufficient.

Nowadays, a great number of countries are seeking to pursue the path of reform without really knowing exactly what they want. Their references originate from the relationships cultivated between their ministries and the major public-sector corporations within the fields of energy or telecommunications. Local experience is quite often lacking in these types of situations. The challenge faced by other countries looms even larger. They emanate from a centralized system that leaves little room for the market, and current trends are attracting them to proceed towards a market economy within a decentralized institutional environment.

The example of Caracas demonstrates well the importance of this context and the magnitude of the difficulties involved. From the outset, a breakdown in confidence impacts the public-sector model discussed earlier on, while at the same time, instability creeps into the ground rules laid out:
- uncertainty over the service's financing and over the rate-setting policy; it's clear at this juncture that the problem is fundamentally political in nature as previously-held perceptions are being dramatically altered - given the change from 1 Bolivar/m^3 of water to roughly 36 Bolivars/m^3.
- lack of choice in the service's overall regulation - applicable legal code, standards, rate-setting guidelines, etc.
- uncertainty over the appropriate jurisdictional level of authority for the service: from the nationwide level all the way down to the municipality.
- need for clarification in assigning responsibilities between the public authority and the firm; as a result, the firm's work gets relegated to a short-run outlook, becomes disjointed with politicians meddling all too often in their attempts at settling problems.

So many issues go unresolved that the partners to the service contract are not able to dialog smoothly and this privatization effort ends up as a failure. Beyond each of these unsettled difficulties which are representative of negotiation roadblocks, the experience was confronted with an incompatible set of practices which all together form a system. In seeking to reform the water distribution service, a seemingly technical procedure, the actors were in fact organizing to a certain extent a redistribution of revenue within the country, were adjusting a delicate balance between civil society and politics, and between lifestyle choices. Ultimately, it was this density and complexity of social relationships that doomed the Caracas initiative.

Such resistance to the system in place, that tends to focus primarily on the rate structure, can also be found in other countries - Ivory Coast, Guinea, Mali and even Italy. The "right" solution would be to charge an appropriate price in order to reduce wastage and to generate operating revenue. Yet, no single actor has the political clout to impose this kind of measure. Obtaining payment of the water service rates charged proves difficult in cases where incomes are too low or where free services have become customary. The Italian setting reminds us of the significance of the political element.

So, what's to be done? What can be done when ownership rights have not been established? or when financial conditions have not been fixed over time? or when the local population, at all rungs of society, considers that water should be provided free of charge? or when too few households are connected to the network?

The Guinean example highlights the necessity of managing over the long run and of allowing for institutional and technological transitions:
- institutional transitions: In light of potential risks and poor rates of return on investment, there will be no service privatization through sale of assets but rather delegated management - meaning the granting of use rights by the public authority. One of the institutional roles will be to modify behavior patterns, to explain the dual nature of water - public service component vs. industrial commodity - and to set an example. Time must be allocated for the training of local-level decision-makers. Financing arrangements could be set up such that the cost of billings is reduced by imputing part of the financial charges onto the subsidies accorded.
- technological transitions: Might not it be somewhat illusory to seek to reproduce the Occidental model for household water distribution everywhere and all at once? Between household water delivery services and water-carriers, the appropriate solution lies in quality networks and in water fountains managed by an operator actually selling water at a price, as displayed in Mali, the Ivory Coast and Guinea.

Methods for organizing cooperation

The cases presented in this book, by virtue of their diversity, serve to instruct us on the methods for establishing a partnership between public authority and service provision firm. Once a set of minimal preliminary conditions has been specified, actors are presented a choice between two approaches for developing a satisfactory long-term relationship; we often speak herein of a system calibration. This calibration may be performed before the signing of the contract, a step which orients us towards several recent experiences often influenced by English and American examples. On the other hand, actors may elect to adopt a more basic contract and to calibrate the system during its execution, a situation more closely resembling French-styled pragmatism such as it has been applied over a long period of time.

Between these two techniques, the contrast is not necessarily absolute; rather it's a question of the proper dosing with respect to the point in time when the effort to clarify contractual terms is actually exerted: prior to vs. during execution. From an observation of those experiences yielding satisfactory results, there is clearly no one single approach. The field of urban services management is situated too close to an overlapping of a variety of moral grounds, customs and political regimes to be structured around one distinct framework.

TABLE 1
To organize cooperation

System Calibration	Preliminary Conditions		
	Good	**Minimal**	**Insufficient**
Before	Sydney, Buenos Aires	Gdansk, Conakry	Indonesia, Caracas 2
During	Lyons 2, Bordeaux, Nimes, Macao	Lyons 1, Abidjan	Caracas 1

Good preliminary conditions and calibration before action. The Sydney experience without question illustrates this type of scenario. It combines preliminary conditions of a particularly strong quality with high-level professionalism in conducting the final selection process. From the beginning, the Water Board created a very professionally-oriented task force. The procedure was laid out into three stages that allowed smoothly moving from an initial step of formulating a statement of interest all the way to the final step of signing a contract. The various stages enabled refining project definitions as well as reducing the number of competitors from 17, down to 10 and ultimately to 5 with whom more detailed negotiations were conducted. This outcome can also be explained by the amount of time devoted to the proposal review process. The entire process lasted almost two and a half years; the decision to build four water treatment plants was taken by the Water Board at the beginning of 1991, and it was in September 1993 that the contract for the Prospect plant, the largest of the four, was signed.

In Buenos Aires, all observers concur that the operation's success should be attributed to the government, which was able to direct a global privatization program without any previous experience. The Argentine government was largely assisted by a group of experts contracted by the World Bank and company teams of specialists. The climate of trust that surrounded these privatization programs served to instill credibility in the eyes of the financial community for this water project. In other words, the quality of the prerequisite conditions for action did facilitate the efforts to delegate water services. The construction work carried out between the 1991 privatization decision and the concessionary contract award at the end of 1993 enhanced the level of preparedness.

Minimal preliminary conditions and calibration before action. This scenario describes a situation wherein the conditions for implementation prove more complicated owing to weaknesses in the overall institutional environment. Actors have specifically set aside their time in order to develop an appropriate institutional framework. The Gdansk case concerned the first ever experience of service delegation in a former Eastern bloc country. And even if the preparation process in this case was less international in scope than for Sydney or Buenos Aires, a whole year would nonetheless be required to complete direct contract negotiations along with another eight months for negotiating the statutes of the company. In Guinea, the task at hand was immense considering the delays engendered as well as the practices adopted under the previous regime. The World Bank and its team of experts played a tremendous role in assisting the government, both in managing the entire negotiation process and in participating during the project period that followed.

Minimal preliminary conditions and calibration during action. The French experience provides us with another interpretation. At the beginning of these privately-run operations, or around the turn of the century, the preliminary conditions were at a minimum, a good number of elements remained unknown and yet the calibration of the authority-firm relationship would occur during the execution of the contract. Herein were combined the actors' poor state of preparedness with flexible contracts. System learning took place in the field under real operating conditions and not without its moments of difficulties as illustrated by the Lyons example from the past (Lyons 1). "Operating conditions have proved unsatisfactory for both parties involved...; while the rates they're charging are excessive, the company is still complaining about the City's wastefulness in its use of water for street cleaning purposes." A lack of preparedness can provoke distrust of the elected officials; again in the Lyons case, this would correspond with the City's water department taking over responsibility for service provision in 1900, and the creation of the suburban intermunicipal syndicate in 1928, intended to present a united front opposite the power of the private operator.

Satisfactory preliminary conditions, calibration during action. Later on in the French cases, the presence of well-qualified actors in technical, legal and financial areas along with the practice of working together would serve to authorize the quick implementation of contracts. Action programs relied on a climate of trust. Falling into this category would be the examples of Lyons in 1986 (Lyons 2), Bordeaux in 1992 and Macao in 1985. It could be added that the contracts signed in French cities also consist of this type. In comparison with Sydney or Buenos Aires, preparation time is significantly less.

Macao is an extremely interesting case that functions in some respects according to a French-styled pattern: selection of the firm Sino-French without an actual international competitive tender; quick decision-making process; and global level of responsibility held by the operator over both production and distribution. This example aptly demonstrates the advantages of a flexible action framework:
- speed in implementing the capital investment program (the initial contacts date back to the summer of 1984), the contract was signed in the middle of 1985, and the first four-year works plan took effect at the beginning of 1986.
- mobilization of the firm's human resources right from the start in order to define solution strategies.

As a result of this classification, the following points are to be retained:
- When preliminary conditions are lacking, it becomes most unlikely to reach a result no matter what approach had been adopted. Solutions always run into obstacles at one point or another.
- When preliminary conditions are minimal, actors can get involved directly, but they run the risk of paying, during the course of the action being carried out, the cost of system calibration that they would have avoided at the contract's entry into application. Taking the time to insure preparedness therefore proves its worth, especially in cases of "total delegation"[1]. However, it's the nature of the mission that's determinant; at this point, the gradient of contract forms is going to enter into significant consideration. Actors can compensate for a weak level of preparedness by a "limited delegation" contract - operations & maintenance, operations contract, "contracting out" formula, incentive management contract or fixed-fee management contract -

---

1. See the introduction chapter for these terms- limited delegation, total delegation.

which provides them with the possibility of system learning during actual service operations.

- When preliminary conditions are good, it is then possible to establish the relationship on a professional footing; the chances of success are strong; the approach will depend on customary practices and particularly on how well the partners know one another. An initial choice requires adequate preparation time to reach a high level of calibration. The familiarity of working together enables a rapid signature of the contract.

Several questions remain regardless of the approach adopted.

What is the cost of careful preparation? It is most certainly rather high. Does the effort undertaken at the outset of the contract's application protect the partners from unexpected events, or even crises, over the course of the contractual period? It's well understood that the strategic question consists of knowing just how far one should go in calibrating the system prior to the action phase, given that beyond a certain time frame, forecasts tend to lose their predictive power.

When preparation time is shorter like in France or Macao, what are the guarantees provided to the public authority? What are the contractual clauses that serve to protect the authority in case of a serious crisis?

Ultimately, one question remains: what is the cost of inaction?, a question that takes us back to Caracas. In following the description presented to us, this experience has been marked by two successive stages. The first, discrete phase (Caracas 1), during which the government negotiated with the local electric company, that was being supported by French firms. This phase was not seen through to fruition and was heavily criticized for its lack of rigor. The reform process thereby entered into a new phase (Caracas 2), accompanied by design studies and an international tender that likewise wasn't followed through to completion. The strategic question that comes to the fore in this light is to know whether it wouldn't be more beneficial, after all, that the initial negotiation is taken to completion even if it does have imperfections. Once the actors were committed and the problems arose, they would have been obliged to seek compromises and move on at any rate.

Where are the risks and for whom?

The fact that a local authority would enter into a long-term contractual relationship with a major firm - who, in addition, is foreign - can't help but arouse inquiry. Can the relationship existing between the two parties be a balanced one and under what conditions? Where are the real risks located? Let's take a closer look at a few points.

- Can the market be contested? Is it possible to turn back the clock? The fear expressed is that the dearth of expertise on the part of the public-sector partner makes any alternative to the private operator simply impossible. To resolve this problem the public authority has the choice between two fundamental solutions. The first solution is to maintain a more atomistic market which moves us closer to the cases of "limited delegation" as presented in the introduction, since the number of potential market entrants is high. However, this solution doesn't resolve the given problem because it eliminates the possibility of benefitting from the economic advantages associated with the large firm.

In this case, the solution is found in part at the level of the organizing authority through the inclusion of specific contractual clauses. It would seem to us that this solution is definitely not in line with maintaining an alternative expertise in service operations at the local authority level. It's a costly solution and undoubtedly an illusory one. For the most part, any contestability of these markets is structured at the national level. The State, by virtue of its global regulatory power over infrastructure markets, must maintain a competitive oligopolistic structure with a mix of public and private operators. In the case of a serious crisis, a public operator from another network or a direct competitor could always step in for a deficient service firm.

- Is the risk being run of a monopoly earning excessive profits? It's the most commonly-voiced argument, taking us back to the notion of a situation rent as taught according to economic tradition. Empirical measurements have led us to believe that the profit margins of these major firms are not necessarily high, as the goal of the large urban services firm is not to maximize short-term profit. Instead, this goal is more centered on generating a stable long-term cash flow situation, which incites limiting profitability so as not to jeopardize the firm's long-term position, thus an argument essentially of reputation, and hence the stake of its entire strategy.

The problem should not be couched in terms of profit but rather in terms of prices and of the consumer. Is the price paid by the consumer justified by the service rendered? Are the investments programmed really necessary? If the public authority seeks to be in a position to pass judgement, other than a moral judgement, on this point, it would be incumbent upon the authority to develop its observation capabilities, wherein the importance of yardstick competition. Yet, these observation tools should be implemented more on a nationwide basis than on the city level.

- Are the services provided by a large integrated firm always charged at market prices? Is the public authority aware of the rate's transfer carried out inside the firm? On this particular point of transfer mechanisms being applied by firms, it is essential to clearly indicate the intended market structure being sought. This feature is unquestionably part and parcel of the global regulation of these markets: "limited delegation" and competitive markets for all ancillary components - construction work, services - and "global delegation" to an integrated firm. Each framework has its own set of advantages, and the organization centered around the large firm engenders its productivity factors (see the arguments presented in the introduction). However, if reliance on major integrated firms is ultimately opted for, the rate equalization argument would then lose its purpose, with this choice becoming an internal one concerning the firm's own organizational patterns. The public authority has to be able to evaluate results, and once again the issue of observation techniques draws our attention.

- The risk of proximity. The large firm has the capacity to encompass the entire urban infrastructure market. It is constantly seeking growth; it reads the markets and keeps in touch with elected officials. Its internal dynamic directs it towards development strategies. French history of the 1970's and 1980's illustrates this type of development through proximity and through interconnectedness with its associated risk of confusion. Yet, it's not a rule that's completely inflexible. Action is interactive; firms adapt to the rules defined by the public authority. It's for the public-sector actors to comprehend that signing contracts is merely one step within a much wider dynamic. They must, in addition, observe markets, remain informed about corporate strategy and react through their vested regulatory powers whenever they feel certain limits have been surpassed. As is the case for any action executed, risks exist and they're shared. For example, for the firm operating over a long-term cycle, the risk is encountered that political changes cause contract reevaluation at the very time equilibrium is reached.

o
o   o

Put otherwise, collective action is completely interactive. The quality of the results obtained greatly depends on the level of investment each party will have placed into their actions.

BOX
Strategic points

1. Combine a minimum of conditions preliminary to action:
- legitimacy for the organizing authority,
- a definition of the public domain,
- a legal system,
- a capital market,
- stability in the legal and institutional framework.

2. System calibration: before or during?

Time must certainly be devoted to analyzing problems and refining the contract; it's the guarantee for simpler implementation. But just how far should this calibration go?
- Acknowledging a time for political input in urban affairs leads to accepting a margin for the unexpected.
- Long-term contracts cannot forecast all eventualities. Actors are not necessarily made aware of all parameters "before the fact"; they discover problems through moving forward.

In order to resolve this problem of limited rationality, theories regarding collective action and institutional learning must be integrated. Under specific conditions, exposing all the problems both complicates and heightens the fervor expressed by both parties. In such a case, it's advisable to orient the action around problems and plan for the possibility of a gradual transformation of the action framework.

3. To carry this step out, actors can utilize the gradient of contracts available.

4. The necessity of laying out an easily-comprehensible structure.

Even though the system is naturally complex and always involves various institutional jurisdictions, nonetheless a pilot is still needed to steer the ship.

Our preference tends to unquestionably favor the local public authorities, vested with electoral legitimacy and aware of problems, due to their level of proximity. Since urban utility services include a political dimension, then it's only normal that the politician be part of the action framework.

These authorities will be assisted by a national-level regulatory body, which serves as much in promulgating regulations as it does in acting as a resource center.

5. A few basic principles must be respected.
- the organizational autonomy of operators,
- a measurement of consumption,
- a financial equilibrium.

If the population's income levels make it impossible to pay the service's cost, at least the complementary subsidies can be computed in light of the given parameters of the situation.

Authors' biographical notes

Jean Roland Barthélémy, Graduate of the ESSEC Business School, Ph.D. in Geography, Director of the organization "Fondation des Villes". Has worked for twenty years on various aspects of city management and urban development at both the local and the national levels. Mr. Barthélémy has, in particular, conducted several research missions on water supply services in France and elsewhere.

Eric Baye, Ph.D. in Economics along with an advanced degree in political science, Researcher with the organization "Economie et Humanisme" since 1988, specialist in the management and financing of urban services in the Asian Pacific Rim region; involved in the scientific side of organizing seminars focused on city management issues in Asia and in France (World Bank, Asian Productivity Organization, ...). Mr. Baye is author of several articles on Asian infrastructure.

Alain Cadiou, Hydrogeologist. From 1966 to 1968, was part of the team assigned by the French government to set up the Seine River Basin Agency. Thereafter, Mr. Cadiou headed this Agency's Upper Normandy delegation, then managed its studies / research office. Since 1990, he has held the post of Director of International Relations for the Seine-Normandy Water Agency, and has been rather heavily involved with Latin American countries.

Henri Coing, Professor at the Paris Planning Institute. Among his noteworthy achievements is the work "La ville marché d'emploi" ("The city as a market for employment"), published by the Grenoble University Press. Mr. Coing has been concentrating over the past fifteen years on the evolution taking place in management methods of urban services within developing nations, especially in Latin America.

Daniel Faudry, Economist with the CNRS National Research Center; has directed scientific and technical research / exchange programs with Latin America on water supply and wastewater service problems for the French Ministry of Public Works and Housing on behalf of the Worldwide Federation of Sister Cities. Mr. Faudry has headed research at the National Institute of Public Works Engineering and is currently working in the area of local environmental policy.

Jean-Claude Lavigne, Ph.D. in Economics and in Geography, Director of Research with the organization "Economie et Humanisme", international consultant. Mr. Lavigne has led the research and study program on urban services and on African and Asian cities for the CNUEH (Housing), the CNUCED as well as the various French Ministries concerned.

Hugues Le Masson, Civil Engineering graduate from the School of Mines, Geological Engineering graduate from the Petroleum Engineering School, and alumnus of the Harvard Business School. Mr. Le Masson is President of the Sahel Aqua Viva Foundation. After twelve years spent within a wide range of both French and foreign firms, he has been working ever since 1974 with the "Caisse Française de Développement". He is also author of "Faut-il encore aider les Pays en Développement?" ("Should we still be financially assisting the developing nations?"), published by Le Félin, 1992.

Dominique Lorrain, Graduate of the Paris Political Science Institute (Institut d'Etudes Politiques de Paris), Economist, Ph.D. in Sociology, Researcher with the CNRS National Research Center (C.E.M.S.), Member of the organization "Fondation des Villes" since 1975. Mr. Lorrain has published many articles on city government and on urban services both in France and abroad. He has recently directed the work, "The Privatization of Urban Services in Europe" in collaboration with G. Stoker, Pinter, London 1997; has also completed a special issue of "Sociologie du Travail" entitled "La Ville (gouverner, habiter)" ("The City (a place to govern, to live)"), Dunod, 1995.

Claude Martinand, Engineering graduate from the "Ponts et Chaussées" Civil Engineering School, Director of International and Economic Affairs within the Ministry of Regional Planning, Public Works and Transportation. Mr. Martinand has performed a variety of functions both in the field and with the central administration in Paris pertaining to infrastructure, transportation, planning and housing. He has also led the working group that produced "Le génie urbain" ("Urban public works engineering"), published by La Documentation Française, 1986, along with the collective work entitled, "Le financement privé des équipements collectifs, l'expérience française" ("Private Financing of Public Infrastructure: The French Experience"), Economica, 1993.

Zbigniew Maksymiuk, Environmental Engineering graduate from Gdansk Polytechnic. From 1983 to 1990, Mr. Maksymiuk held several engineering positions within OPWiK, a municipal enterprise responsible for providing the city's water and wastewater services. At the beginning of 1991, he was named its Managing Director; in July 1992, became Managing Director of SNG, a joint venture company created between the City of Gdansk and the French company SAUR.

Jack Moss, Oxford graduate, Geographer. Mr. Moss began his professional career in the construction industry and possesses experience in applying the principles of public / private partnership within the sector of infrastructure development. For the past ten years, he has been utilizing this experience in the area of water supply and wastewater services in Europe, Australia, New Zealand and Turkey. Since 1994, he has held the post of Commercial Director for Asian operations with the Lyonnaise des Eaux Group, where he has been directly involved in the development of these concepts towards the expanding economies of Asia.

Didier Rétali, Engineering graduate of the School of Mines, initially held several managerial posts in the field of environmental protection, economic development and energy planning within the French Ministry of Industry. In 1989, Mr. Rétali joined the Lyonnaise des Eaux Group, where he has successively been Head of Projects for the Southern Paris Division, Delegated Administrator of the SAAM (1991-94) and Director of Operations for the territory of China, Hong Kong and Macao (1993-94). Since 1995, he has occupied the position of Director of International Projects with the Group's International Water Division.

Franck Scherrer, alumnus of the Ecole Normale Supérieure; Ph.D. in Geography, currently holds the post of research professor at the Lyons Urban Planning Institute (Université de Lyon II). Mr. Scherrer's specific fields of research concern the long-term evolution of urban services and utility networks, and in particular the relationships existing between a city's technical staff, its political officials and its territorial jurisdiction.

Marco Venturini, Law Degree from the University of Turin. Since 1989, Mr. Venturini has been assigned a special mission by the Commercial Department of the Générale des Eaux company, in its capacity as administrator of two Italian water distribution subsidiaries. He is also member of the ANFIDA (Italian Association of Private Water Distributors) Steering Committee. He participated directly in the book, "La gestione ottimale del ciclo completo delle acque", Il sole 24 Ore, Milan, 1992.